PERGAMON INTERNATIONAL LIBRARY
of Science, Technology, Engineering and Social Studies

The 1000-volume original paperback library in aid of education,
industrial training and the enjoyment of leisure

Publisher: Robert Maxwell, M.C.

Population Geography
and the Developing Countries

THE PERGAMON TEXTBOOK
INSPECTION COPY SERVICE

An inspection copy of any book published in the Pergamon International Library will
gladly be sent to academic staff without obligation for their consideration for course
adoption or recommendation. Copies may be retained for a period of 60 days from
receipt and returned if not suitable. When a particular title is adopted or recommended
for adoption for class use and the recommendation results in a sale of 12 or more copies,
the inspection copy may be retained with our compliments. The Publishers will be
pleased to receive suggestions for revised editions and new titles to be published in this
important International Library.

PERGAMON OXFORD GEOGRAPHY SERIES

General Editor: W. B. FISHER

Other Titles of Interest

CLARKE John I.
Population Geography 2nd Edition

CLOUT Hugh D.
Rural Geography—An Introductory Survey
The Geography of Post-war France—A Social and Economic Approach

COOKE R. U. and JOHNSON J. H.
Trends in Geography—An Introductory Survey

COPPOCK J. T. and SEWELL W. R. D.
Spatial Dimensions of Public Policy

DENNIS R. and CLOUT H. D.
A Social Geography of England and Wales

DEWDNEY J. C.
A Geography of the Soviet Union 3rd Edition

GOODALL B. and KIRBY A.
Resources and Planning

JOHNSON J. H.
Urban Geography—An Introductory Analysis 2nd Edition

KERR A. J. C.
The Common Market and How it Works (revised reprint)

McINTOSH I. G. and MARSHALL C. B.
The Face of Scotland 3rd Edition

MATTHEWS J. A.
Quantitative and Statistical Approaches to Geography—A Practical Manual

O'CONNOR A. M.
The Geography of Tropical African Development 2nd Edition

SUNDERLAND E.
Elements of Human and Social Geography—Some Anthropological Perspectives

TREWARTHA G. T.
The More Developed Realm: A Geography of its Population

Population Geography
and the
Developing Countries

JOHN I. CLARKE
Professor of Geography, University of Durham

PERGAMON PRESS

OXFORD · NEW YORK · TORONTO
SYDNEY · PARIS · FRANKFURT

U.K.	Pergamon Press Ltd., Headington Hill Hall, Oxford OX3 0BW, England
U.S.A.	Pergamon Press Inc., Maxwell House, Fairview Park, Elmsford, New York 10523, U.S.A.
CANADA	Pergamon Press Canada Ltd., Suite 104, 150 Consumers Rd., Willowdale, Ontario M2J 1P9, Canada
AUSTRALIA	Pergamon Press (Aust.) Pty. Ltd., P.O. Box 544, Potts Point, N.S.W. 2011, Australia
FRANCE	Pergamon Press SARL, 24 rue des Ecoles, 75240 Paris, Cedex 05, France
FEDERAL REPUBLIC OF GERMANY	Pergamon Press GmbH, 6242 Kronberg-Taunus, Hammerweg 6, Federal Republic of Germany

---

First edition 1971
Reprinted 1974, 1977, 1979, 1981

Library of Congress Catalog Card No. 74-135413

Printed in Great Britain by A. Wheaton & Co. Ltd., Exeter

ISBN 0 08 016445 5 hardcover
ISBN 0 08 016446 3 flexicover

To Dig, Gemma, Anna & Lucy

CONTENTS

LIST OF ILLUSTRATIONS

PREFACE

THE germ of this volume dates back nearly twenty years to the time when the author, supported by a French government bursary, went to Tunisia as a young researcher to study human migrations in that country. The study stimulated an interest in population distribution and dynamics in the poorer, so-called "developing" countries, an interest which has since been sustained by sojourns in Sierra Leone, Cameroon, Libya and Iran, as well as visits to numerous other developing countries, notably in Africa and South-west Asia. This interest, however, is not merely academic, for nobody studying developing countries can remain indifferent to the great magnitude of human problems faced by them. This volume makes a humble attempt to explain some of those problems.

Many visits to developing countries have been made possible by the generosity of the University of Durham, and in particular its Centre for Middle Eastern and Islamic Studies, whose sponsorship has permitted extensive fieldwork. The author must also take this opportunity to thank the many undergraduates and research students in the Universities of Durham, Sierra Leone, Wisconsin, Cameroon and Libya who have patiently endured my impassioned propositions for population geography. The modest success of my excessively succinct textbook (Pergamon, 1965) on this subject has encouraged me to attempt this volume, despite the danger of accusation of over-compression. Once again, the task has been facilitated by the constant support of my wife, who married a sedentary academic, only to find that he was a seasonal nomad.

Finally, I wish to thank Mr. A. Corner, Cartographer in the Department of Geography, University of Durham, for the excellence of his illustrations and Mrs. P. Blair for typing (and re-typing) the text.

Durham,   Jоhn I. Clarke
1969

ACKNOWLEDGEMENTS

The author and the publishers are grateful to the following people who have kindly given permission for the use of copyright material:

Professor G. J. Butland, for the map of the frontier in South America, from his article in *Revista Geografica*, 1966; Colin Clark for a diagram of the growth of Chinese population since 500 B.C. from *Population Growth and Land Use*, Macmillan, 1967; Professor A. T. A. Learmonth and Professor O. H. K. Spate for maps from *India and Pakistan*, 3rd edition, Methuen, 1967; J. P. Lippincott and Company for map of Rural Population in South West Asia by G. B. Cressey in *Crossroads*, 1960; The Longman Group Ltd. for map of The Peoples of Africa by John I. Clarke in R. J. Harrison Church *et al.*, *Africa and the Islands*, 1964; The Odyssey Press for a redrawn and unified version of maps of ethnic composition of Latin America in Preston James, *Latin America*, 3rd edition, 1959; R. Mansell Prothero for map from *Migrants and Malaria*, Longmans, 1965; E. A. Schmidt and P. Mattingly for the maps of Rural and City Populations of Africa from their article in *Geographische Rundschau*, 1966; The Times Newspapers Limited for a simplified version of the population density map of South America from Plate 6 of *The Times Atlas of the World*, 1968; D. Van Nostrand and Company for map of Frontiers of Agriculture by H. Boesch from *A Geography of World Economy*, 1964.

Every effort has been made to trace and acknowledge ownership of copyright. The author and the publishers will be glad to make suitable arrangements with any copyright holders whom it has not been possible to contact.

I

INTRODUCTION

Population Geography and Population Dynamics

Over the past few years more and more geographers have turned
their attention to the study of population. Their interest as geographers
has been primarily directed toward the analysis of areal variations in
the distribution, composition, migrations and growth of populations,
and the ways in which these relate to the nature of places. It may be
postulated that the significance of population geography as a branch
of geography has grown concomitantly with an increasing awareness
of the dynamism of populations. Earlier geographers were often content
to examine patterns of population distributions as more or less static
phenomena, relating them particularly to the patterns of the physical
environment. It is true that population distributions always demonstrate some inertia, present distributions reflecting to a greater or
lesser extent past distributions, but such is the dynamism of populations
that demographic processes in progress at the moment are likely to
modify substantially present distributions. It follows, therefore, that
geographers must be aware of population dynamics, as well as their
causes and consequences. Geographers can no longer regard population
as a final effect of economic processes, themselves conditioned by the
physical environment, an end product rather than a causal element.
They must see how it influences geographical patterns.

The most notable demographic process in the world today is growth.
Over recent decades the rate of world population growth has increased
in a startling fashion. At the end of 1972 there were about 3800 million

1

people on earth, but during that year about 125 million babies were born and some 49 million persons died, so the total increased by 76 millions in one year alone. Indeed, the 1972 total is 800 million more than the 1960 total, nearly 1300 million more than in 1950, and over twice as many as at the time of the First World War. Moreover, it is confidently expected that if present trends persist there will be 4900 million people living on earth by 1985.

It is true that these figures are only rounded estimates, and that we cannot provide precise numbers and rates of increase, especially for those many countries where population enumeration is poor or absent. Nevertheless, it has become obvious that the less advanced, under-developed or developing countries are accounting for the bulk of world population growth. The developing countries, here crudely defined as Latin America, Africa and Asia (except Japan and the USSR), in-creased annually by 2.1 per cent during the period 1950–65, while the developed countries grew by only 1.2 per cent. In other words, during this period the developing world accounted for 78 per cent of the world population growth, so that by 1965 it contained nearly 70 per cent of the world's population. Unfortunately the developing countries shared only about 20 per cent of the world's gross national product. If present projections prove accurate, the developing countries may contain about four-fifths of mankind by the end of this century. We should remind ourselves, however, that population projections have a long history of false assumptions and erroneous conclusions, even over short periods of a decade or so in advanced countries with sophisticated data, so we must not rely on guesses as to the future population of the developing world.

Rapid population growth in developing countries is closely associated with very youthful population structures and high age-dependency ratios, which contrast markedly with those of the developed countries and can severely retard increases in *per capita* production. Most develop-ing countries, but by no means all, face pressures of population upon resources, and find it extremely difficult to overcome the problem of raising productivity; and in many countries the pressures may worsen before they improve. In addition, the internal patterns of population in developing countries are undergoing radical transformation, particu-larly as a result of the impact of modernity upon traditional societies.

One aspect of this impact is urbanization, a widespread phenomenon which affects developing and developed countries alike, but which is more parasitic and less economically justifiable in developing countries. Rapid urbanization is also indicative of the diminishing influence of the physical environment upon the pattern of population distribution.

The aim of this volume is certainly ambitious, and perhaps presumptuous, because it attempts to depict the broad patterns in the population geography of the developing countries and the way in which they differ from the developed countries. Obviously, the broad view masks a myriad of complexities, owing to the great variety of physical environments, cultural traditions and economic activities, so emphasis is given to the diversity of patterns, pressures and problems of population at continental and subcontinental levels, but also in particular countries and regions. In any one volume, however large, it is impossible to look at all these complexities, but we can try to see how the situation varies from one major region to another, and how it is changing with time.

What are Developing Countries?

The irony of the term "developing countries" is that it is used with reference to those poorer countries of the world which are generally growing economically at a slow or intermittent rate, and cannot rely on their growth to be a continual or self-generating process, but whose populations are expanding rapidly. Indeed, the term "developing" is often one of aspiration rather than achievement. These are the countries experiencing a "revolution of rising expectations", as the American Assistant Secretary of State, Harland Cleveland, described the situation; the countries which want to develop rapidly, to bridge the gap between them and the select minority of countries which can be labelled "developed". The term "developing" was considered preferable to other terms like "underdeveloped", "less developed" and "backward", which were distasteful to countries so described. These terms were regarded as too pessimistic, implying a permanent status of backwardness for countries which had won political independence from European control. It was this political emergence which had partly inspired the growing concern with "underdevelopment"; other causes were the publicity given to two major social discoveries of our time: that the majority of mankind suffered from poverty, hunger and illiteracy, and that the number of people living in poor countries was growing at a faster rate than the number living in rich countries. Public concern over these matters has mostly manifested itself during the period since the Second World War, in association with the decline of colonialism and the dissatisfaction with the social and economic disparities among the peoples of the world.

Unfortunately, the revolution of rising expectations has not proved as successful as many would have hoped, and the 1960s have brought disappointment and disillusionment. As Horowitz explains, there was far too much optimism and misunderstanding. Development cannot be equated with industrialization or externally induced transformation. Superimposition of the technology of advanced countries does not provide an answer. Many developing countries are now aware of the failures of the 1950s and are much more realistic about the magnitudes of their tasks. Nevertheless, Horowitz rightly distinguishes between those countries which have no consciousness of being underdeveloped and those which have a concept of emergence and characterize themselves as being developed socially and culturally and of being underdeveloped economically and technically.

Developing countries, which are in general politically non-aligned and diversely committed, are sometimes collectively known as the Third World, in order to distinguish them from the capitalist and socialist worlds. Although the term "Third World", first used by Frantz Fanon, has gathered an emotive connotation and considerable acceptance, it is not clearly definable, for some developing countries may also be included in one of the other two categories. Moreover, it may be argued that the economic and social contrasts between developed and developing countries are probably greater than those between capitalist and socialist countries, and that the economic contrasts arising from the differences between capitalist and socialist countries are generally wider among developed countries than among developing ones. Taken literally, therefore, the term "Third World" is rather too restrictive for all those countries experiencing disharmony between slow economic growth and rapid population growth, for neither phenomenon is the prerogative of the Third World; both also occur among capitalist and socialist countries.

There can be no simple acceptable definition of developing countries, which exhibit diverse relationships between economic and population growth as well as diverse prospects for development. In essence, these are the poorer countries of the world, which experience a variety of common features: low standard of living, low average income, low food consumption, low energy consumption, low literacy level, high unemployment and underemployment, poor health, rapid population growth, youthful age composition, high age–dependency ratio, high proportion engaged in agriculture, under-utilization of resources, limited capital equipment, limited industrialization, poor communications and monoproduction of foodstuffs or minerals. (Not all are confined to developing countries; Stamp has suggested with reason that the temperate lands of North America contain some of the most under-utilized areas.) It must be obvious, therefore, that no single criterion is satisfactory for the definition of developing countries. All the above-mentioned phenomena are interrelated, forming a matrix of socio-economic and demographic factors, so that if one factor undergoes modification others must also change at one time or another. Attempts to classify developing countries on the basis of one criterion have been consequently inconclusive, whether we use *per capita* income, *per capita* GNP, *per capita* consumption of energy or any other index. If we look at the cases of Kuwait and Libya, for example, we find that both enjoy high and rising *per capita* incomes owing to massive monoproduction of oil, indeed Kuwait has the highest *per capita* income in the world, yet in many other senses both countries are underdeveloped. It is therefore preferable to consider combinations of criteria, like Scheidl, who suggests seven: (1) rapid population growth, (2) one-sided exploitation of resources, (3) lack of capital, training and effective social and political administration, (4) ancient and conservative traditions and attitudes, (5) poor and limited industrial development, (6) expensive and cumbersome system of distribution, and (7) low *per capita* income (Fig. 1.1) and standard of living.

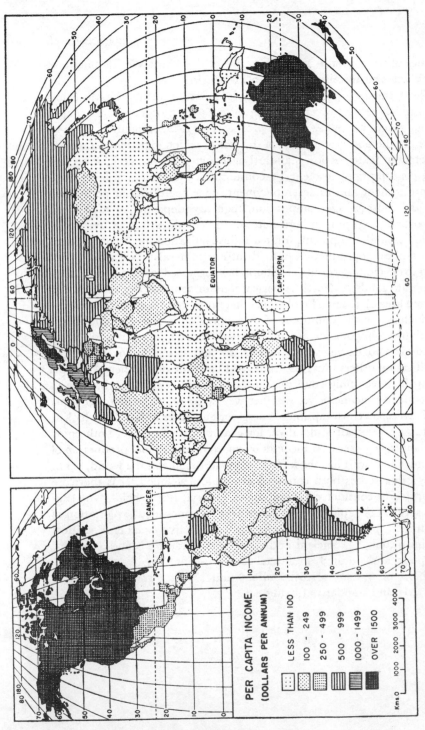

Fig. 1.1. *Per capita* income (dollars per annum). Although *per capita* income is an imperfect index of levels of economic development, this map highlights the contrasts between the developing and developed countries.

Which are the Developing Countries?

A further difficulty of definition arises from the fact that no inherent clear-cut division exists between developed and developing countries. Between the highly developed and the poorly developed there is a wide spectrum, which is not easily divisible, because countries may experience development in one sector but not in another and because the relative position of countries in the spectrum is not static. In this sense, J. K. Galbraith's analogy to developing countries as beads on a string, capable of movement along the string, may be misleading by implying an immutable hierarchy, an unchanging rank order. Such immutability is contradicted by the rise of a country like Japan.

In these circumstances it is not surprising that the designations "developing countries" and "underdeveloped countries" have been variously interpreted by different authors and organizations. The United Nations Organization, for example, incorporated within its definition all of Africa except the Republic of South Africa, the Americas except Canada and the United States, Asia except Japan, Turkey and the USSR and finally Oceania except Australia and New Zealand. On the other hand, the OECD definition added several European countries (Greece, Spain, Yugoslavia, Gibraltar and Malta) and Turkey, but subtracted a number of communist countries (Mainland China, Tibet, North Korea, North Vietnam and Mongolia) for which data are not easily available. Both definitions are admittedly crude, for countries like Argentina, Uruguay and Israel can with justice claim a place in the list of developed states.

The difference between these two particular definitions merely highlights the problem of distinguishing classes within an array, and the problem is not simplified by increasing the number of classes. Fryer, for example, uses four types of economic development—highly developed, semi-developed, underdeveloped and planned economies—while Russett uses five stages of economic and political development, namely traditional primitive societies, traditional civilizations, transitional societies, industrial revolution societies and high mass-consumption societies. In both examples, however, anomalies of categorization or terminology arise through inevitable limitations in the criteria used for classification.

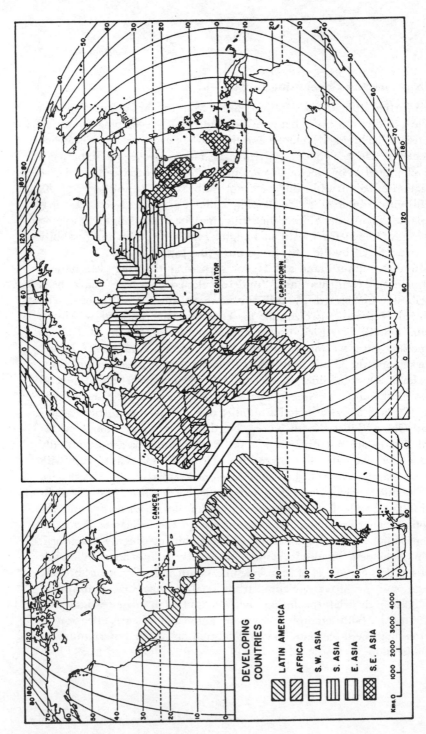

FIG. 1.2. Developing countries. This map distinguishes the various major regions of the developing world considered in this volume.

For our purposes, therefore, it is appropriate to retain the term "developing countries" despite its imperfections and with the full realization that the term is only arbitrary. In this volume our attention will be focused on three large geographical areas—Latin America, Africa, Asia except Japan and the USSR (Fig. 1.2)—containing nearly 70 per cent of the world's population (Table 1.1) and occupying over 56 per cent of the world's land area. Within these areas there are a few states which should undoubtedly be classed as developed, but in this volume it is perhaps better to include them with the developing countries, partly because they are integrated parts of geographical wholes and partly because they offer contrasts and comparisons with less developed countries.

Classification of Developing Countries

The ninety or so developing countries exhibit a great variety of sizes, shapes, situations, climatic conditions, cultures, population densities, natural increase rates, productions and so on, so that it is not easy to classify them, except on a broad geographical basis, as in this book.

We may note, however, that developing countries vary in population size from a few thousand inhabitants to many hundreds of millions, and that many, like Pakistan and Indonesia, are fragmented into separate land masses. The factor of population size of a country certainly affects population growth and its relationships to economic growth, and so is an important consideration. If three arbitrary size categories of states are established, as in Fig. 1.3, with large states having more than 50 million inhabitants, medium-size states 5–50 million and small states less than 5 million, it is found that seven of the thirteen large states in the world are developing countries (China, India, Pakistan, Indonesia, Bangladesh, Nigeria and Brazil) and contain nearly half the world's population. At the other end of the scale are the numerous pocket-size developing countries, many of which result from colonial rule or are still colonial vestiges; in these smaller states population dynamics may be greatly accelerated by sudden changes in fertility, mortality or migrations. But these states play a small part in total world population growth, and it is expected that the larger states of the developing world will gain an increasing proportion of the total world population. Of the

TABLE 1.1. REGIONS OF THE DEVELOPED AND DEVELOPING WORLD

Regions	Area (km²)	Population (millions)		Density (per km²)	
		1970	1980	1970	1980
DEVELOPED COUNTRIES	61,315	1090	1195	18	19
Northern Europe	1,636	81	81	49	50
Southern Europe	1,314	128	133	98	101
Eastern Europe	989	104	114	105	115
Western Europe	992	149	152	149	153
USSR	22,402	243	278	11	12
Northern America	21,515	228	262	11	12
Australia and New Zealand	7,973	15	18	2	2.3
Temperate South America*	4,124	39	46	10	11
Japan	370	103	111	280	300
DEVELOPING COUNTRIES	73,814	2,545	3,075	34	42
Middle America	2,512	67	90	27	36
Caribbean	235	26	32	109	136
Tropical South America	13,666	151	205	11	15
Northern Africa	8,484	87	116	10	14
Western Africa	6,165	101	150	16	24
Middle Africa	6,607	36	41	5	6
Eastern Africa	6,301	98	113	15	18
Southern Africa	2,670	23	30	8	11
South-west Asia	3,968	77	102	17	26
Middle South Asia	6,774	762	900	113	133
South-east Asia	4,492	287	364	64	81
East Asia (Mainland)	11,097	765	850	69	77
Other East Asia	259	61	77	237	297
Melanesia	539	3	3.1	5	6
Polynesia and Micronesia	45	1	1.7	41	57
WORLD	135,129	3,632	4,270	27	32

SOURCE: *UN Provisional Report on World Population Prospects as Assessed in 1963*, New York, 1964 and *U.N. Demographic Yearbooks*.

* Temperate South America is included among the developing countries in this volume.

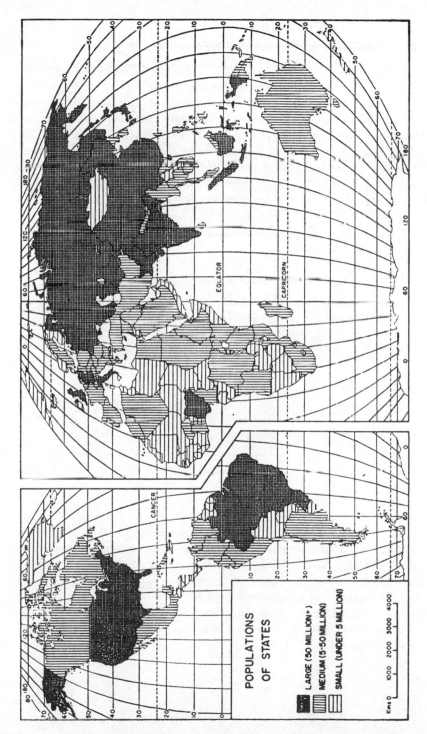

FIG. 1.3. Populations of states, 1965. Large, medium and small populations are distinguished.

POPULATIONS
OF STATES

LARGE (50 MILLION+)
MEDIUM (5-50 MILLION)
SMALL (UNDER 5 MILLION)

Kms 0   1000 2000 3000 4000

76 million extra people on earth this year, most are Asians, especially Chinese, Indians, Pakistanis and Indonesians.

We have already indicated the problems of classifying developing countries in terms of a hierarchy of development. Many classifications have been based on levels of national income, which in general are more variable among developing countries than developed ones. Lacoste further introduced the factor of population growth into his classification of developing countries, because of the fairly close relationship between national incomes and population growth (Table 1.2).

TABLE 1.2. TYPES OF UNDERDEVELOPMENT (AFTER LACOSTE)

	Per capita Income ($ p.a.)	Annual population growth (%)	Examples
A	Under 100	Under 1.8	Some countries of Tropical Africa, like Guinea, Upper Volta, Chad
B	Under 100	Over 1.8	Congo, Nigeria, Afghanistan, South Korea, Indonesia
C	100–200	Over 1.8	North Africa, Middle East, Ecuador, Bolivia, Paraguay
D	200–350	Over 1.8	Many Latin American countries
E	200–350	Under 1.8	Barbados

SOURCE: Y. Lacoste, *Géographie du Sous-Développement*, Paris, 1965, with some modifications of examples.

He used three thresholds of *per capita* income ($100, $180 and $350 per annum, which are now too low, but were satisfactory in the early 1960s) and one of population growth (1.8 per cent per annum) to produce a five-fold classification, whose fifth category is not normally considered as underdeveloped. However, he insisted that this classification should not be regarded as a classification of levels of underdevelopment, for which we should know something about the rates of population growth and economic growth of the modern and traditional sectors over a period of time.

Unfortunately, data for such knowledge are often lacking. Lacoste's choice of 1.8 per cent as the threshold of population growth may also seem arbitrary, but in fact it is about the recent world average, and the developing countries nearly all experience more rapid rates of population growth, while the developed countries are increasing more slowly. Few developing countries have only moderate rates of population increase, and the numb of countries in categories A and E are dwindling annually. In ther words, rapid population growth may now be a significant criterion of underdevelopment, but unless consideration is given to elements influencing rapid population growth it helps little in distinguishing between groups of developing countries.

Rapid Population Growth

Rapid population growth has accentuated the economic problems of developing countries which many in the past have either regarded as a natural state of affairs or have attributed to such factors as climatic disadvantages, "the shackles of colonial rule", racial inferiority, backward social structures (e.g. slavery, serfdom, feudalism, tribalism), social inequalities between rich and poor, the lack of a middle class, and disparities in land ownership. These and many other factors have been proposed as root causes of underdevelopment, but there can be no doubt that the fundamental reasons vary from country to country, and from region to region. What is certain is that the situation has changed remarkably in recent years owing to the phenomenal increase in population growth in developing countries.

As is well known, the main cause of rapid population growth in many developing countries is the abrupt decline in mortality, particularly infant mortality, which has occurred especially since the Second World War. While the growth in knowledge of the causes and cures of diseases was a slow process resulting in a gradual decline of mortality in developed countries during the nineteenth and twentieth centuries, many less-developed countries have received the benefit of this accumulated knowledge only during the last few decades. The result has been sudden declines in death rates from formerly high levels in nearly every developing country for which reasonably reliable data exist, and these declines have frequently been of a magnitude unprecedented in the

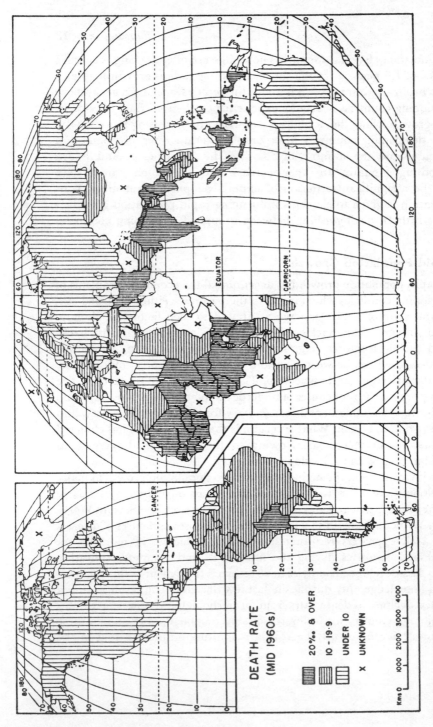

FIG. 1.4. Death rate (mid-1960s). Owing to substantial declines in the death rates of developing countries, and older age structures in developed countries, no clear distinction exists between the death rates of the two sets of countries.

history of population growth in developed countries (Fig. 1.4). In countries like Algeria, Sri Lanka, and Mauritius, mortality diminished more during a decade after the Second World War than during a century in the earlier mortality decline of West European countries. The death rates of some countries dropped by more than 50 per cent during the two decades 1940–1960, sometimes to levels below 10 per thousand (Table 1.3). In Ceylon, a classic example, the extermination of malaria by DDT spraying after the Second World War, helped the death rate to tumble from about 22 per thousand to 10 per thousand in a period of 10 years. In other islands and small countries, like Hong Kong, Singapore, Mauritius, Taiwan, Kuwait, Puerto Rico and Trinidad, mortality has also plunged to levels well below those of developed countries because of the youthful age-structures, and life expectancy has increased from about 30 years to well over 50. The decline in mortality has been neither simultaneous nor universal in developing countries; some countries of tropical Africa, such as Guinea, Mali and Upper Volta, at the time of writing, have experienced little mortality decline. Moreover, within any particular country there are usually marked variations in mortality, influenced not only by geographical patterns of disease, but also by the distribution of medical facilities and establishments, which are most frequently localized in towns.

Under the influence of a mesh of social and biological factors, birth rates also vary among developing countries, usually within the range of 30–55 per thousand (Fig. 1.5), but in general fertility levels are high and have rarely declined over the last few decades. As a result there is a sharp division between fertility in developing and developed countries, so that fertility is one of the better socio-economic variables distinguishing between them. On the other hand, there is a low correlation between fertility and levels of economic development among developing countries; those with higher *per capita* incomes, for example, do not necessarily have lower fertility. Only in temperate Latin America, a few of the smaller countries of south-eastern Asia (Taiwan, Singapore, Ryukyus, South Korea, Hong Kong and Malaya) and some islands of Central America, the Indian Ocean and the Pacific have there been clear signs of a decline of fertility. In some countries, such as Venezuela, it has actually risen, partly because of reductions in infant mortality and maternal mortality, producing a prolongation of reproductive

TABLE 1.3. CHANGES IN BIRTH, DEATH AND NATURAL INCREASE RATES FOR SELECTED COUNTRIES, 1940-70

	Birth rates per 1000				Death rates per 1000				Natural increase per 1000			
	1940	1950	1960	1970	1940	1950	1960	1970	1940	1950	1960	1970
Singapore	45.0	45.4	38.7	23.3	20.9	12.0	6.3	5.3	24.1	33.4	32.4	18.0
Malaya	40.7	42.3	37.7	35.2	20.1	15.9	9.5	7.6	20.6	26.4	28.2	27.6
Sri Lanka	35.8	39.7	37.0	32.0	20.6	12.4	9.1	7.9	15.2	27.3	27.9	24.1
Taiwan	43.7	42.5	39.5	28.1	19.7	11.3	6.9	5.1	24.0	31.2	32.6	23.0
Egypt	41.3	44.4	42.9	44.1	26.3	19.1	16.9	16.5	15.0	25.3	26.0	27.6
Mauritius	29.9	49.7	38.9	26.7	25.5	13.9	11.3	7.8	4.4	35.8	27.6	18.9
Venezuela	36.0	42.6	49.6	40.9	16.6	10.9	8.0	7.8	19.4	31.7	41.6	33.1
Chile	33.4	34.0	33.4	26.6	21.6	15.0	11.9	9.0	11.8	19.0	23.5	17.6
Costa Rica	44.6	45.9	42.9	45.1	17.3	12.2	8.6	7.6	27.3	33.7	34.3	37.5
Mexico	44.3	45.5	45.0	41.3	23.2	16.2	11.4	9.2	21.1	29.3	33.6	32.1
Jamaica	30.8	33.1	42.8	32.9	15.4	11.9	8.9	7.1	15.4	21.2	33.9	25.8

SOURCE: *UN Demographic Yearbooks.*

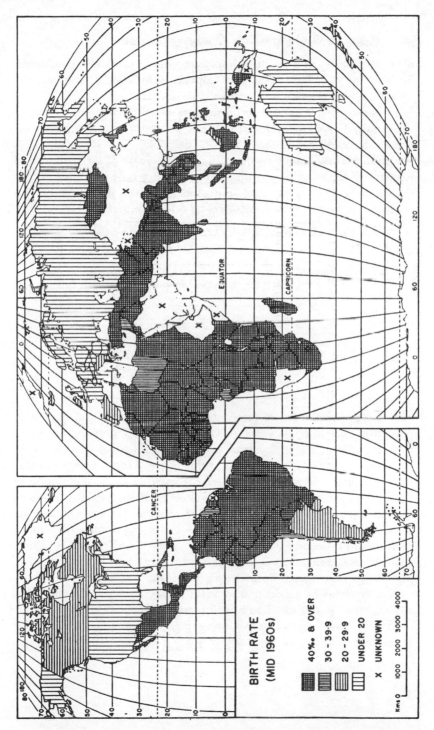

FIG. 1.5. Birth rate (mid-1960s). Fertility is one of the best differentials between developed and developing countries.

lives, and partly as a result of improvements in economic conditions. So in many developing countries, especially in Middle America, the birth rate is more than four times the death rate.

In consequence, natural increase rates of the developing countries are usually above 20 per thousand (i.e. 2 per cent per annum) and may rise as high as 40 per thousand in a few cases like Costa Rica (Fig. 1.6). We should recall that the rates of natural increase of the countries of western Europe during the nineteenth century only exceeded 10 per thousand in exceptional cases. The startling effect of these recent increase rates may best be understood by reference to Table 1.4. If they

TABLE 1.4. TIME TAKEN FOR POPULATIONS TO DOUBLE AT CERTAIN RATES OF INCREASE

Percentage annual increase	Years taken for population to double
0.5	139
1.0	70
1.5	47
2.0	35
2.5	28
3.0	23
3.5	20
4.0	18

persist, the populations of many developing countries will double in population size in 20–35 years. A 3 per cent annual increase rate, common in tropical Latin America, means a doubling of population in 23 years, and a century of growth at this rate will multiply the population 18 times. Ansley Coale has demonstrated that the population of Brazil, for example, which had 84 million in 1966, would increase at the current rate of 3.1 per cent to 1700 million by the year 2066. In contrast, most developed countries, even in conditions of fertility revival, will take 35–100 years to double, a few, like Sweden, Belgium, Austria and Hungary, will take much longer, while East Germany's population is static and Berlin experiences natural decrease.

The interplay of mortality and fertility provides considerable diversity in national and district natural increase rates, which are difficult to classify, but it appears that four types may be distinguished among developing countries at the moment:

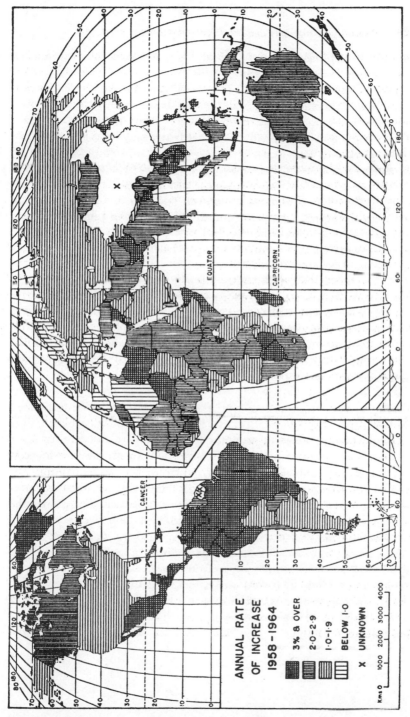

ANNUAL RATE OF INCREASE 1958–1964

- 3% & OVER
- 2·0–2·9
- 1·0–1·9
- BELOW 1·0
- X UNKNOWN

Kms 0 1000 2000 3000 4000

Fig. 1.6. Annual rate of increase, 1958–64. There is no simple pattern of annual increase, although it is usually high in developing countries.

(1) *Fairly rapid natural increase (about 15–25 per thousand) resulting from persistently high fertility and mortality.*

This is the case for much of tropical Africa, as well as Indonesia, Laos, Burma, Haiti and Bolivia. In some African countries, where birth rates are reportedly over 50 per thousand (e.g. Mali, Niger and Togo), natural increase rates may be as high as 30 per thousand.

(2) *Very rapid natural increase (over 30 per thousand) resulting from unabated or rising fertility and declining or low mortality.*

Many Latin American countries fall into this category, along with some of the smaller countries of Africa and Asia, and many islands in the Pacific and Indian Oceans.

(3) *Fairly rapid natural increase (15–25 per thousand) resulting from gradually falling fertility and mortality.*

India, and perhaps China, may be included within this group, partly owing to their efforts in family planning.

(4) *Fairly rapid natural increase (15–25 per thousand) resulting from declining fertility and low mortality.*

A number of Latin American countries, such as Uruguay, Cuba, Puerto Rico and Barbados, and some small Asiatic countries, like Singapore, Hong Kong and Israel, are of this type.

Obviously, these types and their present component countries are far from static, and in particular we can expect considerable changes in group (1) as a result of declining mortality.

At this stage we should strike one or two warning notes. Data of population dynamics in developing countries are notoriously unreliable, and it is dangerous to use countries with relatively good data as representative samples of developing countries as a whole. In general, the quality of mortality data, the key variable, is closely related to the efficiency of the health services, and so Venezuelan data must not be construed as typical of Ecuador or Bolivia, nor Egyptian data as typical of Libya or Mali. Furthermore, natural increase rates may undergo considerable annual oscillations, because they are dependent upon two variables, birth rates and death rates. Consequently, mean annual rates of increase for a 5-year period may be more indicative of general trends than figures for an individual year. It is also necessary to recall that all three rates—birth, death and natural increase rates—are crude measures, making no allowance for the age composition of the population, and so they must not be used as an indication of future population growth. In fact, nearly all sophisticated attempts to predict future growth in highly developed countries like the United States have proved very unsuccessful, even over a short period such as a decade.

TABLE 1.5. MEDIUM ESTIMATES OF WORLD POPULATION, 1750–2000

	A. Numbers in millions					
	1750	1800	1850	1900	1950	2000
WORLD	791	978	1262	1650	2515	6130
DEVELOPING			*919*	*1088*	*1682*	*4742*
Asia (except Japan and the USSR)	468	600	770	881	1290	3336
Africa	106	107	111	133	222	768
Latin America	16	24	38	74	162	630
DEVELOPED			*343*	*562*	*834*	*1388*
Europe (except the USSR)	125	152	208	296	392	527
USSR	42	56	76	134	180	353
North America	2	7	26	82	166	354
Japan	30	30	31	44	83	122
Oceania	2	2	2	6	13	32

	B. Annual rate of increase				
	1750–1800	1800–1850	1850–1900	1900–1950	1950–2000
WORLD	0.4	0.5	0.5	0.8	1.8
DEVELOPING			*0.3*	*0.9*	*2.1*
Asia (except Japan and the USSR)	0.5	0.5	0.3	0.8	1.9
Africa	0.0	0.1	0.4	1.0	2.5
Latin America	0.8	0.9	1.3	1.6	2.8
DEVELOPED			*1.0*	*0.8*	*0.9*
Europe (except the USSR)	0.4	0.6	0.7	0.6	0.6
USSR	0.6	0.6	1.1	0.6	1.4
North America	—	2.7	2.3	1.4	1.5
Japan	0.0	0.1	0.7	1.3	0.8
Oceania	—	—	—	1.6	1.8

SOURCE: J. D. Durand, The modern expansion of world population, *Proc. Am. Phil. Soc.* **111**, 137 and 143 (1967).

Small wonder, therefore, that population projections for developing countries have only the most limited validity.

Despite these cautions, there is no doubt that this massive increase in the population growth of developing countries has ushered in a new phase of demographic history, in which the developing countries of Latin America, Africa and Asia will increase their total numerical superiority *vis-à-vis* the developed countries. If their membership remains unchanged over the next few decades, there is good reason to believe that the developing countries may contain nearly four-fifths of the world's population by the end of this century, instead of under two-thirds as at mid-century.

Durand among others has expressed the contrast in population growth between the developed and developing worlds in quantitative terms (Table 1.5) and has projected these populations to AD 2000 in accordance with the expected rising rates of growth during the next few decades. Although the developing countries increased by only one-fifth during the first quarter of this century, it is believed that they may double in population during the last quarter. The populations of the developing countries of Asia are expected to rise to three-fifths of the world's total, and those of Latin America and Africa to just under one-tenth each. The population of Latin America should soar the most rapidly; in 1900 Latin America had 74 million people, in 1972 there were 300 million, and by 2000 there may be 638 million, more than eight times as many inhabitants as at the beginning of the century. But rapid as these Latin American increases are, they do not involve such mammoth numbers as in Asia, where, for example, the population increase during 1960–75 in Indonesia may be 44 million, in Pakistan 50 million, in India 177 million and in Mainland China 380 million.

Some Problems of Population Growth

It is reasonable to suppose that most developing countries will enjoy improved mortality and morbidity conditions over the next few decades, and this will mean very low death rates, because they have extremely youthful age structures. In most developing countries 40–50 per cent of the total populations are under 15 years of age, whereas in developed countries only about 20–33 per cent are within this age

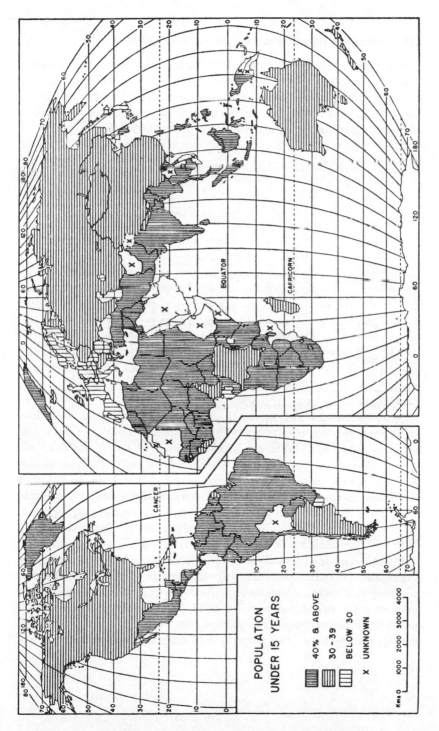

Fig. 1.7. Population under 15 years. More than two-fifths of the populations of most developing countries are under 15 years.

group (see Fig. 1.7 and Table 1.6). Nicaragua, Dominica and Honduras, for example, have more than twice the proportion of children found in western European countries. Moreover, reduced mortality has the initial effect of broadening the base of the population pyramid, so that in succeeding decades the fertility potential is high.

TABLE 1.6. PERCENTAGE AGE COMPOSITION OF THE WORLD AND MAJOR REGIONS, 1960

	Per cent of total population in certain age-groups				
	0–14	0–19	15–59	20–59	60 and over
WORLD[a, b, c]	36.2	45.1	56.0	47.1	7.8
East Asia[a]	36.0	45.3	57.1	47.8	6.9
South Asia[b]	40.7	50.5	54.2	44.4	5.1
Africa	43.1	53.5	52.3	41.9	4.6
Latin America	41.7	51.6	53.0	43.1	5.3
Europe	25.8	32.9	59.6	52.5	14.6
Soviet Union	30.8	37.2	59.5	53.1	9.7
North America	31.3	38.8	55.7	48.2	13.0
Oceania[c]	31.7	39.6	56.9	49.0	11.4

[a] Not including North Korea and Ryukyu Islands.
[b] Not including Israel and Cyprus.
[c] Not including Polynesia and Micronesia.
SOURCE: *UN Provisional Report on World Population Prospects, as Assessed in 1963,* New York, 1964.

With high proportions of children, developing countries inevitably experience high dependency ratios (Fig. 1.8), usually expressed as children and aged: adults, and a large part of the available supplies of labour and capital must be devoted to feeding, clothing and educating the youth. This is a great drain on resources. Some idea of the scope of the problem may be drawn from the fact that in 1960 India had about 100 million children of school age (5–14 years), and that this number may increase by 50 per cent by 1975, giving a total of about 150 million. In China, there may be more than 290 million children of school age by 1975. The provision of school facilities for all these

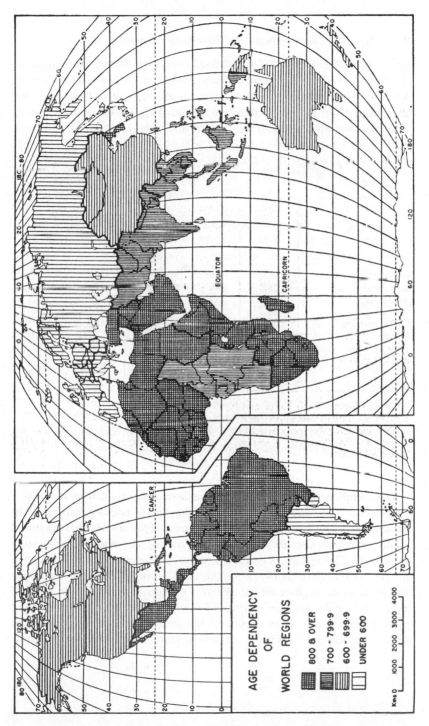

FIG. 1.8. Age dependency of world regions. The major regions of the developing world suffer from a heavy age-dependency burden.

children is extremely costly, especially in communist China which receives little outside aid. Of course, the majority of the adults of developing countries are either illiterate or have had only minimal schooling, and many of the children of school age do not attend school. In a few developing countries, especially of Latin America, the situation has vastly improved in recent years, but in some cases the type of education is ill-adapted to the need for social and economic development, and in others the level of education attained by many schoolchildren is insufficient to have important sociological results, such as the reduction of fertility. Moreover, in many countries of Africa and Asia, the increase in literacy is slower than the increase in population so the problem intensifies.

One of the most crucial problems of developing countries is that it is extremely difficult to force an economy to grow faster than its rate of population increase. When this rate is about 3 per cent per annum, a great amount of saving and of capital accumulation is necessary in order to maintain the existing structures, let alone invest for development. As Keyfitz states: "A country which saves ten per cent of its income and is growing at three per cent per annum will just about be able to prevent a fall in the average income of its citizens; it will hardly be able to change its industrial structure in the direction of economic development." With some notable exceptions, like Puerto Rico and Kuwait, developing countries have not experienced very much economic growth in the generation since the Second World War, and partial development has invariably meant mortality decline and increased population growth, with intensifying effects upon the distribution of population and the distribution of wealth.

The contrasts between the developed and developing worlds and the disparities of wealth within the developing world are now widely realized, and have engendered heightened aspirations and expectations which may be achieved in a number of different ways. One way is through the large-scale supply of capital assistance from the wealthy nations, but as yet few of the latter have accepted this need. Even if they did, it is doubtful whether all developing countries would be able to maintain their populations at present living standards in the land areas available to them. Many developing countries heavily dependent upon intensive agriculture, often based on irrigation (e.g. Egypt,

Philippines, China and Indonesia), experience great population pressure in considerable portions of their cultivable areas.

In circumstances like these, it would seem that fertility control can have a positive influence upon economic development. Coale has demonstrated in quantitative terms how a 50 per cent decline in fertility over 25 years can have great effects upon a population with a 3 per cent annual increase. In the short run it sharply reduces the dependency burden and permits much greater investment. As all developing countries have a high density of population in relation to capital, fertility control can therefore bring some relief. It cannot immediately reduce the size of the labour force or the population density—these are only possible in the long run. But population density in itself is not necessarily disadvantageous. Only in subsistence economies are resources in relation to labour an important element in productivity. The growth of commerce can greatly diminish the effect of limited resources. In Hong Kong, for example, 4 million people live at a density of about 10,000 per square mile, yet there has been a substantial increase in *per capita* incomes since the Second World War. In support of his advocacy of fertility control, Coale calculated that in the long run a population undergoing 50 per cent decline in fertility over 25 years would experience a reduction in the growth of the labour force and a massive increase in *per capita* incomes.

The issue of fertility control varies in importance from one country to another. It is a moral issue upon which fervent views have been propounded. Countries, religions, peoples react differently to the issue. Latin American and Muslim countries may not accept birth control as readily as some Asiatic countries, yet religion alone has not prevented fertility decline in a number of Catholic countries of Europe or in Argentina. The matter is a complex one. Some methods of family planning which are acceptable in one part of the world may not be acceptable elsewhere; induced abortion was a major check on Japanese fertility, and sterilization is common in India, but neither of these methods may be acceptable in parts of Africa. Acceptance of family planning will come quickly in some countries, but not in others, for it is no light matter to abandon traditional practices and ideals which have served for generations, ideals which are associated with family ties and economic power. Because children in traditional agricultural societies mean power. For many people of developing countries family planning is an alien ideal, a Western ideal, which should receive scant respect; some would like more people, not less. Indeed, in some communist countries Western family planning propaganda is regarded as a neo-Malthusian trick to keep the proletariat in check, to deny the underprivileged masses the one advantage they have over the West, namely numerical superiority. Although in countries like China and the USSR it is very difficult to reconcile Marxist demographic ideals with reality, and consequently there has been considerable heart-searching over population policies, it is doubtful whether family planning will be an immediate, universal solution. Certainly, it is gaining ground in some societies, through the efforts of a number of international and Western agencies, but even today there are national economic plans which say little or nothing about population, save total numbers and crude distribution. Many countries in the developing world have no precise notion of their population growth, and no declared policy toward it, except for the need for death control. In many African countries, for instance, it is still not accepted at government level that population size and growth are key factors in economic development, and that governments should be aware of the factors and adopt an attitude toward them. Of course, development is not merely a matter of population control; development plans necessitate the close inter-relationship of social, economic, political and demographic processes. Economic development itself can bring about a decline in fertility through rising levels of living, and educational advances can bring similar results. But in existing conditions of international economic aid, only immediate fertility control can bring short-term alleviation of urgent population problems, such as those in the populous countries of South and East Asia, where they are the dominant socio-economic fact.

Momentum of Past Population Distribution

The preponderance of Asians has been mentioned, and it is important to remember that the present distribution of world population reflects past patterns, in particular three overlapping phases:

(1) the pre-industrial concentration of population in Eurasia;

(2) nineteenth-century expansion of Europeans overseas to the so-called "empty continents"; and

(3) twentieth-century growth and urbanization of population within the established political framework.

If we accept Durand's estimates of pre-censal populations (see Table 1.5), we find that in about 1750, prior to the Industrial Revolution, approximately 63 per cent of the world's population of 791 million lived in Asia and 84 per cent in Eurasia. Here the main civilizations had evolved, based on sedentary peasant cultivation, especially in the lowland areas where water supplies enabled high-yield cereal crops to be grown intensively. Consequently, more than half of mankind lived in China and the Indian subcontinent alone, while outside of Eurasia the only continent with a sizeable population in the mid-eighteenth century was Africa (over 106 million), but its numbers had been severely checked by slavery and disease as well as by the great extent of inhospitable deserts and tropical rain forests.

During the late eighteenth and nineteenth centuries the growth of industry and commerce in Europe encouraged the growth of population and urbanization as well as the dispersal of people to other parts of the world, especially the temperate regions of North and South America, Africa, Australasia and Inner Asia. Here Europeans occupied huge areas at low densities of population, and mostly settled in cities or peripheral clusters in good contact with Europe. These patterns of population distribution have persisted despite the great reduction in large-scale migration streams during the twentieth century.

In the nineteenth century the abandonment of the slave trade, which was such a prominent and evil feature of the sixteenth, seventeenth and eighteenth centuries, was followed by the recruitment of contract labourers from South and East Asia for work on estates (and sometimes mines and railway projects) in other colonial countries of Africa and Asia and islands of the Caribbean, Pacific and Indian Ocean. Many Chinese and Indians became peasant planters, traders and government employees, and the result was a rash of plural or multiracial societies, where peoples of contrasting races, languages, religions and customs came to live side by side, sometimes mixing but more often retaining their cultural identity. On islands like Fiji and Mauritius, the divisions are drastic, but the problems are also severe in countries like Kenya where the Indian community is numerically small but economically important.

Most of the countries of "Europe overseas", decolonized or otherwise, now have policies which make large-scale migration impossible, especially from Asian countries for some of whom it might have acted as a safety valve. As a result, the nineteenth-century process of world population redistribution was partially arrested, and so there is still great unevenness in distribution as between continents. In spite of their rapid population growth, the Americas, Africa and Oceania contain less than one-quarter of mankind while Eurasia contains more than three-quarters. In present political conditions it seems extremely unlikely that those continents, which are relatively empty, will receive large numbers of either Europeans or Asians. The superimposition of a mesh of political boundaries over the earth's surface has had a stabilizing influence upon world population distribution. Boundaries have in many cases become barriers to human movement, so that populations and their relationships to resources have become nationalized. Consequently, it is perhaps fanciful to speak about a world population or a world food supply, when the political divisions of mankind impede the free movement of men and goods. Present population problems of countries must in general be solved within national boundaries; while emigration can relieve population pressure and bring welcome remittances for West Indian islands and small states like Lebanon and Lesotho and immigration can substantially modify the population sizes of Kuwait and Israel, international migration can have no major influence upon the large populous nations of Asia. Some Westerners have felt that the numerical superiority of one of these states, Mainland China, presents a threat to less densely peopled countries, and point to the example of former Japanese expansionism in the Far East. The future dangers of population politics are difficult to assess, but they should never be discounted, for historical examples of demographic expansion are numerous.

The Ecumene and the Negative Areas

Although the developing countries contain about 70 per cent of the world's population, they also include a large part of the uninhabited or sparsely inhabited areas, referred to by Dudley Stamp as the negative areas.

The majority of mankind live on only a small part of the earth's land area; over three-quarters live in South and East Asia, Europe and the north-eastern parts of the United States and adjacent areas of Canada. Despite considerable redistribution of population over the last two centuries, the inhabited area or ecumene has advanced little. At present not much more than one-tenth of the land surface is used as arable land (Fig. 1.9) and less than one-fifth as permanent meadows and pastures. In all, only three-tenths of the land area is permanently inhabited, the exact percentage depending on what population density one accepts as the threshold of habitation.

The seven-tenths of the earth's land surface which may be classified as negative environments for human occupation comprise particularly those with extreme climatic conditions: the polar and sub-polar lands, the high mountains, the hot and mid-latitude deserts and parts of the tropical wet-lands in Africa and Latin America. All except the first are widespread in the developing countries, which have more than their fair share of such physical environments.

These areas pose difficult climatic problems to human existence, but this does not mean that they are perpetually committed to emptiness. The adaptation of primitive peoples to deserts, polar lands and mountains has demonstrated that absolute environmental limitations to human survival are few. Among peoples like the bedouin, eskimos and Andean indians the environment has influenced physiology, psychology, vital rates and modes of life, but in more advanced cultures the direct influence of the physical environment is considerably diminished, especially in cities. Nevertheless, the problems for cultivation, livestock farming, route construction and so on differ substantially from those in temperate climates, and cannot be discounted. It may also be argued that the problems of settling these negative areas on a large scale are quite different from settling small groups, because not only are these areas often physiologically unattractive but they are also expensive to develop. Costs are an important deterrent unless there is a considerable incentive such as major resources of minerals, power or water.

The uses and values of environments change with time and with the

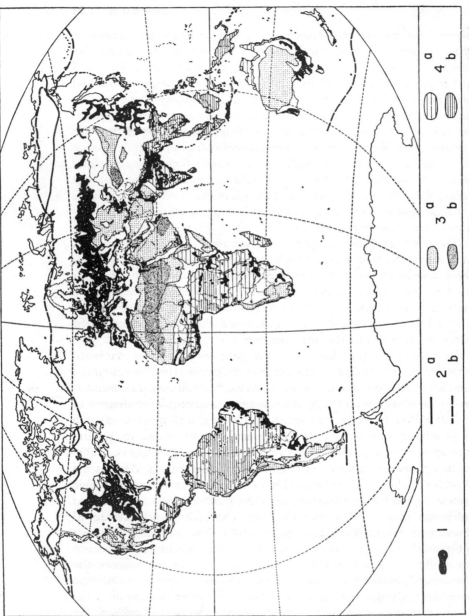

Fig. 1.9. Frontiers of agriculture (with kind permission of H. Boesch). (1) Extent of cultivated land; (2) cold frontier—(a) southern limit of permanently frozen soils, and (b) poleward limits of forest; (3) arid frontier—(a) arid lands and (b) extremely arid lands; (4) humid tropical frontier—(a) more or less periodically wet lands and (b) more or less permanently wet lands.

type of human occupancy. Indeed, the density of human occupation greatly reflects the modes of economic activity, which in turn are affected by cultural traditions. Moreover, different peoples view and utilize similar environments in diverse ways. Therefore environmental potential is not enough to ensure human occupancy; many social, economic and political factors come into play. In any case environmental potential cannot easily be quantified; nor, for that matter, can optimum population density. They depend such a lot on the advance of technology and human ideals, which vary considerably across the world. Habitability increases in time and space as technology advances and is disseminated to larger parts of the world.

Predictions as to the future habitability of the earth's surface contrast greatly. Some are cautious about the prospect of expanding the world's cultivated area, at present about 1400 million hectares, and suggest that the tendencies towards intensification of land use and concentration of population will continue. Some, like the Paddock brothers, and Borgstrom forecast imminent famine as a result of the "population explosion". Such views are particularly current in the United States and other Western countries, and among institutions like FAO, and are one of the *raisons d'être* of family planning movements.

In contrast, some authorities have much more faith in man's ingenuity and in the technological revolution, and feel that the cultivated area is capable of massive expansion. Clark, for example, has estimated on the basis of climate alone, that the earth contains the equivalent of 10,700 million hectares of standard land, that is land which is capable of producing one crop a year or substantial quantities of grazing throughout the year. He claims that this land could support 47,000 million people at current American dietary standards. In 1965, at the World Population Conference, Malin estimated the total cultivable area as high as 2670 million hectares merely by extension of the present cultivable area with existing methods, but with additional capital investment he suggested it could be 5490 million hectares, and with substantial capital investment and new methods of cultivation it could rise to 9330 million hectares. In terms of solar energy resources, the present cultivable area could feed 143,000 million people, while the potential cultivable area could feed 933,000 million, an astronomical figure in comparison with the present world total of 3500 million. He goes on to say that if the resources of the oceans were fully utilized and the nature of plants modified to use solar energy more fully, then potential food resources could "sustain several million million people".

In other words, there are widely differing answers to the question of the expansion of the ecumene and the number of people who can live on earth. They range from pessimistic gloom to optimistic visions. Some are worried about the next decade, others are thinking of the next century. At the moment there is no great trend for the settlement of the negative areas; in fact, some are even suffering from out-migration. The principal areas where the "pioneer fringe" might experience most advance are where there is adjacent high pressure of population, or in localities where there is wealth to be extracted. In parts of Africa and Latin America population pressure and capital availability are insufficient to induce agricultural expansion into difficult environments. Consequently, under present conditions of political division and uneven population distribution, it is not easy to envisage a major invasion of the world's open spaces, except for the intensive production of power, minerals, industrial products and crops. This would probably mean small concentrations of population at high densities. Yet, such is the speed of technological advance that it would be unwise to make predictions for the future.

Population and Resources

In developed countries land and resources are accounting for a smaller part of the increase in output, while scientific discovery, technology and education are playing greater roles, expanding the stocks of fuel, minerals and other resources. One of the challenges facing the world today is to expand discovery, technology and education in developing countries. Unfortunately the economic and political organization is frequently a deterrent to progress.

It has become customary to talk of population as a problem, in developed or developing countries, whether one considers it in social, economic or political terms. It is as if there are always too many or too few people, and never the elusive and undefinable optimum. This problemistic approach toward population has often emphasized that population–resource disequilibrium is a population problem which may be rectified by influencing the numbers of people, particularly through migration or fertility control (sometimes wrongly termed population control). But population represents only one side of the ratio, and it is within the capacity of man to expand the resources and to make great changes in their utilization through economic development, social change and political transformation. There can be no general panacea for all developing countries. Indeed, the topic has been the subject of far too much generalization, against which there is now a strong reaction. For example, it is now evident that no simple generalization is tenable about the effects of population growth on economic development in developing countries.

Discussion of population growth in developing countries, of rising numbers resulting from declining mortality and stable fertility, has tended to conceal the fact that at local level there are immense variations in population distribution, density and dynamics as well as in development, expectation and in the relationship of population to resources. While in eastern China, Bangladesh and in Egypt rural population pressures are exceptionally high, large expanses of the southern continents are capable of sustaining much larger populations than at present. Rice production of the Asiatic type, for example, is possible in many areas, but has not evolved because the sparse populations could be fed by extensive agricultural systems without great capital investment in land development and migration. High rates of population growth make it essential to find alternatives to traditional systems of agriculture. Extensive systems like pastoral nomadism, hunting and collecting, and shifting cultivation with long and medium periods of regeneration cannot sustain rapidly increasing densities of population. The first reaction to this situation is to utilize additional land, but if no such land is available then fallows are generally shortened and the land used more intensively. Unfortunately, intensification of land use may result in a decline in yields unless methods are used to arrest deterioration of land and livestock, such as fertilizers, terracing, irrigation and the growth of fodder crops. As Boserup has suggested, the change from extensive to intensive types of land use offers more potential for increased food production than the achievement of higher yields for a given crop or the substitution of one crop for another. She also emphasizes that the replacement of extensive patterns of land use necessitates not only an increase in capital per worker but also an increase in man-hours of labour per unit of output. Less land is needed per family, but greater investment and more work are required, as in the rice fields of Monsoon Asia. In many areas of developing countries the supply of labour is all too readily available; in some areas it is not. Less generally available is the supply of capital to bring into operation radical changes in existing systems of agriculture. In developing countries far too little is invested in agriculture: in land improvement, mechanization, irrigation works, marketing facilities, research establishments and training. Only by such investment will the flow of rural–urban migration be staunched and food supplies augmented.

The changes which are taking place in rural areas of the developing world—the introduction of new crops, dams, roads, schools, hospitals and houses—and the changes which are needed to accommodate future population growth, make assessments of the relationship between population and resources extremely hazardous. Population density has no meaning for such a relationship, and any formula for the population–resource ratio must always suffer from difficulties in calculating resources. It will be seen that most parts of developing countries have transitional rather than traditional economies; and in such circumstances population–resource ratios which regard areas and societies as closed and self-subsistent have little real relevance to the present-day facts of the developing world. Therefore we should not envisage an index like Allan's CDP (critical density of population) as a measure of universal utility; it was never intended as such, being devised only as conservationist's tool for discovering critical population pressures among subsistence economies. Similarly, concepts like environmental potential and population carrying capacity must be used with caution. They should not be considered in abstract, without reference to investment possibilities, levels of mechanization, types of crops, market prices, cultures and desires of the local population, remittances from migration, etc. In other words, the environment should not be considered without reference to man and his advancing techniques.

Internal Disequilibrium

It has been emphasized that developing countries experience a disharmony or disequilibrium between economic growth and population growth, but disequilibrium also manifests itself in many other ways within developing countries, with great influences upon population geography. In essence, developing countries tend to have greater heterogeneity of human geography than is normally found in developed countries. This heterogeneity results from

(a) the persistence of traditional contrasts;
(b) the introduction of a modern sector; and
(c) the widespread effects of the modern sector upon traditional areas, inducing transition.

Traditional contrasts in developing countries have survived largely through the persistence of closed subsistence economies and technical or cultural limitations upon human movement. They are evidenced especially by the enormous ethnic diversity of the developing world. Whereas most of the developed world is European in culture and origin, the developing world exhibits an almost unbelievable array of ethnic groups, languages and cultural complexes. This is particularly true for those parts of the developing world which have known long periods of human habitat without the emergence of great civilizations. Tropical Africa and the Pacific Islands may be cited as examples demonstrating the complexity of traditional groups, posing very difficult puzzles for ethnologists and anthropologists to unravel. And yet even in countries like India and Iran, whose civilizations are among the oldest in the world, there survive a multiplicity of ethnic, linguistic and religious groups. The *UN Demographic Yearbook* for 1956 lists 283 languages in India alone, including nineteen with more than one million speakers and twelve with more than 10 million speakers.

Contrasts in traditional economies have undoubtedly contributed to ethnic complexity. The distributions of nomadic pastoralism and sedentary cultivation, for example, have greatly influenced the patterns of population in Asia and Africa. When pastoralists held sway over great expanses of these continents, cultivators were often confined to oases, irrigated valleys and mountain fastnesses. Such localities offered varied environmental conditions for economic utilization, and engendered contrasting cultures, with widely different social structures, systems of land-ownership, technical equipment and settlement forms. Mortality and fertility varied from one group to another, according to such factors as climatic conditions, economic prosperity, salubrity, political stability and social customs, but only rarely were mortality and fertility anything but high.

The pre-colonial world therefore exhibited great human variety, although many of its patterns and movements are so shrouded in historical mystery and so affected by later events that they are difficult to decipher. Slavery and colonial conquests had extremely disruptive effects, and missionary activity brought great social changes. Yet despite these events, many traditional contrasts have persisted in the human geography, which inspired the concept of "mode of life" dear to earlier French human geographers. It is the study of the activities of a group, on the assumption that the group finds its cohesion and coherence in its production. The productive activity polarized and organized the group, which tended to be studied in isolation in a specific environment. Harmony, balance and order were found in traditional societies, and classifications of modes of life were produced which sometimes bore little resemblance to reality. For example, many traditional societies were either categorized as sedentary or nomadic, whereas in fact there exists a wide range of societies which are partly sedentary and partly nomadic, partly cultivators and partly pastoralists. Nowadays, they are generally loosely termed semi-nomadic, and they are symptomatic of great changes in the world of pastoral nomadism. The "mode of life" concept is suitable to balanced situations in isolated regions, but such situations are increasingly rare. One of the most prominent characteristics of developing countries is the breakdown of isolation and balance.

The geography of developing countries, especially the population geography, is one of increasing disequilibrium. Largely responsible for this internal disequilibrium was the introduction of a modern sector into the economy, generally localized geographically in the major towns, the mining centres and the zones of commercial agriculture. Invariably it incorporates only a small porportion of the total population, providing them with regular employment and stable incomes. They include the salaried officials, professional classes, employers, technical staff, wage-earners, traders and artisans, of whom a considerable proportion may be aliens, sometimes so numerous as to provoke the problems of a plural society. Chinese traders in Malaya, Indian traders in East Africa, Lebanese traders in West Africa exemplify alien prominence in commerce, but even more widespread are Europeans, especially in colonial territories and in countries which have recently gained independence. The modern economic sector is usually dependent upon foreign initiative and markets, whose purchases and prices fluctuate markedly. Fluctuations are particularly detrimental to countries such as Sudan, Senegal, Egypt and Brazil, which are heavily reliant upon the export of one or two agricultural products. Countries relying on the large-scale export of minerals like Venezuela, Chile, Liberia, Saudi-Arabia and Libya, are not exempt from the dangers of monoproduction but are usually in a slightly more fortunate position, as there is normally no chronic overproduction of mineral products. On the other hand, the economies of such countries may be dominated or excessively influenced by foreign companies, and may suffer from inflation and speculation to the disadvantage of local productive activity. Moreover, mineral resources are not renewable, and production may cease abruptly before the mines are exhausted owing to competition from other states possessing more profitable deposits. The modern sector may therefore provoke considerable economic instability, at both national and regional levels. The developing world has many examples of moribund mines and ports, which have known brief phases of intense activity.

Whether agricultural or mining products are concerned, the main modern commercial production is for export, and consequently the economies are externally orientated. Regions of modern agricultural development are especially located near the coast, where export is easy. Moreover, unless mineral deposits are of exceptional size and quality, they are only developed when good access to the sea is available. Plenty of examples exist in Latin America, Africa and Asia of remote and undeveloped mineral deposits, which are at the moment too costly to exploit.

Export-orientated colonial-type economies have particularly encouraged the growth of ports, which dominate the distribution of urban centres in much of Latin America and Africa, where port capitals abound, often in better contact with developed countries than with each other. These coastal cities concentrate many of the industries which occur in these countries, as well as a high proportion of the foreigners and those employed in the service sector. In much of Asia urban civilization is older, and precedes the superimposition of colonial-type economies. Consequently, urbanism in Asia is usually more scattered and not so peripheral as in Latin America or Africa.

Mines, regions of intense commercial agriculture and cities constitute "islands" of modern economic activity, which sometimes cover only a small proportion of the total area of a developing country. Their presence provokes enormous disparities in regional development, which aggravate problems of political integration in large newly emergent countries, such as Nigeria and Sudan. Another example is the disastrous effect of the development of the Mediterranean zone in the Maghreb upon the traditional northward movement of nomads and their flocks during the summer drought. Regional disparities of this type may be positive checks to social and economic development. Regional disparities are not merely economic; these "islands" localize most of the hospitals, clinics and schools, and therefore enjoy much lower mortality and sometimes slightly lower fertility than other regions. As a result, they experience more rapid natural increase. They are also the poles of labour migration, the magnets for migrants from far and wide, and this process is accentuated by the fact that in many developing countries, these are the only areas served by railways, airports and surfaced roads, all of which canalize migration streams. Source areas for migrants are not evenly spread. The environs of "islands" of the modern sector are generally most affected, often adversely, but sizeable migration streams may come from distant areas suffering from high population pressure upon resources. Most migrants are moving for economic motives, although the "push" and "pull" factors at origin and destination and the intervening obstacles to migration may vary greatly. Among the important push factors are rural poverty, lack of land, natural increase of population, improved communications and the spread of information about the towns. But so many economic, social and psychological factors intermingle that it is impossible to isolate them quantitatively. Whatever their reasons, migrations generally cause increasing concentration of population, for the colonization of sparsely peopled lands is now much less significant than the attraction of existing "islands" of modern activity.

Migrations show abundant evidence of disequilibrium in developing countries. Many are only temporary, and most are sex-selective. Young men form the majority of migrants in the developing world, with the exception of parts of Latin America and South-west Asia. The result is wide discrepancies in age and sex composition between source areas and destinations of migrants, causing considerable social and economic difficulties. Labour migrations sometimes have grave effects upon agriculture, and encourage social ills in cities, such as prostitution, alcoholism and drug addiction.

We should not think of the geography of developing countries in terms of local modernity and widespread tradition, for the effects of the "islands" of modern economic activity are far-reaching. Their influence has extended over large areas of the developing world, for which the term "transitional" is more appropriate than "traditional". This transitional sector includes the majority of the population, but it represents only a small proportion of the national revenue. No longer reliant on subsistence agriculture, its development is blocked by the development of the modern sector. Furthermore, it is not fully adjusted to the needs and limited growth of the modern sector, which is too often restricted by imports of foreign consumer goods and the lack of investment in industry and agriculture.

Before leaving the topic of internal disequilibrium, it is important to note that this feature is not the sole prerogative of developing countries. It is also found in developed countries, where it may be heightened by racial contrasts, as in South Africa. The above arguments have merely been presented with a view to showing how developing countries suffer from special problems of internal unbalance.

Urbanization

Rapid urbanization epitomizes the disequilibrium of developing countries perhaps better than any other aspect of their population geography. Of course, it is not confined to developing countries, but the character of their urbanization differs in general from that of developed countries, as it owes little to industrial development.

Between 1800 and 1960 the number of people in the world living in localities of 20,000 inhabitants or more rose from about 22 million to

TABLE 1.7. GROWTH OF WORLD URBAN POPULATION, 1800–1960

	1800	1850	1900	1950	1960
TOTAL WORLD POPULATION (millions)	906	1171	1608	2400	2962
Localities of 20,000+: *World population*	22	50	148	502	803
Percentage	2.4	4.3	9.2	20.9	27.1
Localities of 100,000+: *World population*	16	28	89	314	590
Percentage	1.7	2.3	5.5	13.1	19.9
Asian population	10	12	19	106	204
Percentage	1.6	1.7	2.1	7.5	12.3
African population	0.3	0.3	1	10	20
Percentage	0.3	0.2	1.1	5.2	8.1
American population	0.1	2	19	75	170
Percentage	0.4	3.0	12.8	22.6	42.0
European population[a]	5	13	48	118	189
Percentage	2.9	4.9	11.9	19.9	29.6
Oceanic population	—	—	1	5	7
Percentage	—	—	21.7	39.2	43.3

[a] Including the USSR.
SOURCE: G. Breese, *Urbanization in Newly Developing Countries*, Englewood Cliffs, New Jersey, 1966, pp. 19 and 22.

TABLE 1.8. ESTIMATED INCREASE IN WORLD URBAN POPULATION,
1950–60, BY REGIONS

	% In localities of 20,000 +		
	1950	1960	% Increase
WORLD TOTAL	21	24–25[a]	12–17[a]
Less developed regions:	14	17–18[a]	17–28[a]
Africa	10	13	37
North Africa	21	26	23
Sub-Saharan Africa	6	9	50
Asia	14	16–18[a]	11–26[a]
Excluding China	17	19	15
China	10	10–15[a]	0–50[a]
Latin America	25	32	28
Argentine, Chile, Uruguay	47	56	19
Remainder	21	28	33
More developed regions:	37	41	10
North America	43	46	6
Europe	37	40	8
USSR	31	36	17
Oceania	46	53	15

[a] Range of estimated values corresponding to alternative estimates for Mainland China.

SOURCE: G. Breese, *Urbanization in Newly Developing Countries*, Englewood Cliffs, New Jersey, 1966, p. 33.

803 million, from 2.4 per cent of the total population to 27.1 per cent. If we accept the estimates in Table 1.7, we shall see that in 1960 nearly three-quarters of the urban population (defined here as the population living in localities of 20,000 inhabitants or more) lived in large cities with 100,000 inhabitants or more, and that since 1800 such cities have always contained more than one-half of the world's urban population. In 1800 Asia accounted for nearly two-thirds of the world's urban population and a similar proportion of the world's population living in large cities, but during the nineteenth century this proportion declined as urbanization progressed in Europe, North America and Oceania. During the twentieth century the developing countries have witnessed massive urbanization. Between 1900 and 1960 the large city population

of Asia rose from 19 million (2.1 per cent) to 204 million (12.3 per cent), and that of Africa from 1 million (1.1 per cent) to 20 million (8.1 per cent). Urbanization is undoubtedly gathering momentum in developing countries, and during the 1950s proceeded more rapidly than in developed countries (Table 1.8). Projections of the world urban population by Hoyt (Table 1.9), Davis and others assume a great

TABLE 1.9. PROJECTED INCREASE IN WORLD URBAN POPULATION 1960–2000, BY REGIONS

	Population (in millions) in localities with 20,000+		% In localities with 20,000+	
	1960	2000	1960	2000
Asia	355	1934	21	50
Africa	38	165	15	32
Latin America	92	355	45	60
North America	166	281	84	90
Europe	341	682	54	70
Oceania	10	19	63	65
WORLD	1002	3416	34	54

SOURCE: H. Hoyt, *World Urbanization*, Washington, 1962, p. 48–9.

growth of towns in the developing world, so that by AD 2000 the proportion of the population living in towns, though probably lower than in the developed world, should be as high as in the developed world today

Naturally, these generalizations by continent mask great variations between countries (Fig. 1.10). Whereas 2.5 per cent of the population of Uganda live in localities of 20,000 and over, the percentage is 45 in South Africa and 38 in Egypt. Similarly in Asia, only 3 per cent of the population of Nepal are town-dwellers, but 78 per cent of Israel's population were classed as urban in 1961. These variations will certainly persist for some time, but accelerating urbanization is fast becoming a general fact of developing countries. It results from a combination of (a) rapid natural increase, caused by declining mor-

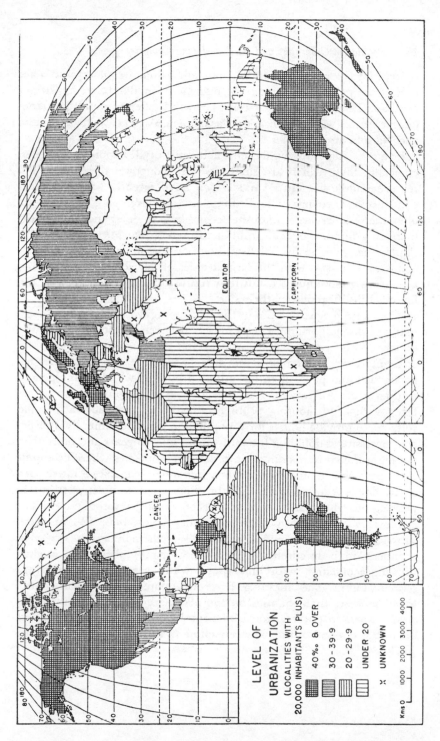

FIG. 1.10. Level of urbanization (localities with 20,000 inhabitants or more). Although most developing countries are still feebly urbanized, the level of urbanization is rising rapidly.

tality, and (b) powerful rural–urban migration. In many cities over half of the population were born elsewhere; in Bombay over 70 per cent, and Douala over 80 per cent. Growth is often so rapid that cities double in size within a decade; Casablanca, Algiers, Delhi, Kinshasa and Nairobi are examples.

Primate cities are highly characteristic of developing countries, especially those which are small (where economies of scale do not require middle-size cities) and which have recently achieved independence from colonial rule. Primate cities of developing countries are often many times larger than the second largest cities, and some of the increasing number of multi-millionaire cities, like Buenos Aires, São Paulo, Shanghai, Seoul, Calcutta, Bombay, Casablanca and Cairo, are comparable in size with the largest cities of developed countries and are growing more quickly, but they frequently lack the economic and financial justifications for their size.

The morphologies of cities in the developing world are also symptomatic of disequilibrium. The contrasts between the spaciousness and luxury of modern residential suburbs and the congestion and squalor of shanty-towns are tangible reminders of the great discrepancies between rich and poor, often accentuated by the lack of an indigenous trading class. All rapidly growing cities of developing countries are faced with acute housing problems. As Mme. Beaujeu-Garnier has stated: "to provide houses for a population growing annually at 5 per cent necessitates doubling the built-up area in 18 years and more than doubling the corresponding equipment. In countries where economic progress is difficult and consequently investment capacity limited, such a rhythm is insupportable. All the more so because investment in housing though socially beneficial is economically unproductive." The result is a mammoth growth of shanty-towns, *bidonvilles*, *barracas*, *barriadas*, *favellas*, etc. In many large cities their inhabitants may be numbered in the hundreds of thousands. Generally, they are located on the edges of cities, with inadequate water supplies and sewerage services, but in some cities (e.g. Freetown) slums are found in central locations more than shanties on the periphery. But all shanty-towns bear witness to poverty, to insufficient public investment, and above all to the disequilibrium between city and country in the developing world.

The populations of cities in developing countries are also frequently unbalanced in age and sex composition. Generally, they are youthful; three-quarters of the population of Mexico City, for example, are under 30 years of age, and in many African cities the proportion is four-fifths. The main reasons are (a) the influx of young migrants, (b) the persistence of rural high fertility habits in cities, despite the practice of family limitation by certain social groups, and (c) the recent abrupt decline in urban mortality to low levels, owing to improved sanitation and increased medical facilities. In Asia and Africa the preponderance of male migrants has meant male surpluses in cities, an aspect of disequilibrium which is much more rare in Latin America, where many more women migrate to the cities.

Unemployment and Underemployment

With swelling populations and stunted industrial growth, many cities of developing countries are consumption centres rather than production centres, for although they have experienced a marked expansion of the tertiary sector they suffer from inadequate growth of manufacturing industries, in spite of the fact that industries have been given priority over agriculture in the investment policies of many newly emergent countries. The result is unemployment and underemployment, both of which are common features of large cities in developing countries. Neither are easy to measure in such environments, but both are serious social maladies whose prevention and cure are urgently required.

The unemployed in some cities, as in Egypt, comprise a third of the active population, especially newcomers and youngsters at school-leaving age. Chronic lack of employment affects particularly those looking for their first job in a city, and failure to obtain jobs leads to crime and political agitation, but it also means that many survive by petty employment or casual labour or by scrabbling a living among the refuse heaps and junk yards. The expansion of the tertiary sector should not confuse. It does not merely mean the increase in the number of administrators, soldiers, schoolteachers, professional men, shopkeepers and traders; it also implies the profusion of domestic servants, street-sellers, taxi-drivers, boot-blacks, porters, night-watchmen and gardeners. Frequently there are three for the work of one, and yet the three are supporting large families, relatives and friends on pitifully low wages. Poverty and malnutrition are sores of the cities, the visible signs of economic inadequacies and maldistribution of population.

The great difficulty is that rural–urban migration has preceded or exceeded industrialization. However, unemployment and under-employment also exist in various forms in agricultural areas: seasonal unemployment, periodic unemployment, underemployment through excessive labour supply or lack of mechanization. Many seasonal migrations start through seasonal unemployment in agriculture and finish by becoming permanent migrations, which may have an adverse effect upon rural areas. They may cause a decline in agricultural pro-duction, a rise in the prices of foodstuffs and an inflationary spiral which is most acute in the cities, affecting particularly the migrants. Un-employment and underemployment in both cities and rural areas should therefore attract the attention of all population geographers, as they are at the heart of the population problems of developing countries.

Conclusions

This introduction has merely highlighted some of the salient changes which have taken place in the population geography of the developing world during the last few decades. Geographers must no longer be content to examine the patterns of population distribution of developing countries and their relationship to the physical environment: we must study also the patterns of population dynamics (migrations, fertility, mortality, natural increase) as well as their causes and consequences, for the dynamics are radically altering the distributions. It is true that the present population distribution map of the developing world demonstrates the momentum of past distributions. The high population densities in Monsoon Asia, for instance, can only be explained with reference to the past; they represent a distributional inertia. Yet there are demographic processes in progress at present which will undoubtedly greatly modify the population map, and these processes vary less than the populations and environments which are being affected. We must therefore look at the various world regions—in particular Latin America, Africa, and the component parts of the populous continent of Asia—where there are contrasting physical and social environments, contrasting population densities and distributions and contrasting economic activities, but high rates of population growth and increasing mobility are common to them all. Inevitably, the approach will vary according to the salient features of each region, and in the case of politically fragmented continents like Africa it will be impossible to say much about individual countries. Nevertheless, in future years political units are going to exert a greater influence upon population dynamics, through policies and attitudes toward the control of fertility, mortality and migrations. Even the size of a state affects these processes. Consequently, it is also extremely important to examine the population geographies of separate countries and their component regions, but unfortunately this is a task which cannot be tackled here owing to limitations of space.

Population distribution, dynamics and disequilibrium are the key topics of this volume. On the whole, it is more difficult to study instability than stability, especially in countries where data are often limited and inaccurate, but any other orientation would be unrealistic.

Select Bibliography

ACKERMAN, E. A., Population, natural resources and technology, *Ann. Am. Acad. Polit. Soc. Sci.* **369,** 84 (1967).

AGARWALA, A. N. and SINGH, S. P., *The Economics of Under-development,* New York, 1963.

ALLAN, W., *The African Husbandman,* Edinburgh, 1965.

BEAUJEU-GARNIER, J., *Geography of Population,* London, 1966.

BERELSON, B. and others, *Family Planning and Population Programs,* Chicago, 1966.

BOGUE, D. J., *Principles of Demography,* New York, 1969.

BORGSTROM, G., *The Hungry Planet,* New York, 1967.

BORGSTROM, G., *Too Many,* London, 1969.

BOSERUP, E., *The Conditions of Agricultural Growth: the Economics of Agrarian Change under Population Pressure,* London, 1965.

BOURGEOIS-PICHAT, J., Population growth and economic development, *International Conciliation,* 556 (1966).

BREESE, G., *Urbanization in Newly Developing Countries,* New Jersey, 1966.

BREESE, G., *The City in Newly Developing Countries,* New Jersey, 1969.

BROWN, L. R., The world outlook for conventional agriculture, *Science* **158,** 604 (1967).

CLARK, C., *Population Growth and Land Use,* London, 1967.

CLARKE, J. I., *Population Geography,* Oxford, 1965.

CLARKE, J. I., *Population and food resources: a critique,* IBG Special Publication No. 1, Sir Dudley Stamp Memorial Volume, 53 (1968).

COALE, A. J. and HOOVER, E. M., *Population Growth and Economic Development in Low Income Countries,* Princeton, 1958.

DAVIS, K., Population policy: will current programs succeed? *Science* **158,** 730 (1967).

DAVIS, K., *World Urbanization 1950–1970,* University of California, 2 vols., 1969.

50   *Population Geography and the Developing Countries*

DURAND, J. D., The modern expansion of world population, *Proc. Am. Phil. Soc.* **111**, 136 (1967).

FREEDMAN, R. (Ed.), *Population: The Vital Revolution*, New York, 1964.

FRYER, D. W., World income and types of economies, *Econ. Geog.* **34**, 283 (1958).

FRYER, D. W., *World Economic Development*, New York, 1965.

GALBRAITH, J. K., *Economic Development in Perspective*, London, 1963.

GEORGE, P., *Questions de Géographie de la Population*, Paris, 1959.

GEORGE, P., *Géographie de la Population*, Paris, 1965.

GINSBERG, N. S. (Ed.), *Essays on Geography and Economic Development*, Chicago, 1960.

GINSBERG, N. S., *Atlas of Economic Development*, Chicago, 1961.

HAUSER, P. M. (Ed.), *The Population Dilemma*, New Jersey, 1963.

HODDER, B. W., *Economic Development in the Tropics*, London, 1968.

HOROWITZ, I. L., *Three Worlds of Development: The Theory and Practice of International Stratification*, Oxford, 1966.

HOYT, H., *World Urbanization*, Washington, 1962.

JAFFE, A. J., Population trends and controls in underdeveloped countries, *Law Contemp. Prob.* **25**, 508 (1960).

KUZNETS, S., *Modern Economic Growth: Rate, Structure and Spread*, New Haven, 1966.

KUZNETS, S., Population and economic growth, *Proc. Am. Phil. Soc.* **111**, 170 (1967).

LACOSTE, Y., *Géographie du Sous-Développement*, Paris, 1965.

MOUNTJOY, A. B., *Industrialization and Underdeveloped Countries*, London, 1963.

MOUNTJOY, A. B., Million cities: urbanization and developing countries, *Geography* **53**, 365 (1968).

MYINT, H., *The Economics of the Developing Countries*, London, 1964.

MYRDAL, G., *Economic Theory and Underdeveloped Regions*, London, 1957.

OHLIN, G., *Population Growth and Economic Development*, Paris, 1967.

PADDOCK, W. and P., *Famine 1975*, London, 1967.

ROSTOW, W. W., *The Stages of Economic Growth*, Cambridge, 1960.

RUSSETT, B. M. *et al.*, *World Handbook of Political and Social Indicators*, New Haven, 1967.

SAUVY, A., *Fertility and Survival*, London, 1961.

SCHEIDL, L. G., Some problems of developing countries, *Tijdschrift voor Economische en Sociale Geografie* **55**, 250 (1964).

SPENGLER, J. J., The economist and the population question, *Am. Econ. Rev.* **56**, 1 (1966).

STAMP, L. D., *Our Developing World*, London, 1960.

THOMPSON, W. S. and LEWIS, D. T., *Population Problems*, New York, 1965.

TROLL, C., Plural societies of developing countries: aspects of social geography, in *20th International Geographical Congress, Congress Proceedings*, 9 (1967).

UN, *World Population Prospects, as assessed in 1963*, New York, 1966.

UN, *World Population Conference, 1965*, New York, 4 vols., 1965-8.

ZELINSKY, W., *A Prologue to Population Geography*, New Jersey, 1965.

ZELINSKY, W., The geographer and his crowding world: cautionary notes toward the study of population pressure in the "developing lands", *Rev. Geograf.* **65**, 7 (1966).

2

LATIN AMERICA

Population Size

The part of the Americas found south of the United States, unsuitably but universally called Latin America, has not a large population. Its principal interest to students of population is that it has a faster rate of population growth than any other major region in the world. In 1972, the United Nations estimate of the total population of Latin America was 300 million, equivalent to only 35 per cent of the population of Mainland China, one-half of that of India, and only a little more than that of the USSR. With 15.2 per cent of the total land area of the earth, Latin America contained only 7.9 per cent of the total population. However, this latter proportion is growing quickly owing to an annual increase of 2.8 per cent or about 8.4 million—almost equal to the annual growth of the African continent, although Africa has a larger total population. The rate of growth has accelerated so rapidly in the twentieth century that whereas the population total of 1900 took 40 years to double, that of 1972 will probably double in 25 years. And if present rates of increase continue Latin America will contain 435 millions by 1985, and according to the "medium growth" hypothesis, by the year 2000 it will have more people than Europe and the Soviet Union, and 9.4 per cent of the projected world population.

These rounded figures should not lull the reader into a false sense of statistical security, for records of population in Latin America are recent. Despite a variety of attempts to determine population size and growth in different parts of Latin America in colonial times, it was only in the closing decades of the last century that records were sufficiently accurate in the main countries to give a reasonable indication of population size in the region. But patchy population distribution, ethnic contrasts and illiteracy resulted in under-enumerations and underestimates. It is probable that Humboldt's estimates of the population in the early nineteenth century are also low, and in recent years there has been a tendency to elevate earlier estimates of colonial Latin America. Durand, for example, has made new estimates of Latin American population growth since 1750, which exceed earlier figures by Carr-Saunders and Willcox (Table 2.1).

TABLE 2.1. ESTIMATED POPULATION GROWTH IN LATIN AMERICA, 1650–1965 (*numbers in millions*)

	Carr-Saunders	Durand	UN
1650	12		
1750	11	16	
1800	19	24	
1850	33	38	
1900	63	74	
1920			91
1930			108
1940			130
1950			163
1960			213
1970			283

SOURCE: A. M. Carr-Saunders, *World Population*, Oxford, 1936, p. 42, J. D. Durand, The modern expansion of world population, *Proc. Am. Phil. Soc.*, **111**, 1967, 137, and UN *Demographic Yearbooks*.

Whatever the estimates, there is no doubt that this region of the world has never been a large cradle of humanity, and its present position as leader of the demographic growth table has only recently been achieved. Indeed, the rapidity of growth has only recently been realized, for prior to the 1950 round of censuses, largely sponsored by the Pan American Union, demographic data for Latin America were unreliable, unavailable or sporadic. Now the situation is greatly improved, and Latin America has better data than most of Africa and Asia. As Miro states: "By early 1963, 14 Latin American countries, including the three most populated of the region and comprising around 82 per cent of the estimated population of the 20 republics, had taken a census of population".

Ethnic Diversity

Before examining the population growth of Latin America, its rapidity, regional variations and economic implications, we must first look at its great ethnic diversity and the way that it has evolved, for Latin America is one of the main melting-pots of humanity. In particular, there are three main ethnic elements of diverse and widely separate origins, namely the American Indian, European and Negro populations who have undergone a great deal of mixing (Fig. 2.1). Broadly speaking, the autochthonous Indian population is found in southern Mexico, the highlands of central America, the Andean countries, Chile, Paraguay and the remote interior of Amazonia. Whites of European origin are located in rural areas of southern Brazil, Uruguay, Argentina, Cuba and Costa Rica as well as in most cities of Latin America. Negroes are preponderant in north-east Brazil, interior Haiti and in a number of West Indian islands. Elsewhere, great intermixture of peoples causes difficulties for ethnic classifications. Data of the proportions of national populations of "pure Indian stock" and of "Indian blood" must therefore be regarded with suspicion. It is true that many censuses ask questions concerning race, but often the decision is left to the individual, and this usually means exaggerated numbers of whites. This is because of the persistence in many Latin American countries of social differentiation according to races, with whites as the landowners and governing class, Negroes and Indians as peasants, artisans, and labourers, and *mestizoes* either in the latter class or as professional and business elements. Such social stratification is far from universal, it is not rigid and the strata have no clear-cut horizons; it arises more from cultural differences than from colour, and an Indian may be able to change his status merely by adopting western dress and habits.

The pre-colonial indigenous Indian populations were heterogeneous and scattered, being mainly located in Middle America, the Caribbean,

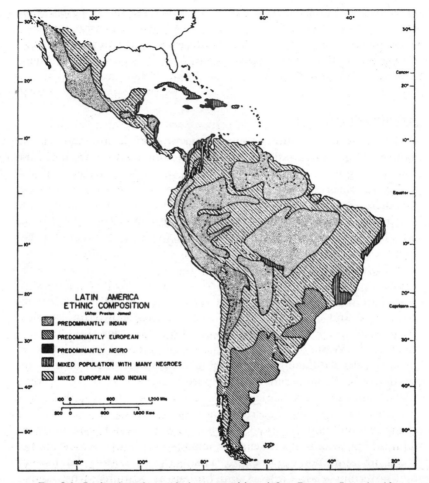

Fɪɢ. 2.1. Latin America: ethnic composition (after Preston James). Although very much simplified, this map portrays the general pattern of ethnic groups.

the northern and central Andes and the Amazon Basin. The temperate southern part of South America and the vast Brazilian plateau were virtually uninhabited. Estimates of the total Indian population prior to the arrival of Europeans have ranged from 4 to 100 million, and at present there is much investigation into the demographic history of the region. One major difficulty is that the early impact of the Europeans, from 1492 onwards, was disastrous, especially in the Caribbean, where the Antillean aboriginal Indian population numbering at least 400,000 was almost completely annihilated by killing or by disease. The more advanced Indian population of mainland Middle America, probably numbering over 11 million, was also drastically reduced, and only began to recover as a hybridized population from the mid-sixteenth century. Fortunately, the early impact of Europeans upon the size of the Indian populations of South America was far less severe, and there Indian populations of greater racial homogeneity have survived, although on the whole the Indians have made few efforts to maintain their racial purity.

The round of censuses held in Latin America during the 1950s gave rise to an estimate of about 16 million people of pure Indian stock, or one in thirteen of the total population. The proportions of pure Indian stock and of Indian blood varied greatly, with main concentrations in Guatemala, Honduras, El Salvador, Mexico and the Andean countries of Bolivia, Ecuador and Peru. High proportions of Indian blood, but not of pure Indian stock, can also be found in Panama, Nicaragua, Costa Rica and Paraguay. It is certain that the Indian population, which now suffers from low economic status in Latin America and is still primarily rural, is going to form a larger proportion of the total population.

The early immigration of Europeans in the sixteenth and seventeenth centuries was not on a large scale. During the sixteenth century only 60,000–70,000 arrived, and peasant colonization was confined to a few localities, including the lowlands of Colombia and central Chile. Everywhere fusion with the Indian population was strong, so that by the end of the eighteenth century the mixed population probably exceeded the white population by ten to one. The European immigrants came mainly from the populous parts of the Iberian peninsula, and spread out in Latin America from a few primary areas of settlement. Spaniards were attracted by areas with relatively concentrated Indian settlement; they went to the Caribbean, central Chile (which has a Mediterranean type of climate), the lowlands of northern Colombia and to the coastal zone of Peru, but established no frontier of settlement of the North American type. On the other hand, the Portuguese established themselves in the eastern part of South America, especially the north-east along the Pará River and in south-eastern Brazil around São Paulo, from which they moved progressively south and west. The forested lowlands of the Amazon basin and Middle America, the Venezuelan llanos and the Argentinian pampa were all neglected by early European colonists (Fig. 2.2).

During the nineteenth century, the volume of migration from Europe to Latin America rose considerably. Indeed, during the period 1801–1950 the net immigration of Europeans was about 12 million, and, in addition there was substantial seasonal and periodic migration, especially to Argentina. The arable and grazing lands and the growing cities of temperate South America—Argentina, Uruguay, southern and central Chile—attracted the majority of these later migrants, and these countries experienced a distinctive and moving frontier of colonization, although as Preston James has described, in all except south Brazil the frontier was "hollow" owing to abandonment of over-utilized land. After the Second World War Venezuela also attracted numerous European immigrants with the advent of oil exploitation there. Only in these countries of Latin America has European immigration played a vital role in population growth, but even here it is unlikely that more than one-tenth of the increase during any decade resulted from the immigration of Europeans or Asians. In the period 1821–1945 the total number of white immigrants into Argentina was only 6.7 million and the number entering Brazil was 4.7 million. In other words, Latin America never received a flow of European immigrants comparable with that entering North America during the nineteenth and early twentieth centuries. Climatic difficulties in tropical areas, the prevalence of disease and modest levels of living tended to deter major migration streams and to encourage counter-streams.

Although Spanish and Portuguese cultures (in which Catholicism plays an important role) prevail over much of Latin America, European immigrants into Argentina and Brazil, the main white immigrant countries, have also numbered many Germans, Italians and East Europeans. Italians, for example, have migrated in considerable numbers to Brazil during this century, especially after the imposition of immigration quotas by the United States in the early 1920s. However,

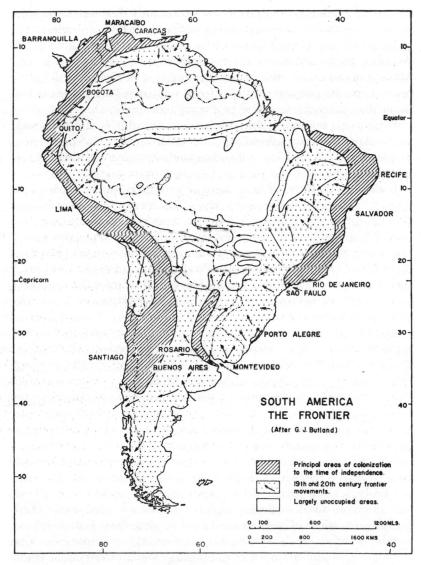

FIG. 2.2. South America: the frontier (after G. J. Butland). The pattern of European occupation has greatly influenced economic development and population distribution.

Italian emigration to South America has recently diminished since the social and economic developments resulting from Italian participation in the Common Market. Spaniards are also migrating less to South America, partly because of the availability of work in the Common Market countries but also because emigration is discouraged by the present Spanish government. In order to sustain its Portuguese culture, Brazil has encouraged a flow of Portuguese immigrants, but whites constitute only one-half of the population of Brazil in contrast to nearly the total population of Argentina. Other countries with high proportions of whites are Puerto Rico and Cuba, both of which are about three-quarters white.

It should also be noted that there is a cultural distinction between foreign-born whites and creoles,* who are in theory Europeans born in Latin America. Obviously they differ in the degree of cultural assimilation. Moreover, nearly every European nation is represented and, sometimes groups from European countries retain cultural features of their homeland. For example, the Welsh community of the Chubut valley in central Patagonia, established there in the mid-nineteenth century, retains its Protestant religion, "eisteddfod" and even, to some extent, the Welsh language.

During the colonial period Negroes were taken to Latin America as slave labour for the development of plantation agriculture. The first slaves reached the Caribbean, the main slave market, in the early sixteenth century, and Brazil did not receive its first consignment until 1535. Estimates of the number of slaves taken to Latin America vary widely, the maximum being of the order of 20 million. By the beginning of the nineteenth century, however, there were probably no more than 3 million, their numbers being limited by low fertility (caused by adverse sex-ratios), high mortality and much fusion. Since the abolition of slavery the number of Negroes in Latin America has increased markedly, and by the mid-1950s they probably numbered 13 million, half of whom lived in Brazil, particularly in the north-east. Much higher proportions of Negroes are found in some West Indian islands, notably Haiti, where they account for over 95 per cent of the total population, in contrast to the neighbouring Dominican Republic whose population is only about 15 per cent Negro, 70 per cent mulatto and

* The term "creole" has a variety of connotations in different parts of the world.

15 per cent of European origin. Other West Indian islands with a high proportion of Negroes are Jamaica, the Bahamas and Trinidad. In Panama, Nicaragua and Colombia they constitute smaller but important minorities.

The Asian element in Latin America is very much smaller than the three ethnic elements already mentioned. Chinese are found in sizeable communities in Peru, Cuba and other Caribbean islands. Indo-Pakistanis are also common in these islands and in Guyana, and in Brazil there are more than 250,000 Japanese who have played an important role in the opening up of parts of São Paulo and Paraná. They have been welcomed in Brazil, and in smaller numbers in Paraguay and Argentina, particularly in default of numerous European immigrants.

In many parts of Latin America there has been fusion between the various ethnic elements, producing many contrasting types: *mestizo* (mixed Indian and white, known in Brazil as *mameluco*), *mulatto* (mixed Negro and white), *zambo* (mixed Negro and Indian), *chigro* (mixed Negro and Chinese), etc. The degree of racial miscegenation varies greatly, although it is rarely small. If one can speak of a typical Latin American he would be mestizo, but the variety of indigenous Indians has even resulted in diverse types of mestizo. States where the mestizo is preponderant include Mexico, Honduras, El Salvador, Nicaragua, Panama, Venezuela and Colombia. In the Andean states of Peru, Bolivia and Ecuador the *mestizo* population is about one-third of the total. But nowhere is racial intermixture more evident than in Brazil where all the basic ethnic elements are present and where all types of miscegenation have occurred. It has been referred to as "the world's great laboratory for racial experiment", for fusion of such widely separate racial elements on a large scale has been previously unknown in the world.

Far from being a part of the world receiving large numbers of immigrants, Latin America now has a greater volume of emigration, notably to the United States and Europe. Mexicans, Puerto Ricans, Cubans, Virgin Islanders and many South Americans have been attracted by the high living standards and job opportunities in the United States; at the time of the 1960 US census, 1,736,000 Mexicans were counted, mostly in California, Texas and Arizona, and about 40,000 are admitted annually, excluding *braceros* or seasonal farm workers. Some of the overcrowded colonial or Commonwealth territories of the Caribbean have long been reservoirs of migrants to Europe; migrants from Martinique and Guadeloupe go to France, while those from Jamaica, Barbados, Trinidad and Tobago go mainly to the United Kingdom, where they concentrate in the conurbations and major industrial cities.

Although immigration into Latin America is now generally of little importance, except in Venezuela, a good case can be made for encouraging the immigration of professional manpower, qualified technicians and highly skilled workers from European countries in order to increase the skills available and give greater impetus to social and economic development.

Population Distribution

Over two-thirds of the total population of Latin America live in South America and well over half in the tropical part of that continent, but the density of population in South America is very much lower than that of Middle America, particularly the Caribbean region, which is the smallest in area and population of the four major regions of Latin America, but its overall density of population is about ten times that of tropical or temperate South America and four times that of mainland Middle America (see Table 1.1).

There is also great unevenness of population size among the twenty-three independent states and eighteen colonial territories of Latin America. Brazil (98 million in 1972) has one-third of the total population of Latin America and half the population of South America. Brazil and Mexico (54 million in 1972) together have over half of the population of Latin America, and if the next three largest populations (Argentina, Colombia and Peru) are added it is found that the big five have 72 per cent of the total population. At the other end of the scale there are over a dozen independent countries each with less than 5 million inhabitants, while most of the colonial dependencies have only pocket populations; in 1972 a dozen had less than 100,000 inhabitants each.

A population distribution map of Latin America demonstrates even greater unevenness (Figs. 2.3 and 2.4) in particular a striking tendency

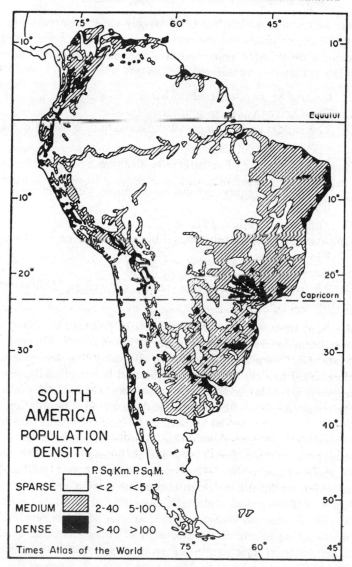

FIG. 2.3. South America: population density (after *Times Atlas of the World*). The patchy, largely peripheral distribution of population is clearly apparent.

toward clustering, which has been largely caused by past phases of economic development and the evolution of core areas, being intensified at present by massive urbanization. The main regional clusters of population may be enumerated as follows:

(1) Central Mexico, centred on Mexico City.

(2) The Oaxaca valley in southern Mexico.

(3) The valleys and hillslopes of the mountains of Middle America between Mexico and Panama.

(4) Many islands in the Caribbean, including the republics of Cuba, Haiti and Dominica.

(5) The Andean highlands from north-central Venezuela to southern Bolivia.

(6) The central valley of Chile.

(7) A wide zone in south-eastern Brazil, centred on São Paulo and Rio de Janeiro.

(8) North-east Brazil, centred on Recife.

(9) The surrounds of the Plate estuary, centred on Montevideo and Buenos Aires.

Apart from these main regional clusters of population, many major cities of Latin America are foci of more localized population clusters, as, for example, Caracas (Venezuela), Barranquilla and Cartagena (Colombia), Lima (Peru), Porto Alegre and Belém (Brazil), Asunción (Paraguay) and Bahia Blanca (Argentina). One of the difficulties which sometimes arises from the marked clustering of population is that national cohesion may be impeded, for some clusters are widely separated by large, sparsely inhabited or quite uninhabited areas. Such areas cover one-half of South America, including most of the Amazon basin, the Guianas, the Mato Grosso, the Atacama desert and Patagonia, all of which are hostile environments at the present time.

Many of the population clusters, especially in South America, have a peripheral location, owing to the character of European territorial occupation, the economic development of areas accessible to the sea and the external orientation of economies toward the developed countries. The main areas of population in South America lie within 300 miles of the coast, and it is only since the Second World War that there has been more extensive penetration of the interior, especially along river valleys. Epitomizing the significance of a coastal location are the Caribbean islands, some of whose lowlands are among the few parts of the western hemisphere where rural over-population is obvious. But these islands have wide differences in population densities, from 32 per square mile in the Bahamas to 1480 per square mile in Barbados. Even the rural population density of Barbados is more than 750 per square mile.

Coastal influence must not be exaggerated, for the plateaus and inter-montane basins of the Andes, the Central American Cordillera and Mexico are centres of population concentration, because high altitudes

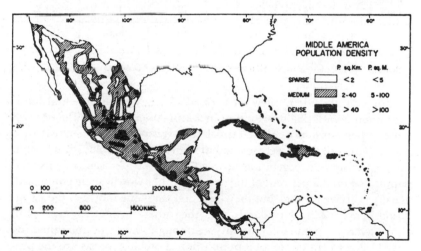

Fɪɢ. 2.4. Middle America: population density. Densities are generally higher on the Caribbean islands than in mainland Middle America.

offer considerable climatic amelioration. In Peru and Bolivia large populations live between 3000 and 4000 metres, despite diminished supplies of oxygen, which reduces fecundity (possibly even among Indians) and induces respiratory ailments among peoples moving into such high land. Early Spanish colonizers were greatly affected. In the northern Andes and Middle America large populations are found at rather lower altitudes, between 2000 and 3000 metres, which are nevertheless sufficiently elevated to transform climate and vegetation.

TABLE 2.2. POPULATION DISTRIBUTION AND VEGETATION TYPES IN LATIN
AMERICA

Vegetation type	Area (km²)	Population (millions)	Persons (per km²)	% of total area	% of total population
Mountain	1,690	38.8	23	8.2	18.6
Dry	5,226	41.4	8	25.3	19.7
Forest	9,843	100.2	10	48.0	48.0
Savanna	2,573	5.2	2	12.5	2.5
Grassland including Pampa	1,243	23.1	19	6.0	11.2
	20,575	208.7	10	100.0	100.0

SOURCE: J. P.Cole, *Latin America, an Economic and Social Geography*, 1965, p. 49.

Although altitude is often mentioned as a key environmental influence upon population distribution in Latin America, this influence was more important in pre-colonial times than it is today, for the great Inca and Aztec civilizations were located at high altitudes. Cole estimates that areas of mountain vegetation now contain 18.6 per cent of the total population on 8.2 per cent of the area. In other words, their population density is above average but they have less than one in five of the population (Table 2.2). Grasslands are the other vegetation type with above-average population density, although they are inhabited by only 11.2 per cent of the total population. Lowland forests are the predominant vegetation type of Latin America, and covering nearly half of the total area they contain a similar proportion of the total population. In contrast, dry lands have one-quarter of the area and one-fifth of the population, and savannas one-eighth of the area and only one-fortieth of the population. Savannas therefore have unusually low densities. Obviously, Cole's table masks many local differences, as, for example, among the forested areas; whereas Amazonia is very sparsely inhabited, forested islands are generally densely peopled. Moreover, the proportions living in the various vegetational zones are changing, for in several parts of South and Middle America there has been a redistribution of rural population through a downhill movement from populous highlands to less inhabited plains. It may be seen in Guatemala, El Salvador, Honduras, Nicaragua, Costa Rica (where it has been well documented by Sandner), as well as in the Andean countries of Colombia, Peru and Bolivia, where downhill migration is largely orientated toward the interior.

Latin America contains a considerable proportion of the unutilized land of the world. Huge areas of Mexico, Colombia, Venezuela, Peru, Bolivia, Paraguay and above all Brazil are either uninhabited or very lightly peopled. However, there are diverse opinions on the habitability of such areas, especially among Latin Americans. There are those who believe that the centres of civilization will return to the tropics, while others, particularly climatic determinists, doubt the feasibility of extending a pattern of close settlement over much of these areas. The question is most pertinent in Brazil, half of which is virtually uninhabited. Its pioneer fringe of settlement has only been extended markedly in recent years "in the north-western part of the state of Paraná, the north-central portion of the state of Maranhão, the sections of the Goias which are fairly close to the new national capital (Brasilia), the northern portions of the state of Minas Gerais, and the extreme north-western part of the state of São Paulo" (T. Lynn Smith). Between 1940 and 1964 the population of Paraná state rose from 1,236,276 to 5,625,000, indicating the great speed of occupation of newer frontier lands; but Amazonia still remains largely untouched. There is no doubt that many regions of Latin America are sparsely inhabited because of the small population sizes of countries and because technology and capital have been inadequate to master environmental difficulties. However, if present population growth persists, greater extension of the inhabited area may be expected, at least in South America. Some of the uninhabited areas may be the scenes of localized colonization and urbanization, especially where minerals or power are available. In almost every country of Latin America, with the possible exception of Costa Rica, rural colonization is greatly exceeded by migration to cities.

Urbanization

The urban history of Latin America stretches back beyond the

Spanish and Portuguese conquests, especially in the sedentary and densely peopled areas of the Middle and South American highlands. Unfortunately, many pre-Columbian Indian cities fell into ruins, especially in the sixteenth century when Indian peoples were decimated and scattered. European cities in Latin America were established with different terms of reference, being related to reorientated economies and to transatlantic trade. Consequently, many cities were located at the coast, and had few interrelationships.

The character of Portuguese and Spanish urban settlement was considerably influenced by patterns prevailing in the Iberian peninsula at the time. Portuguese colonial towns were agro-commercial and coastally located, with haphazard or "natural" layouts, whereas Spanish colonial towns were agro-military with chessboard layouts, closely resembling cities of the central Meseta of Spain. Colonization was by urban-minded peoples who set up towns, from which departure for rural settlement proceeded; the population movement was centrifugal. Not all towns were wisely sited or firmly established, and some had only brief hey-days followed by abandonments. Nevertheless, a new urban pattern evolved, which gained strength during the eighteenth and nineteenth centuries when a number of cities began to assume a metropolitan importance: Mexico City, Lima, Guatemala, Bogotá, Quito, Buenos Aires, Rio de Janeiro and Havana.

The present rapidity of urban growth is one of the most astonishing features of Latin America. At the beginning of this century there were only ten cities with more than 100,000 inhabitants and none had more than 700,000. If we take the threshold of 20,000 inhabitants as the lower limit of urban status, urbanization was of little importance in the early decades of this century, except in Cuba, Panama and the countries of temperate South America. Even by 1940, most other Latin American countries were less than one-fifth urbanized (Table 2.3.).

So in most of Latin America rapid urbanization is recent. In some countries like Venezuela and Chile, urban growth has been quite mercurial; only in Costa Rica and Paraguay has it been slow. The overall result is that Latin America has a higher degree of urbanization than any other major region of the developing world. Between 1950 and 1960 the urban population (in localities with 20,000 inhabitants or more) rose from 25 to 32 per cent, a proportion which is even higher

TABLE 2.3. LATIN AMERICA: PERCENTAGE OF POPULATION BY SIZE OF LOCALITY, 1940-1 and 1960-1, IN SELECTED COUNTRIES

	Percentage in places with 20,000 or more		Percentage in places with 100,000 or more	
	1940-1	1960-1	1940-1	1960-1
Brazil	15.3	28.1	10.7	18.8
Peru	14.2	28.9	8.4	18.5
Venezuela	18.1	47.2	11.8	30.0
Mexico	18.1	29.6	10.2	18.6
Honduras	6.1	11.6	—	7.2
Nicaragua	7.5	23.0	7.5	15.2
Panama	26.6	33.1	19.5	25.4
Puerto Rico	18.8	28.0	10.1	23.3
Chile	36.4	54.7	23.1	33.3

SOURCE: C. A. Miro, The population of twentieth-century Latin America, in J. M. Stycos and J. Arias (Eds.), *Population Dilemma in Latin America*, 1966, pp. 15–16.

than that of southern Europe (27 per cent). It is extremely difficult to be precise about the rate and level of urbanization in individual Latin American countries, but the highest levels appear to be in Argentina (63.2 per cent in 1970), Chile (54.7 per cent in 1967), Uruguay (62.2 per cent in 1963), Venezuela (47.2 per cent in 1961) and Cuba, and many large cities have grown annually at more than 5 per cent over the past 30 years: Mexico City, Santo Domingo, San Juan, Caracas, Barranquilla, Medellin, Bogota, Lima, Belo Horizonte.

The most spectacular aspect of urbanization is the growth of large cities (Fig. 2.5), which are absorbing a great deal of the population growth. In 1940 there were only four cities with more than one million inhabitants; today there are sixteen, and four of them—Buenos Aires, Rio de Janeiro, São Paulo and Mexico City—are multi-millionaire agglomerations which may be ranked among the twenty-five largest in the world. At the same time there is a growing profusion of cities with 100,000 inhabitants or more; the 1970 *Demographic Yearbook* lists thirty-two in Brazil, twenty-four in Argentina (amounting to about half of the total population) twenty-three in Mexico, twenty-one in Colombia, nine in Venezuela and Cuba and eleven in Chile. But the important point is the high degree of urban primacy, sometimes called "hyper-

Fig. 2.5. Large cities in Latin America. Large cities are peripherally located and are often in clusters.

cephalism". This refers to the concentration of population within a single city, which is usually the capital. Such cities also invariably concentrate a large proportion of the administrative, economic, educational and cultural functions, and may contain more than one-fifth of the total population. An extreme case is Montevideo (1,158,000 in 1963) which comprises 45.9 per cent of the total population of Uruguay. Other notable examples are Buenos Aires (Fig. 2.6), in whose agglomeration live 8 million people or one-third of all the population of Argentina, and Santiago, Panama City and San José each of which contains about one-quarter of the population of its country (see Table 2.4). It is fairly common for the capital to contain over half of the urban population and to be over five times larger than the second city. The main exceptions to marked "hypercephalism" are Brazil where São Paulo (5,187,000 in 1970) and Rio de Janeiro (4,252,000) are keen rivals, Ecuador where similar rivalry exists between Quito (400,000) and Guayaquil (650,000), and Colombia where Bogotá is little more than twice the size of the next largest city Medellín.

Unlike the centrifugal movements of the colonial period, modern population movements in Latin America are centripetal, to large cities.

TABLE 2.4. GROWTH OF CAPITALS IN LATIN AMERICA

City	Country	1960–4 percentage of		Estimated growth in last inter-censal period
		Total population	Urban population	
Montevideo	Uruguay	45.9	—	—
Buenos Aires	Argentina	33.8	58.8	2.9
Santiago	Chile	25.9	47.3	4.2
Panama City	Panama	25.4	76.7	5.2
San José	Costa Rica	24.0	100.0	4.6
Havana	Cuba	21.8	—	2.7
San Juan	Puerto Rico	18.4	65.6	1.9
Caracas	Venezuela	17.7	37.6	6.8
Asunción	Paraguay	16.8	—	3.3
Managua	Nicaragua	15.3	66.3	5.4
Lima	Peru	14.5	50.2	4.9
Mexico City	Mexico	13.4	26.4	4.9
Santo Domingo	Dominican Republic	12.2	65.1	7.3
Quito	Ecuador	11.2	41.4	5.2
San Salvador	El Salvador	10.2	57.6	4.3
Bogotá	Colombia	7.6	—	6.8
Tegucigalpa	Honduras	7.1	61.5	5.9
Rio de Janeiro[a]	Brazil	4.5	16.2	4.3

SOURCE: C. A. Miro, The population of twentieth-century Latin America, in J. M. Stycos and J. Arias (Eds.), *Population Dilemma in Latin America*, Washington, 1966, p. 21.

[a] Capital until 1957, when Brasilia was established.

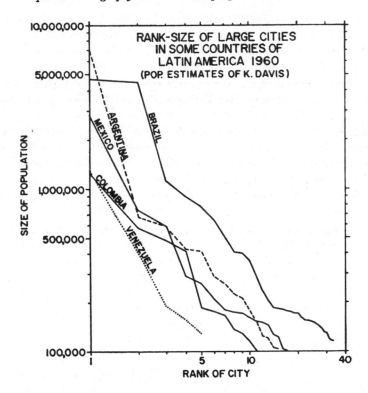

FIG. 2.6. Rank-size of large cities in some countries of Latin America, 1960. All except Brazil exhibit striking urban primacy.

Attitudes toward this concentration of urban population differ. While the Mexican government has encouraged the growth of Mexico City, the Chilean government has not always favoured the growth of Santiago. Moreover, while some hold the view that concentration of urban services within one large city, like Montevideo, is a useful economy in a small developing country, others promote decentralization.

Internal Migrations

In general, urban growth in Latin America results more from internal migration than from natural increase. Unfortunately, only a

limited amount of information is available on the volume and characteristics of internal migration, and most of it depends upon indirect
estimates from census data on birthplace, age and sex. For example,
rural–urban migration in Latin America has caused high proportions
of females in towns and of males in rural areas (Table 2.5). This feature
is somewhat unusual in the developing world and contrasts greatly with
Africa.

Male migrants to towns are mainly in their twenties, while female
migrants are usually younger and in some countries are mostly in their
teens. Many women migrate as part of a family and do not have independent motives for migration. Although migrants to towns are fairly
youthful by the standards of developed countries, they do not appear so

TABLE 2.5. SEX-RATIOS OF URBAN AND RURAL POPULATIONS IN SELECTED
COUNTRIES OF LATIN AMERICA

	Census year	Number of males per 100 females		
		Total	Urban	Rural
Costa Rica	1963	100.7	88.4	107.7
Chile	1960	96.3	88.0	115.3
Dominican Republic	1960	102.0	89.2	108.1
El Salvador	1961	97.4	88.3	103.7
Honduras	1961	99.2	90.7	103.2
Mexico	1960	99.5	94.6	104.8
Panama	1960	103.0	92.9	110.9
Paraguay	1962	97.2	89.2	101.9
Peru	1961	99.1	98.3	99.9

SOURCE: C. A. Miro, The population of Latin America, *Demography* **1**, 25, 1964.

in the age-structures of Latin American cities, where often the majority
of residents are under 15 years of age. Moreover, the impression should
not be retained that migration to the large cities is entirely from rural
areas. In fact, there is considerable stepped migration, and studies of
migration into the cities of Buenos Aires, San Salvador and Santiago
give reason to believe that many male migrants to Latin American
cities do not come directly from rural areas, but from small towns of
5–20,000 inhabitants. Many small towns are not very effective as

administrative, market or service centres, and are losing some of these functions. As leaders leave for the big cities, some small towns become moribund and "ruralized", and in Peru some have become more Indian because of out-migration.

The growth of cities and of migration streams in Latin America has been facilitated by great social and economic changes which have taken place during this century. The functional changes in cities have been instrumental, for the modern Latin American city is quite unlike its colonial predecessor. Whereas the latter had mainly military, administrative and residential functions, the twentieth century has brought increased port, commercial and industrial functions. Most cities have acquired industries, industrialization being seen by some government leaders as a panacea for social and economic problems, but the rate of urbanization is not a function of the rate of industrialization. Rural–urban migration exceeds the employment opportunities in urban industry, and the secondary sector in most Latin American cities is much smaller than the tertiary or services sector, in which too many are employed in petty services, domestic service or casual work. Urban growth, particularly port growth, has been also induced by the close dependence of many Latin American economies upon markets in North America and Europe, and by the presence of foreign companies and personnel. So nowadays some sizeable cities in Latin America have little administrative importance: Barranquilla, Belém, Buenaventura, Callao, Porto Alegre, Manaus, Recife, Rosario and Valparaiso.

Urbanization has also been encouraged by the development of modern means of communication: cars, lorries, buses, railways, radio, television ... all have intensified the urban attraction upon rural populations, which seek employment and education in cities. Companies scour the countryside for workers, the wealthy search for servants, and youngsters are usually not too unhappy to leave the countryside for the city. It is not merely a move to modernity, but also a move to higher incomes and better working conditions: legislation concerning hours of work, minimum wages, security of tenure, paid vacations, terminal pay, etc., has been much more effective in cities than in rural areas, where discontent with social structures and archaic systems of land tenure has further encouraged migration. It is often not realized that 5–10 per cent of the landowners in Latin America control 70–90 per cent of the agricultural land, and that most of the large farms are traditional in type, being characterized by extensive land use, limited machinery, little expenditure and absentee ownership. At the other end of the scale, in some Latin American countries *minifundia* is so marked that 20–50 per cent of farms are less than 5 acres in size. The family incomes of *minifundistas* are small, but probably higher than for most wage labourers, who provide many of the migrants. In addition to many social and economic influences upon migration, civil disorder must rank as a primary factor, as for example in Guatemala and particularly Colombia, where the terrorism of bandits made people seek the safety of cities.

Although Latin America's rural population is growing by about 1.6 per cent annually, rapid urbanization has frequently provoked a dearth of labour in rural areas. It is very difficult to persuade workers to remain on the farms once they have seen Lima, Buenos Aires or Mexico City. Yet the process of settling in the city is hard, for the flow of migrants often exceeds the availability of jobs. Cities have inadequate organization and private investment to cope with the influx. Migrants have crowded into tenements and shack-yards (*coralones, jacales*) near the city centres, but these have not been enough, so other migrants have had to build their own cities. Around every city are shanty-towns or squatter camps, "bands of misery" called *favelas* in Brazil, *ranchos* in Venezuela, *callampas* in Chile, *barriadas* in Peru; a generic name is *población* or *barrio "marginal"*. These marginal (in many senses) settlements are jungles of shacks with little or no sanitation, lighting, heating or piped water. It has been estimated that between 4 and 5 million families in Latin America, one in ten of the total population, live in shanty-towns. In general, the problems are less severe in countries where the people have a more secure subsistence from the land (e.g. Bolivia), or where there is fairly rapid industrialization (e.g. Buenos Aires or São Paulo), or where both these conditions exist (e.g. Mexico), but the shanty-town populations of Caracas, Bogotá and Santiago are growing more rapidly than the cities as a whole. Rio de Janeiro's is growing three to four times as fast, from 203,000 (8.5 per cent of total) in 1950 to 600,000 (16 per cent) in 1964, and Lima's grew from one-tenth in 1958 to one-fifth in 1964. It is not surprising that disease, petty crime and political agitation flourish in such harsh and squalid conditions, especially where employment opportunities are insufficient and underemployment is excessive. Colin Clarke has graphically described the unemployed and eventually almost unemployable population of Kingston, Jamaica, a case-study which could be repeated many times in Latin America. In some cities like Chimbote in Peru and Buenaventura in Colombia, the shanty-town population accounts for two-thirds to three-quarters of the total. Consequently, there is growing concern to overcome the great housing deficit, particularly localized in the cities.

It would be wrong, however, to assume that shanty-dwellers always have the lowest socio-economic status, and always have great difficulties in adjusting to urban life. While this is often the case in old-established cities like Buenos Aires, it is not so in Lima, Mexico City or Guatemala City, where many immigrants have previous experience of town-dwelling and have similar occupational and educational distributions to non-migrants. Moreover, with organizations to facilitate adjustment to city life as in Lima, squatter camps may be an integrative force in the process of urban development. On the other hand, Lima exemplifies better than most primate cities the acute dangers of parasitism and over-concentration, dominating all spheres of Peruvian national life and utterly dependent upon the provinces for food. It will be interesting to see what success the Cuban government will have in its policy to overcome this type of parasitism by decentralization of the economy and development of small cities at the expense of Havana, the capital.

Population Growth

At the beginning of this chapter reference was made to the astonishing rapidity of population growth in Latin America. Whereas at the beginning of this century the population total was approximately 74 million, by 1972 a total of 300 million had been attained, and the annual increase was about 2.8 per cent or 8.4 million. United Nations experts expect that Latin America will probably continue to have the highest rate of increase of any of the world's major regions during the 1970s.

The rates of population growth of the main sub-regions of Latin America have varied substantially in the twentieth century (Table 2.6).

TABLE 2.6. LATIN AMERICA: PERCENTAGE ANNUAL RATE OF REGIONAL GROWTH, 1920–1975

	1920–30	1930–40	1940–50	1950–60	1960–65	1965–70	Projected 1970–75
LATIN AMERICA	1.8	1.9	2.2	2.7	2.8	2.8	2.9
Tropical South America	1.8	2.0	2.3	2.9	2.9	3.0	3.0
Mainland Middle America	1.4	1.8	2.5	3.0	3.3	3.4	3.4
Temperate South America	2.4	1.7	1.8	2.0	1.9	1.8	1.7
Caribbean	2.0	1.8	1.9	2.0	2.3	2.2	2.2

SOURCE: C. A. Miro, The population of twentieth-century Latin America, in J. M. Stycos and J. Arias (Eds.), *Populatoin Dilemma in Latin America*, Washington, 1966, p. 4, and M. A. El-Badry, Latin American Population Prospects in the next fifteen years, *Population Studies*, **25**, 185, 1971.

TABLE 2.7. FREQUENCY DISTRIBUTIONS OF POPULATION GROWTH RATES OF TWENTY INDEPENDENT LATIN AMERICAN COUNTRIES FOR DECADES 1925–35, 1945–55, 1965–75

Mean percentage annual rate of growth	1925–35		1945–55		1965–75	
	No. of countries	Proportion of total population	No. of countries	Proportion of total population	No. of countries	Proportion of total population
Under 1.5	4	9	—	—	1	1
1.5–1.9	8	30	4	7	1	9
2.0–2.4	6	58	5	24	2	6
2.5–2.9	1	2	8	65	6	17
3.0–3.4	0	1	2	1	6	63
3.5 and over	1	0	1	3	4	4
	20	100	20	100	20	100

SOURCE: C. A. Miro, The population of Latin America, *Demography* **1**, 15–41 (1964).

TABLE 2.8. POPULATION GROWTH OF LATIN AMERICAN COUNTRIES, 1950–70

Countries	Midyear Population (in thousands)		Annual Rates of increase	
	1950	1970	1950–60 (%)	1963–70 (%)
TOTAL: LATIN AMERICA	159,973	283,000	2.7	2.9
Mainland Middle America	34,705	67,000	3.0	3.4
Mexico	25,826	48,377	3.1	3.5
Guatemala	2,805	4,284	3.0	2.9
El Salvador	1,868	2,511	2.7	3.8
Honduras	1,428	1,885	2.6	3.4
Nicaragua	1,060	1,536	3.4	3.7
Costa Rica	801	1,336	3.9	—
Panama	797	1,425	2.9	2.6
Others	120	5,646	1.0	—
Caribbean	16,284	26,000	1.9	2.3
Cuba	5,508	8,553	2.1	2.1
Haiti	3,112	3,097	1.2	2.0
Dominican Republic	2,131	4,012	3.5	3.6
Puerto Rico	2,207	2,690	0.6	1.7
Jamaica	—	1,865	—	2.3
Trinidad and Tobago	—	945	—	—
Barbados	—	238	—	1.1
Others	3,326	4,600	2.5	—
Tropical South America	82,418	151,000	2.9	3.0
Colombia	11,334	17,485	2.2	3.2
Venezuela	4,974	7,524	4.0	3.6
Guianas	700	714	2.2	3.0
Ecuador	3,197	4,650	3.0	3.4
Peru	7,533	9,907	2.9	3.1
Brazil	51,976	92,238	3.0	3.2
Bolivia	2,704	2,704	2.4	2.6
Temperate South America	26,566	67,000	1.8	1.8
Chile	5,790	8,835	2.3	2.4
Argentina	16,970	23,364	1.6	1.5
Paraguay	1,397	1,819	2.4	3.2
Uruguay	2,407	2,596	1.6	1.2
Falkland Islands	2	2	—	—

SOURCE: G. Mortara, Appraisals of census data for Latin America, *Demography and Public Health in Latin America, Milbank Memorial Fund Quarterly*, **42,** no. (2) 59 (1964), and *UN Demographic Yearbook*, 1970.

In the first 30 years, temperate South America experienced the fastest rate of growth, partly because of moderately high natural increase and partly because of immigration. Between 1900 and 1930, gross immigration into Argentina amounted to 2,400,000, into Uruguay 402,000 and into Chile 102,000. At the same time, both Brazil and Cuba grew rapidly. However, in the decade 1930–40 the other three sub-regions of Latin America overtook temperate South America in rate of population growth. In the 1940s, mainland Middle America attained the fastest growth rate, a position which it has maintained, followed by tropical South America and the Caribbean.

The speed of increasing population growth in Latin America has been demonstrated by Miro, by comparing the frequency distributions of the population growth rates of the twenty independent republics of Spanish, Portuguese or French speech for three distinct decades (Table 2.7). In the period 1925–35 twelve countries with 39 per cent of the population had annual growth rates of less than 2 per cent; during the period 1965–75, it is likely that only two countries (with one-tenth of the population) will grow at such a modest rate. Moreover, whereas only one country with one per cent of the total population was growing annually at more than 3 per cent in the period 1925–35, there will probably be ten countries comprising 67 per cent of the population with this fast growth rate in the period 1965–75. The states with the most rapid population growth rates in recent years have been Venezuela and Costa Rica, which have known rates of about 4 per cent. Indeed, Costa Rica has sometimes exceeded this figure. These countries are not wildly exceptional, for several other countries, like Mexico, Honduras, Nicaragua and Dominica, have had annual rates in excess of 3.5 per cent (Table 2.8). Such rates are astonishing, for, as T. Lynn Smith has said: "In all probability throughout the entire history of mankind no other large section of the earth, except the United States during the years 1790 to 1860 has experienced a rate of growth as high as 3 per cent per year."

It must be emphasized here that the rapid population growth of recent decades has been little influenced by immigration. It results mainly from the abrupt decline in mortality, with no corresponding change in fertility. Highest increase rates have been attained in countries where economic advance has been great, social advance small, and

TABLE 2.9. ESTIMATED CRUDE BIRTH AND DEATH RATES AND EXPECTATION OF LIFE AT BIRTH FOR LATIN AMERICAN COUNTRIES, 1945–50 and 1965–70.

Countries	Births per 1000 population		Deaths per 1000 population		Expectation of life at birth	
	1945–50	1965–1970	1945–1950	1965–70	1945–50	1965–70
Middle America and Caribbean						
Costa Rica	44–48	45.1	12–16	7.6	52–58	66.8
Cuba	32–36	26.6	11–15	7.5	52–58	66.8
El Salvador	44–48	46.9	18–23	12.8	40–47	55.2
Guatemala	48–52	43.2	22–27	15.1	37–42	51.1
Haiti	42–50	43.9	25–30	19.7	32–38	44.5
Honduras	45–50	49.0	18–24	17.1	40–46	49.0
Mexico	44–48	43.2	17–20	8.9	45–48	62.4
Nicaragua	45–52	46.0	16–20	16.5	45–52	49.9
Panama	38–42	41.1	14–17	8.8	48–53	64.3
Dominican Republic	48–54	48.5	20–25	14.7	38–45	52.2
Tropical South America						
Bolivia	41–45	44.0	23–27	19.1	36–42	45.3
Brazil	43–47	37.8	17–23	9.5	40–48	60.7
Colombia	44–47	44.6	17–21	10.6	44–48	58.6
Ecuador	45–50	44.9	20–25	11.4	38–43	57.2
Peru	42–48	41.8	18–24	11.1	40–45	58.0
Venezuela	44–48	40.9	16–20	7.8	45–50	63.8
Temperate South America						
Argentina	25–26	22.5	9–10	8.6	61–62	67.1
Chile	34–37	33.2	17–19	10.0	47–51	61.1
Paraguay	45–40	44.6	15–20	10.8	48–52	59.4
Uruguay	20–23	21.3	8–9	9.1	62–65	69.3

SOURCE: C. A. Miro, The population of Latin America, *Demography* 1, 35 and 39 (1964) and M. A. El-Badry, Latin American Population Prospects in the next fifteen years, *Population Studies*, 25, 186–7. 1971.

peaceful conditions have been attractive to immigrants. Costa Rica best exemplifies these conditions.

Mortality

At the beginning of this century death rates in Latin America generally exceeded 25 per thousand and probably reached 30 per thousand in some countries. It is impossible to provide precise figures, as population registers, on which death rates are based, are known to be imperfect. It is certain, however, that there has been a general and continual decline in mortality during this century. Initially the decline was slow, but after 1930 it gathered speed so that by 1960 the death rates of some countries, such as Mexico, El Salvador, Costa Rica, Puerto Rico, Argentina and Chile, were less than half of those prevailing in earlier decades. Infant mortality rates have particularly tumbled in mainland Middle America and the Caribbean, where they are invariably below 100 per thousand and often below 50 per thousand. Indeed the lowest mortality conditions in Latin America are found in some West Indian islands (e.g. Puerto Rico, Trinidad and Tobago, Guadeloupe, Bahamas) and in areas of white settlement, like Mediterranean Chile, Argentina, Uruguay and southern Brazil (Table 2.9).

Mortality decline has been accompanied by a substantial increase in average expectation of life. Eight of the eleven countries returning data report increases of 6–17 years since 1950, although in all countries except Argentina and Uruguay levels are well below those of developed countries. Little information is available on mortality differentials by social class, although evidence from Chile suggest that they exist. In general, Indian populations suffer the worst mortality conditions, especially in countries like Bolivia, Ecuador and Paraguay. In most Latin American countries, especially in Middle America and tropical South America, there is considerable potential for further mortality decline.

Existing mortality levels have been achieved by major health programmes with the advice and assistance of such organizations as WHO and the Rockefeller Foundation. Great advances have been made in the reduction of killer diseases such as smallpox, malaria and dysentery, and in improving sanitation and sewerage systems. All Latin American governments are dedicated to the reduction of mortality and to the increased health of their populations. Urban mortality has declined most, because of improved sanitation and the localization of wealthier classes and medical facilities. In 1965 there were about 100,000 doctors practising in Latin America, about half of the minimum number needed. It has been estimated that in 1966 there were about 5.8 doctors for every 10,000 persons, just over one third of the ratio in the United States. Nurses are also in relatively short supply. Moreover, in 1966 there were only 3.2 hospital beds per 1000 inhabitants, and even to maintain this inadequate ratio a further 170,000 beds are required by 1971. Medical facilities vary greatly by country and by region, but are generally better than in Africa or Asia. Inevitably, most are in the major cities, which usually have five times as many doctors per thousand inhabitants as can be found in rural areas. Yet there is no doubt that these ratios will improve, and that mortality will continue to decline.

Fertility

Only in a few countries of Latin America have there been comparable declines in fertility. At the beginning of this century fertility was high in every country; only in Uruguay was the birth rate below 40 per thousand. By mid-century six countries had rates lower than this—Uruguay 22 per thousand, Argentina 25, Cuba 30, Haiti 35, Chile 37 and Panama 39—but all the other countries of Latin America still had birth rates similar to those in 1900. Since 1950 the general situation has not altered greatly, and the only major Latin American countries which seem to have undergone a permanent change to low fertility are Argentina, Uruguay and to a lesser extent Cuba. But all these three countries had achieved moderately low birth rates by the mid-1930s, partly through the immigration of Europeans with relatively low fertility. Since then the birth rates in these three countries and in Latin America as a whole have not changed much, although there have been minor fluctuations owing to revolutions and civil disturbances as well as to the Second World War, which particularly affected the economies of those countries shipping products to Europe and North America. In most of tropical Latin America low-fertility groups are small and urban, and are being increasingly outnumbered by the large high-fertility groups. In Latin America high fertility owes much to the doctrine of *machismo* among males, who gain pride and prestige through proving their virility, by begetting large numbers of children. Another important influence may be the high incidence of consensual unions, especially in Guatemala and Haiti and to a lesser degree in El Salvador, Honduras, Nicaragua, Panama and the Dominican Republic, though consensual unions are usually less fertile than stable legitimate ones.

In some countries there has been some reduction in fertility which is not apparent in birth rates. In the British Caribbean, for example, Roberts has shown that there has been a reduction in the level of completed fertility during the past four decades, but that this has not materially changed the situation because it has been accompanied by a decline in the proportion of childless females following campaigns to control venereal diseases and yaws. There is also a growing rural–urban fertility differential, large cities usually being pockets of lower fertility owing to the presence of an urban middle class.

Collver's studies of fertility in Latin America demonstrate that differences in the age–sex and marital compositions are enough to produce differences in crude birth rates (see Table 2.9). Crude birth rates are often deceptively low because of the large and growing proportion of children under 15 years, resulting from the abrupt fall in infant and child mortality. In few countries, with the notable exceptions of Argentina, Uruguay, Chile and some Carribbean islands, are less than 43 per cent of the population under the age of 15, or less than 50 per cent under 20 years, and usually the proportion is increasing (Table 2.10). Analysis of standardized birth rates in some countries, including Venezuela and Mexico with fairly advanced and expanding economies, shows that the fertility of women in the reproductive age groups surpasses anything previously known.

In Latin America there is increasing awareness of the significance of high fertility in relation to population growth and economic development, but family planning is a matter of considerable controversy. In opposition to those who advocate birth control are the combined forces of the weight of the Catholic Church, the political ideals of Marxism, the suspicion of American motives in sponsoring family planning, as well as the notion that large areas of Latin America remain under-populated. Only a few countries—Chile, Colombia, Honduras, Peru and Venezuela—officially sanction population programmes, although

TABLE 2.10. CHANGES IN AGE STRUCTURES OF SELECTED LATIN AMERICAN POPULATIONS

	Year	Percentages in age groups		
		0–14	15–64	65 and over
Tropical South America				
Brazil	1950	41.9	55.6	2.5
	1960	42.7	54.5	2.8
Venezuela	1950	42.0	55.3	2.7
	1961	44.8	52.4	2.8
Ecuador	1950	42.5	54.0	3.5
	1962	45.1	51.6	3.3
Mainland Middle America				
Mexico	1950	41.8	54.8	3.4
	1970	46.2	50.0	3.7
El Salvador	1950	41.2	55.9	2.9
	1961	44.8	52.0	3.2
Nicaragua	1950	43.3	53.8	2.9
	1963	48.3	48.8	2.9
Costa Rica	1950	42.9	54.2	2.9
	1963	47.6	49.2	3.2
Temperate South America				
Argentina	1947	30.9	65.2	3.9
	1960	31.0	63.4	5.6
Chile	1952	37.3	58.7	4.0
	1960	39.8	56.0	4.2
Paraguay	1950	43.8	52.5	3.7
	1962	45.2	50.9	3.9
Caribbean				
Dominican Republic	1950	44.5	52.7	2.8
	1960	44.6	52.5	2.9
Puerto Rico	1950	43.2	52.9	3.9
	1960	42.7	52.1	5.2

SOURCE: *UN Demographic Yearbooks.*

most countries accept an affiliate of the International Planned Parenthood Federation. Of the three methods of birth control now in use in Latin America—late marriage, contraception and induced abortion—most noteworthy is the prevalence of induced abortions.

In some countries of Latin America there seems to be an indication of a change in attitude, and this is reflected in an upheaval in the Catholic Church. Studies carried out in Panama, Rio de Janeiro and San José show a marked degree of deviation from the norms of the Catholic Church by church-going married women, the majority of whom use contraceptives. This conflict between religious norms and social realities may expand with increased education. At present one-third of the population of Latin America is illiterate, and the average educational level is only 4 years of schooling. Only one in twelve entering primary school go to secondary school, and nearly half of all teachers are uncertificated. The task of providing even elementary school facilities in Latin America is enormous, as in many countries more than one-quarter of the population is aged 5–14, and this proportion is growing. Government expenditures on education over the past few years range from 7.3 per cent in Brazil to 27.5 per cent in Bolivia. The successes of these educational programmes will have much influence upon attitudes toward fertility and population growth.

Population and Economic Growth

The irony of the Latin American rise in population growth is that it comes at a time when there are great hopes for a rise in standards of living. In 1966 the Alliance for Progress (founded in 1961) announced that the combined *per capita* income gain per annum in Latin America in the period 1961–66 was only 1.1 per cent, well below the target of 2.5 per cent (Table 2.11). The question arises as to how far this slow rise in *per capita* income may be attributed to rapid population growth.

In general, the countries with rapid population growth have high rates of GNP growth and vice versa, but Cabello has shown that a cause-and-effect relationship cannot be established between changes in the rate of population growth, fluctuations in the GNP and increases in *per capita* income. He considers that "there has been a direct though limited connection between the rate of population growth and the rate of increase of the GNP", so it is not certain that a reduction in population growth would be by itself a stimulant to economic development. He concludes that birth control cannot be regarded as the sole key to the solution of development in Latin America, although a reduction in fertility may well facilitate development in some countries. In this view he takes a median path between those who consider birth control a precondition for realistic economic development, and those who believe

TABLE 2.11. POPULATION GROWTH AND ECONOMIC GROWTH IN LATIN
AMERICA, 1960–64

	% Annual rate of population growth	% Annual increase in GNP	% Annual increase in *per capita* GNP
Tropical South America			
Bolivia	2.3	5.0	2.7
Brazil	3.0	3.9	0.8
Colombia	2.8	5.3	2.5
Ecuador	3.1	3.7	0.5
Peru	2.7	6.4	3.7
Venezuela	3.5	5.3	1.7
Mainland Middle America			
Costa Rica	4.0	3.3	−0.7
El Salvador	3.2	8.3	5.1
Guatemala	2.9	5.4	2.5
Honduras	3.5	4.3	0.8
Mexico	3.4	6.2	2.8
Nicaragua	3.5	7.3	3.8
Panama	2.8	5.3	2.5
Temperate South America			
Argentina	1.8	1.2	−0.6
Chile	2.4	4.0	1.6
Paraguay	2.5	3.6	1.1
Uruguay	1.2	0.1	−1.2
Latin America except Cuba	2.9	4.0	1.1

SOURCE: O. Cabello, Housing, population growth and economic development, in
J. M. Stycos and J. Arias (Eds.), *Population Dilemma in Latin America*, 1966, p. 107.

that population size and growth in most of Latin America should not
give great concern because of the availability of natural resources and
the possibilities for their greater utilization. This middle view is based
in particular on the assumption that the relationships between economic
development and population are complex, economic development
being also influenced by other factors such as capital increase, natural
resources, human resources and technical innovations. In such circumstances it is difficult to isolate population growth as an individual factor.

At the moment it is certain that in most of Latin America the population pressure on resources is far lower than in much of South and East
Asia. Many natural resources are underutilized, especially energy and

mineral resources. Although over the past decade almost two-thirds of the increased agricultural production in Latin America has come from extensions to the cultivated area, in most countries there is scope for further agricultural extension by colonization. Costs will be high, however, and extension cannot be carried on indefinitely. For instance, in Middle America it is expected that there will be no remaining pioneer fringe in 5–10 years if current rates of population growth and migration persist. So these countries will have to switch to intensification of agriculture in the drive to increase food supplies.

Latin America as a whole does not suffer from as much poverty and malnutrition as most of Africa and Asia, nor are general living standards so low. Average annual incomes for Latin America as a whole are about three times those for Asia and Africa. While the poorer countries, like Paraguay, Ecuador, Bolivia, Honduras and Haiti, are not at the bottom of the world income-level table, other richer countries, such as Venezuela, Argentina, Chile, Uruguay, Puerto Rico and Cuba, rival South European countries. But these generalizations conceal great internal discrepancies within states, for all Latin American countries exhibit pockets of great wealth and pockets of great poverty. These are features of the social structure, and yet at the same time they have discrete geographic distributions. It is probable that Latin America exemplifies more than any other major region of the world the concept of internal disequilibrium. The prevalence of hypercephalism of cities, the clustering of population, the great voids of Amazonia, the sporadic nature of economic development, the dependence on overseas markets . . . all these factors demonstrate a real imbalance, which gives every sign of continuing. United Nations demographic experts have calculated that practically the entire increase of South America's population in the period 1950–80 is likely to be absorbed by the growth and expansion of existing areas of relatively dense settlement. Like all projections this must be accepted only with reservations, but in the late 1960s it appears to be correct.

The character of the areal imbalance is certain to be greatly affected by the rapidity of population growth. Ansley Coale has made the projection of a population of one million persons with age distribution, fertility and mortality typical of Latin America north of Uruguay, and with mortality rapidly improving. After 50 years the million rises to

5,736,000, and after 150 years the total is 245,500,000. He invites the reader to start the projection at 1960 and multiply the totals by 70.5 for Brazil and by 34.6 for Mexico. Such astronomical numbers may never be attained, but already the pressure of growing numbers is great. As Miro has pointed out, both Venezuela and Chile in 1960 had population totals similar to that of Sweden, but whereas Sweden's natural increase was 0.4 per cent, Venezuela's was 3.9 and Chile's 2.5. It is pressure of population growth rather than pressure of population density which is the characteristic demographic feature of most Latin American countries.

Population growth and areal imbalance are great challenges in Latin America, and there is increasing awareness of both. Pressures for improvement are generally greater in those countries where there are changes underway than in those where stagnation prevails. It is sometimes said that one of the great dilemmas in Latin America is how far countries can afford to finance both social reforms and economic development. In fact, these two phenomena cannot really be dissociated, because obsolete social institutions and class structures inhibit economic development, and the remaking of Latin American society is only possible by the modernization of those institutions and structures.

Select Bibliography

ARRIAGA, E. E., Components of city growth in selected Latin American cities, *Milbank Memorial Fund Quarterly* **46**, 237 (1968).

ARRIAGA, E. E. and DAVIS, K., The pattern of mortality change in Latin America, *Demography* **6**, 223 (1969).

AUGELLI, J. P. and TAYLOR, H. W., Race and population patterns in Trinidad, *Ann. Am. Assoc. Geog.* **50**, 123 (1960).

AUGELLI, J. P. and WEST, R. C., *Middle America; its lands and peoples*, Englewood Cliffs, New Jersey, 1966.

BEAUJEU-GARNIER, J., Les migrations vers Salvador, *Cahiers d'Outre Mer* **15**, 291 (1962).

BEAUJEU-GARNIER, J., La Population de Mexico, *Bull. Assoc. Géog. Français* 1967.

BENITEZ ZENTENO, R., *Análisis Demográfico de Mexico*, Instituto de Investigaciones Sociales. Biblioteca de Ensayos Sociologicos. Cuadernos de Sociologia, Mexico, 1961.

BEYER, G. H. (Ed.), *The Urban Explosion in Latin America*, Cornell Univ. Press, 1968.

BUTLAND, G. J., Frontiers of settlement in South America, *Revista Geografica* **65**, 93 (1966).

CABELLO, O., The Demography of Chile, *Pop. Studies* **9**, 237 (1956).

CASTRO, R. B., El Desarollo de la población Hispano-Americana (1492–1950), *Cahiers d'Histoire Mondiale* **5,** 425 (1959).

CLARKE, C. G. Population pressure in Kingston, Jamaica; a study of unemployment and overcrowding, *Trans. Inst. British Geog.* **38,** 165 (1966).

COLE, J. P., *Latin America, An Economic and Social Geography*, London, 1965.

COLLVER, A. O., *Birth Rates in Latin America: New Estimates of Historical Trends and Fluctuations*, Research Series No. 7, Institute of International Studies, University of California, 1965.

DALE, E. H., The demographic problem of the British West Indies, *Scottish Geog. Mag.* **79,** 23 (1963).

DAVIS, K., The Place of Latin America in World Demographic History, *Milbank Memorial Fund Quarterly* **42,** 19 (1964).

DYER, D. R., Distribution of Population on Hispaniola, *Econ. Geog.* **30,** 337 (1954).

DYER, D. R., Urbanism in Cuba, *Geog. Rev.* **47,** 224 (1957).

DYER. D. R., Growth of Brazil's Population, *J. Geog.* **65,** 417 (1966).

EL-BADRY, M.A., Latin American population prospects in the next fifteen years, *Population Studies*, **25,** 183 (1971).

ENJALBERT, H., La pression démographique au Mexique, *Cahiers d'Outre Mer* **13,** 451 (1960).

GAIGNARD, R., La montée démographique argentine, le recensement du 30 Septembre 1960, *Cahiers d'Outre Mer* **14,** 85 (1961).

GEISERT, H. L., *The Caribbean: population and resources*, George Washington University, Population Research Project, Washington, 1960.

GENDELL, M., Fertility and development in Brazil, *Demography* **4,** 143 (1967).

HAUGER, J., La population de la Guyane francaise, *Ann. Géog.* **66,** 509 (1957).

HAUSER, P. M. (Ed.), *Urbanization in Latin America*, UNESCO, Paris, 1961.

HERRICK, B., *Urban Migration and Economic Migration in Chile*, Massachusetts, 1965.

INTER-AMERICAN STATISTICAL INSTITUTE, *La Estructura Demografica de las Naciones Americanas*, Washington D.C., 1960.

JAMES, P., *Latin America*, New York, 3rd. ed., 1959.

JAMES, W. H., The effects of altitude on fertility in Andean countries, *Pop. Studies* **20,** 97 (1966).

KUCZYNSKI, R. R., *Demographic Survey of the British Colonial Empire, vol. III. West Indian and American Territories*, London, 1953.

LAVELL, C. B., *Population Growth and the Development of South America*, George Washington University, Population Research Project, Washington, 1959.

LOWENTHAL, D., The population of Barbados, *Soc. Econ. Stud.* **6,** 445 (1957).

LOWENTHAL, D., Production and Population in Jamaica. *Geog. Rev.* **48,** 568 (1958).

LOWENTHAL, D., Population contrasts in the Guianas, *Geog. Rev.* **50,** 41 (1960).

MIRO, C. A., The population of Latin America, *Demography* **1,** 15 (1964).

MORSE, R. M., Recent research in Latin American urbanization: a selective survey with commentary, *Latin American Res. Rev.* **1,** 35 (1965).

MORSE, R. M., Latin American Cities: aspects of function and structure, in FRIEDMAN, J. and ALONSO, W. (Eds.), *Regional Development and Planning*, 378 (1964)

MORTARA, G., The development and structure of Brazil's population, in J. J. SPENGLER and O. D. DUNCAN (Eds.), *Demographic Analysis*, Glencoe, 1956, pp. 652–70.

PEACH, C., *West Indian Migration to Britain: A Social Geography*, London, 1968.

PEREZ DE LA RIVAJ, La population de Cuba et ses problèmes, *Population* **22,** 99 (1967).

ROBERTS, G. W., *The Population of Jamaica*, Cambridge, 1957.

ROBERTS, G. W., *The Demographic Position of the Caribbean*, U.S. House of Representatives Committee on Judiciary, Subcommittee No. 1, Study of Population and Immigration Problems, Western Hemisphere (11), Spec. Series No. 6, 1963.

ROSENBLAT, A., *La Poblacion indigena y el mestizaje en America*, Buenos Aires, 1954.

SAUNDERS, J. V. D., *The People of Ecuador; a demographic analysis*, University of Florida Latin American Monographs, No. 14, Gainesville, Florida, 1961.

SMITH, T. L., *Brazil: People and Institutions*, Baton Rouge, 1954.

SMITH, T. L., *Latin American Population Studies*, University of Florida Social Sciences Monographs, No. 8, Gainesville, Florida, 1961.

SMITH, T. L., *Colombia: Social Structure and the Process of Development*, University of Florida Press, Gainesville, Florida, 1967.

SMITH, T. L., *The Process of Rural Development in Latin America*, University of Florida Social Sciences Monographs, No. 33, Gainesville, Florida, 1967.

STYCOS, J. M., *Human Fertility in Latin America*, Cornell University Press, 1968.

STYCOS, J. M. and ARIAS, J. (Eds.), *Population Dilemma in Latin America*, Washington, 1966.

TRICART, J., Aspects de la géographie de la population au Salvador, *Rev. Geograf.* **34**, 33 (1964).

UNITED NATIONS, *The Population of Central America (including Mexico) 1950–80*, Population Studies, No. 16, New York, 1954.

UNITED NATIONS, *The Population of South America 1950–1980*, Population Studies, No. 21, New York, 1955.

UNITED NATIONS, *Human Resources of Central America, Panama and Mexico, 1950–1980*, 1960.

WHETTEN, N. L., *Guatemala: The Land and People*, New Haven, 1961.

WHITEHEAD, L., Altitude, fertility and mortality in Andean countries, *Pop. Studies* **22**, 335 (1968).

ZARATE, A. O., Fertility in urban areas in Mexico: implications for the theory of demographic transition, *Demography* **4**, 363 (1967).

ZELINSKY, W., The Historical geography of the Negro population of Latin America, *J. Negro Hist.* **34**, 153 (1949).

3

AFRICA

Size of Population

The huge continent of Africa, which covers 22.3 per cent of the world's land area, is particularly remarkable for its ethnic diversity and its political fragmentation. Its peoples range from Bushmen to Berbers, from Arabs to Pygmies, from Hottentots to Nilotes, and from South African whites to West African Negroes. Its numerous political units vary in size from tiny enclaves like Lesotho, Gambia, Djibouti and Cabinda to vast areas like Sudan, Algeria and Zaire. And yet despite this diversity and fragmentation, Africa is relatively sparsely peopled; its population density of 11 per square km. is less than half the world average. The current estimate of the population of Africa in 1972 is 364 million, about 9.6 per cent of the world total. This means that Africa has less than half of the population of China, Europe (including the USSR) or the Indian subcontinent. On the other hand, Africa's population clearly exceeds that of either North America or Latin America.

Prior to the nineteenth-century upsurge of world population, the African continent contained a higher proportion of mankind, but it appears that while European, American and Asian populations grew quickly those in Africa remained largely stationary. In fact, there is a slight difference of opinion among experts: Willcox surmised that the population of Africa remained more or less constant at about 100 million until the latter half of the nineteenth century, Carr-Saunders believed that the total declined from 100 million in 1650 to 90 million in 1800, when it started to slowly rise again, and Durand considers that the increase was more prolonged, although slow at first (Table 3.1). However, present estimated population growth in Africa (1965-70 : 2.6 per cent per annum) is more rapid than the world average, and thus the continent has a slightly increasing proportion of the total world population. But it must be emphasized that these are merely estimates, for studies of African populations are plagued by inadequacies of data. It is therefore not surprising that as yet there is no comprehensive study of African demography, although during the 1960s there have been several major edited volumes including those by Barbour and Prothero, Caldwell and Okonjo, and Brass *et al.*

Types of Enumeration

When in 1933 Carr-Saunders estimated the population of Africa at 145 million he merely added together the official estimates for the populations of the various African countries published in the *Statistical Yearbook* of the League of Nations. According to Bourgeois-Pichat, less than one-third (about 31 per cent) of the estimated population of Africa had been enumerated by the Second World War. Few African countries have a long record of census-taking: Mauritius since 1851, Algeria since 1856, Egypt since 1882, Tunisia since 1886, Gambia since 1901, South Africa, Lesotho (formerly Basutoland) and Swaziland since 1904 and Botswana (formerly Bechuanaland) since 1911. In addition, censuses were sometimes taken of towns or of very small territories, like the former colony of Sierra Leone, now only a small portion of the present state of Sierra Leone. Not all these censuses have been complete; in some of the colonized countries of northern and southern Africa early censuses were more concerned with the European and Asian communities than with the "native" or "indigenous" populations, as they were invariably called.

Since the Second World War, the situation has vastly improved, and now well over nine-tenths of the total population of the continent have been enumerated. At the time of writing, enumerations of one sort or another have been held in all parts of Africa save Ethiopia and Somalia. Countries have been stimulated to enumeration by the United Nations, by independence, by improvements in the methods of collecting data,

TABLE 3.1. ESTIMATES OF THE POPULATION OF AFRICA,
1650–1967

	UN[a]	Carr-Saunders[b]	Willcox[c]	Durand[d]
		(A. Numbers in millions)		
1650		100	100	
1750		95	100	106
1800		90	100	107
1850		95	100	111
1900		120	141	133
1920	141			
1940	191			
1960	277			
1970	344			
		(B. Percentage of world total)		
1650		18.3	21.7	
1750		13.0	14.4	13.4
1800		9.9	10.9	10.9
1850		8.1	9.2	8.7
1900		7.4	9.0	8.1
1920	7.8			
1940	8.3			
1960	9.2			
1970	9.5			

[a] *UN Demographic Yearbook*, 1970, p. 103.
[b] A. M. Carr-Saunders, *World Population*, OUP, 1936.
[c] W. F. Willcox, *Studies in American Demography*, Cornell
University Press, Ithaca, NY, 1940, p. 45.
[d] J. D. Durand, The modern expansion of world population, *Proc. Am. Phil. Soc.* **111**, p. 137, 1967.

and by the need to discover the relationships between population
growth and economic growth. Many of these population enumerations
have been far from perfect, but when the 1970 round of censuses of
population and housing is complete, the position will certainly be
better. On the other hand, vital registration is very rare and usually
inadequate, and estimates of natural increase have to be calculated by
other means; Brass and others working under the sponsorship of the
Office of Population Research at Princeton have made great progress
in methods of analysis of inaccurate and limited data.

Africa is the most politically fragmented continent and because of its numerous countries and diverse colonial associations, there have been many different types of population enumeration, which have been classified by Lorimer as follows:

(1) Classic-type censuses, in which there is visitation of all dwellings and collection of information on individuals by special enumerators, have been held in many anglophone countries such as Ghana, Nigeria, Sierra Leone, Kenya and Uganda, as well as in all countries of North Africa (Morocco, Algeria, Tunisia, Libya and Egypt).

(2) Sampling censuses, used in conjunction with population registers, have been employed in some of the former French territories, such as Guinea, Ivory Coast and Niger, as well as in the former Belgian Congo.

(3) Other sampling censuses, without registers, have occurred in Sudan and the two Rhodesias prior to independence.

(4) Censuses by assembly are held decennially by the Portuguese government in its African dependencies.

(5) Administrative surveys and compilations have been the main method of enumeration in most of the francophone territories of Central and West Africa, with the exception of those mentioned under (2).

Some countries, like the United Republic of Cameroon which previously experienced, in whole or in part, German, French and British rule, have had several of these different types of enumeration.

In addition to these official enumerations, estimates of population numbers have sometimes been derived, with varying degrees of success, from taxation figures (e.g. Sierra Leone) and from analysis of numbers of huts in settlements (e.g. Liberia). In both cases, an assumption is made concerning the number of people per taxpayer or per hut, and it follows that estimates are only crude.

Variety of Data

Of course, these various enumerations have never been synchronized and some counts are decennial, some quinquennial, and some intermittent. The amount and character of data collected by census-type inquiries also vary greatly. While most enumerations ascertain information about age, sex, occupation, industry, nationality, literacy and education, many ask no questions about marital status, size of family, languages spoken, tribal or religious affiliation, or membership of a household, so important data are often lacking for population analysis. The 1963 census of Sierra Leone, for example, throws no light on polygamy, the extended family, bilingualism or the distribution of Muslims, Christians and pagans, and for information on these aspects we are limited to the detailed studies by anthropologists of particular societies. Furthermore, some censuses record each person according to his location at the time of the census (i.e. *de facto*), while others record the normal place of residence (i.e. *de jure*); and Libya has used both bases for enumeration.

There is also considerable variation in the quality of data between different types of enumeration and successive enumerations. As Kuczynski has so clearly demonstrated in his voluminous studies of the demographic data of the former British colonial empire, many of the old censuses were no more than reasoned guesses and have low reliability. On the other hand, the 1960 census of Ghana, for example, was very much better than most other previous censuses taken in tropical Africa. Some censuses may be considered inferior to sampling methods, which are usually cheaper and simpler to undertake and require fewer enumerators and less preliminary mapping; but because of the nature of sampling the results are usually less valuable for small regions than for whole countries and less valuable for geographers than for demographers. Many African censuses have suffered in accuracy because of the inadequacies of enumerators and the system of enumeration, but other reasons given include shortage of funds, insufficient and inaccurate enumeration area maps, prevailing illiteracy, lack of vital registration (and therefore doubt about age), problems of communication of all sorts, fear and suspicion of enumeration, and also political intrigue. Resistance and falsification may reach such a pitch that whole censuses become highly suspect, as in the case of those in Nigeria in 1962 and 1963. The Nigerian example demonstrated that money cannot buy a good census, and that censuses should not be entrusted to politicians. The efforts of politicians in publicizing the need for a census as a basis for an electoral register and for economic and social development meant that many people relinquished their fears that the census was for taxation purposes and ensured that they were enumerated, at least twice! Indeed a Nigerian census enumerator was somewhat dubiously defined as "one who goes from house to house increasing the population". In consequence, the difference between the two censuses exceeded 10 million (45.3 million in 1962 and 55.7 million in 1963), the most notable discrepancies being in the populations of Northern Region and Western Region. Most Nigerian demographers feel that the 1963 figure has been grossly inflated by malpractices, and there is now clear lack of confidence in censuses because they seem to the man in the street to be a method of political jobbery. Certainly census-taking contributed to widespread political dissatisfaction which culminated in the 1966 revolution in Nigeria.

Brass has particularly stressed the importance of sampling in view of the fact that in most of Africa there is no comprehensive system of vital registration. Sampling techniques which involve the retrospective recording of vital events can therefore provide very valuable data for the study of the dynamics of population (i.e. fertility, mortality, migration and growth), although it is no simple matter to extract rates of population growth from such retrospective recording. Another difficulty is to overcome errors in age data, upon which so much refined demographic analysis depends. One of the best methods is to construct population models, and to correct data with reference to the models. The quasi-stable population theory, developed by Coale and Bourgeois-Pichat, has also been used to derive demographic measures from very broad age distributions even when there is little additional evidence. They showed that age distributions are not very sensitive to changes in mortality and so can provide information on fertility even when little is known about death rates. There is every indication that improvements in enumeration and in techniques of demographic analysis will broaden and deepen our knowledge of the population of Africa during the next decade.

Ethnic Groups

Classification of the multitudinous ethnic groups in Africa is plagued by considerable difficulties, which seem incapable of resolution

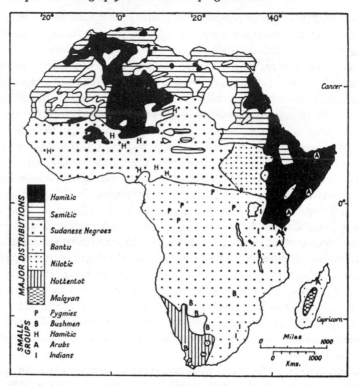

Fig. 3.1. Ethnic groups of Africa. This simplified map based on a classification by Seligman gives only a crude impression of the complexity of African peoples.

(Fig. 3.1). Despite many obvious differences between Africa peoples, especially between the Arabs of North Africa and the Negroes of subsaharan Africa, it is probable that the problems of racial taxonomy are almost insoluble in the present state of knowledge. Some authors, like Livingstone, have denied the concept of race as a valid taxonomic category and have pointed out that the geographical distribution of one variable characteristic in human populations does not correspond to the distribution of another, and this distribution does not correspond to that of a third, and so on. Others, like Garn, stress that "the definition of human racial groups is difficult when the amount of reproductive isolation between them is unknown", and so he considers "racial type" to be an outmoded concept. In particular, he rejects the idea that the darkest skin, the most tightly curled hair and the greatest lip dimensions represent the most "African" characteristics diluted by invaders in varying degrees in different populations. It is certain that classifications like that of Seligman, based on linguistics or assumed migrations, lack accuracy, yet at the same time the little research now being done on the genetic relationships of African peoples is not bringing final answers. Anyone interested in classifying the peoples of Africa is faced with numerous problems, including (a) a wide variety of possible anatomical and social criteria; (b) confusion over the connotation of racial, linguistic and cultural nomenclature (e.g. terms like Hamite, Caucasoid, Bantu, Nigritic, Nilotic, Negrillo); (c) use and misuse of terms like "tribe", "race" and "nation"; (d) variety of names given to an African people (e.g. the Fulani are also known as Fula, Peuhl and Foulbe); (e) paucity of anthropometric, genetic, linguistic, religious and tribal data; (f) uncertain knowledge of past migrations and conquests; (g) mixing of peoples, which has accelerated since the advent of slavery and European rule; and (h) complicated and arbitrary political division of the continent, created by colonialism and adopted by nationalism.

Small wonder, therefore, that population enumerations in Africa usually only distinguish between such broad ethnic groups as Africans, Europeans, Asians, "Mixed" and the like, and are of little or no value in numerical analysis of racial types. Even minority racial groups, like the Bushmen of the Kalahari and its borders, the Hottentots of south-western Africa, and the Pygmies of the Congo and the neighbouring territories, are inadequately enumerated. And no census distinguishes between the various types of Negroes, who are the largest racial group and occupy most of subsaharan Africa. Many of the physical and cultural differences among Negroes arise from the intermixture of Negro and white Caucasoid (or Armenoid) peoples, who migrated southward as pastoralists. The Caucasoid peoples have often been called Hamites and Semites, again linguistic terms; Berbers and Fulani are examples of Hamites, while Arabs are Semitic peoples. Miscegenation of Negroes and Caucasoids has resulted in considerable racial complexity in parts of East Africa, where Nilotic and Nilo-Hamitic peoples are found.

Despite these reservations, it is possible to distinguish in broad terms between White Africa and Black Africa, although in places the division is blurred. Northern White Africa, mostly Arabized and Islamized from South-west Asia and with great cultural homogeneity, contains nearly one-quarter of the continent's population, localized mainly along the Mediterranean littoral and the Nile valley. Black Africa, with much greater racial, linguistic and cultural diversity, contains three-quarters of the total population.

One of the greatest results of cultural contacts between these two great zones of Africa has been the southward advance of Islam, the quasi-universal religion of Africa north of 10°N. Like Christianity, Islam is not indigenous to Africa, and it has spread through immigration, conquest, commerce and cultural assimilation. Apart from the ancient survival of Christianity in Ethiopia, the Christian faith variously taught by many missionary societies is mostly found to the south of Islam in Central and South Africa, the coastlands of West Africa and the interior of East Africa. But in all these regions it competes with tribal religions, and is sometimes modified by them. Indeed, the profusion of religions and sects has made statistical analysis an almost impossible task.

A task of even greater magnitude faces linguists interested in Africa. About 800 languages are spoken in Africa, nearly one-quarter of those found in the world. Even a simplified language map of Africa exhibits a very intricate pattern, owing to the variety of peoples and past migrations as well as to the way that many groups preserved considerable isolation. Many African languages are spoken by small minorities and are little studied, and only in northern Africa is there much linguistic uniformity, because of the wide distribution of Arabic.

In view of the great linguistic diversity of subsaharan Africa, it is not surprising that certain languages have achieved regional importance especially in commerce. Hausa, Ful and Pidgin English are such languages in West Africa, and Swahili fulfils a similar function in East Africa. Moreover, because many African languages are neither written nor modern in so far as technical terminology is concerned and have no international status, European languages have been adopted as the official languages of many subsaharan African states. English and French are the most widespread official languages, and are increasingly important as languages of instruction. Portuguese and Spanish naturally have more restricted distributions. In South Africa, Afrikaans has evolved as a distinct language, based on seventeenth-century Dutch, and with English it is an official language of the Republic.

There is good reason to believe that official and regional languages will expand as communications improve and populations become more literate. In the long run, Arabic, English and French will probably become the main languages of Africa.

Non-Africans

No term adequately embraces the European and Asian elements of the population of Africa, for many of whom Africa is their only home. We call them non-Africans, for want of a better term, partly because they usually retain the appearance of Europeans and Asians, and partly because they are usually regarded as such. Europeans and Asians are not widespread in Africa, but tend to have restricted distributions, with low representation in West Africa. Most are town-dwellers, the proportions living in towns varying from 60 to 90 per cent according to country. These percentages reflect particularly the dominance of employment in the tertiary and, to a lesser extent, secondary sectors of economic activity.

The Asians (Table 3.2) are outnumbered by the Europeans. In 1960 there were 477,000 Indians in South Africa, mostly in Natal where they originally came as indentured labourers for the sugar plantations between 1860 and 1913. In Kenya, Uganda and Tanzania there were until recently some 350,000 Indo-Pakistanis and 76,000 Arabs, many of whom were skilled workers or traders, but the 1970s began with a major exodus from Uganda. The population of Mauritius is also mainly Indian in origin, and an Asian substratum, of Malayo-Polynesian origin, is apparent in Madagascar. Along the west coast of Africa there are also many Lebanese traders. In all, probably less than 1.5 million Asians, of varied cultures and beliefs, live in Africa, but in many countries their presence and economic success is resented by Africans, and so their numbers may diminish.

Towards the end of the 1950s, there were nearly 6 million Europeans

TABLE 3.2. NUMBERS OF INDO-PAKISTANIS IN SELECTED
AFRICAN COUNTRIES, EARLY 1960's

Country	Year	Census or estimate	Number	Approximate % of total
South Africa	1960	C	477,414	2.99 (1960)
Mauritius and Rodrigues	1962	C	455,026	—
Kenya	1962	C	176,613	2.04 (1963)
Tanganyika	1962	E	87,300	0.92 (1963)
Uganda	1962	E	79,900	1.14 (1963)
Zanzibar	1962	E	19,500	6.16 (1963)
Madagascar	1962	E	15,935	—
Mozambique	1955	E	15,235	0.24 (1963)
Malawi	1961	C	10,630	0.33 (1963)
Zambia	1961	C	7,790	0.25 (1963)
Rhodesia	1961	C	7,260	0.19 (1963)

SOURCE: J. Boute, *La Démographie de la Branche Indo-Pakistaniaise d'Afrique*, Louvain, 1965, pp. 33, 44.

living in Africa (Fig. 3.2). Again, they were unevenly spread, the major concentrations being in the northern and southern parts of the continent, especially in the Maghreb and in South Africa and Rhodesia, where their alienation of land was most substantial. Lesser concentrations occurred in Libya and Egypt, and in South-west Africa, Zambia, Mozambique, Angola and Madagascar. In equatorial Africa, where climatic conditions posed difficulties for European settlement except in highland zones, the only sizeable European populations were in Kenya (67,700 in 1960) and the former Belgian Congo (114,000 in 1959).

The wave of political independence has brought considerable changes in the numbers of Europeans in Africa; while in southern Africa they have grown, in East and Central Africa they have diminished, and in North-west Africa they have fallen precipitously. In 1956 there were nearly 2 million Europeans living in North-west Africa, including more than a million in Algeria; massive departures following independence meant that only about 435,000 were left by 1964; 140,000 in Morocco, 137,000 in Spanish North Africa, 70,000 in Algeria, 55,000 in Tunisia and 32,000 in Libya. At the same time, North-west Africa lost nearly

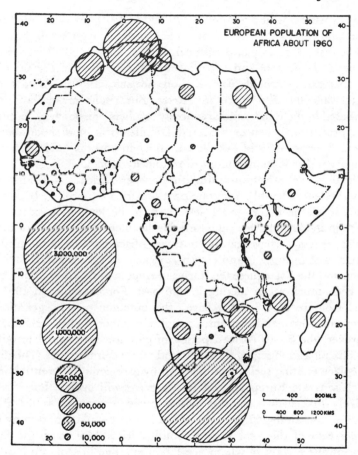

Fig. 3.2. European population of Africa about 1960. The concentration in North Africa has since been dramatically reduced by departures, especially from Algeria.

400,000 Jews through emigration. Today the only African countries (save minor enclaves like the Spanish Plazas de Soberanía of North-west Africa) where Europeans number more than one in twelve of the population are the Republic of South Africa (one in five) and South-west Africa (one in seven). More than half of the European population of South Africa, which totalled 3,779,000 in 1970, are descended from Dutch and German settlers of the seventeenth and eighteenth centuries, but the rest are mainly of British origin, like the 300,000 Europeans in Rhodesia. In Angola and Mozambique the number of Portuguese is also increasing through colonization projects, and in Angola they exceed 300,000. Elsewhere in Africa Europeans are usually only numbered in thousands, and are mostly teachers, missionaries, businessmen, professional men or advisers. Despite their modest numbers in Africa, Europeans have had inordinately important influences upon population distribution, composition and dynamics.

The degree of racial intermingling between Africans and Europeans has varied considerably from one part of Africa to another. In tropical Africa it has been very much less than in the temperate extremities, although in North Africa racial mixing has not been extensive, and its results are less obvious than in southern Africa because of the physical similarity of Europeans and North Africans. In the Republic of South Africa and the Portuguese territories of Angola and Mozambique there has been much racial mixing in the past. For example, in 1961 the Cape Coloureds of South Africa, the outcome of miscegenation of European, Negro and Hottentot peoples, numbered nearly 1.5 million. However, the South African policy of *apartheid* is designed to outlaw this mixing and to segregate black and white communities. The aim is to replace existing social stratification by a regional differentiation, in which separate European and Bantu areas will evolve, but it seems unlikely that such a division will succeed, especially as the Bantu reserves, containing 40 per cent of the Bantu population, occupy only 13 per cent of the total area of South Africa. Moreover, the Bantu town-dwellers, most of whom are labourers, live in separate locations from Europeans, with much poorer housing conditions. It is not surprising that South Africa is one of the main loci of racial tension in the world today.

Low Population of Africa

It has been mentioned that Africa is a relatively sparsely populated continent; its 1970 population density of 11 per square km. is less than half the world average, being roughly the same level as North America and the USSR, but higher than Oceania. This is a crude measure, but even if we look at population per square km. of arable land we still find that Africa's population density is relatively low; in 1970 it was 1792 in comparison with a world average of 3335, while its rural population per square km. of arable land was 1389 in comparison with the world average of 2096. Nevertheless, both figures are higher than those for North America and the USSR.

A host of reasons can be given for the relatively low population total of Africa, some of them environmental, some economic, some social. The east–west width of Africa at the Tropic of Cancer, where north-east trades prevail, has caused the enormity of the Sahara, and although the continent tapers southward and the southern deserts are much smaller, about 34 per cent of Africa may be categorized as desert and another large area as semi-desert, neither of which are conducive to dense populations. At the other extreme, the heat and humidity of the equatorial zone has encouraged luxuriant vegetation, infertile soils, and a proliferation of diseases which have impeded mastery of the environment by man. If we dwell for a moment on the question of pests and diseases, we may note that Africans, their animals and plants have been subject to a stunning variety of impediments. Among a bewildering list of major human diseases we may mention malaria, yellow fever, sleeping sickness (trypanosomiasis), bilharzia, tick fever, filariasis, kwashiorkor, yaws, leprosy and smallpox, all of which have decimated and/or debilitated mankind in Africa. It is true that Europeans in Africa, owing to lack of immunity, have sometimes been more severely affected by these diseases than Africans, but at the same time introduced European diseases (e.g. influenza) have often had more severe effects upon Africans. The major pest of livestock-farming in Africa has been the tsetse-fly, so widespread in the tropical zone and such a curb on the development of large forest areas; but rinderpest, foot-and-mouth and tuberculosis are also common. Plants have also suffered from a wide range of insects, bacteria, viruses and fungi, but the most indiscriminate has been the locust, whose swarms have been known to lay bare vast expanses of the more arid lands.

Environmental difficulties are not only the cause of the low population total. It must also be said that although Africa has been inhabited since the dawn of human history, much of the continent has not witnessed the evolution of peasant civilizations based on irrigation as known to Asia; the Nile valley, as always, is a notable exception. In pre-colonial times urban life was confined to a few widely scattered regions, and traditional social groups were on the whole small, separatist and self-subsistent. Constant inter-tribal warfare caused high mortality, and as Mabogunje has suggested for West Africa, population densities rose mainly where there was security against internal strife or external agression either through environmental isolation, as among the Ibo, or through a highly complex political organization, as in the cases of the Yoruba, Hausa, Mossi and Wolof.

Then there was the scourge of slavery, which according to some authorities meant the exodus of tens of millions, especially Sudanese Negroes and Bantu, to the Americas and to Islamic countries. Recent researches indicate that earlier estimates of the total number of slaves, varying between 25 and 50 million, are excessive but there can be no doubt that slavery had devastating effects in many parts of Africa. Thousands were massacred in the process, and as most slaves were in the reproductive age groups the "birth-deficit" must also be added to the number of departing slaves. Kuczynski, writing in the 1930's, believed that the populations of many West African territories were smaller than before the European slave trade. The Arab slave trade in East Africa had similar drastic consequences, and the Arab slave ports were some of the few urban settlements in that part of the continent in pre-colonial times.

More recently, some European colonial conquests and "pacification" caused considerable losses among African populations, as for example, in Algeria, Libya, Sudan and Ethiopia. Another scourge has been the spread of venereal diseases which have greatly reduced population fertility in many parts of Africa. Romaniuk has stated that in some Negro societies between one-quarter and one-half of the women are infertile through venereal diseases. On the other hand, the colonial introduction of peace and security, medical services and improved sanitation, new crops, new methods of cultivation, transportation routes, modern mining and industries has had very positive effects upon the numbers of Africans, as we shall see.

Population Distribution

The list of reasons accounting for the relatively low population total of Africa might be extended, but to no great avail, for within the African continent there are very great extremes of population density, considered in relation to either total area or arable land (Table 3.3) or resources. Indeed, the population distribution and density maps exhibit remarkable patchiness and complexity (Fig. 3.3). On the one hand, there are a number of widely separate populous areas with densities often over 100 persons per square mile, sometimes including pockets with over 1000 per square mile:

(1) The Mediterranean zone of the Maghreb.
(2) The delta of the Nile and much of its valley in Egypt and Sudan.
(3) Highland Ethiopia.
(4) The environs of Lake Victoria.
(5) The highlands of Rwanda and Burundi.
(6) Northern Nigeria.
(7) The Guinea coastlands of West Africa.
(8) Coastal Natal and southern Transvaal.
(9) Many islands around the African continent.

On the other hand, about half of the continent has population densities of 6.5 per square mile or less, and there are vast areas which are almost uninhabited, including considerable parts of the following:

(1) Sahara desert.
(2) The desert, steppe and swampy plains of south-western Africa.
(3) The desert and steppe of the Horn of East Africa.
(4) Large areas of Central Africa, especially in Gabon, Congo (Brazzaville), Central African Republic and south-western Sudan.

In general, the sparsely peopled areas are more easily explicable than the densely peopled localities. Often the sparsely peopled areas are physically repellent to concentrations of population, and this is particularly true of the arid, semi-arid and much of the dry subhumid zones. The Sahara, Kalahari and Namib deserts and the Horn of East Africa offer conditions of aridity and rainfall unreliability which preclude

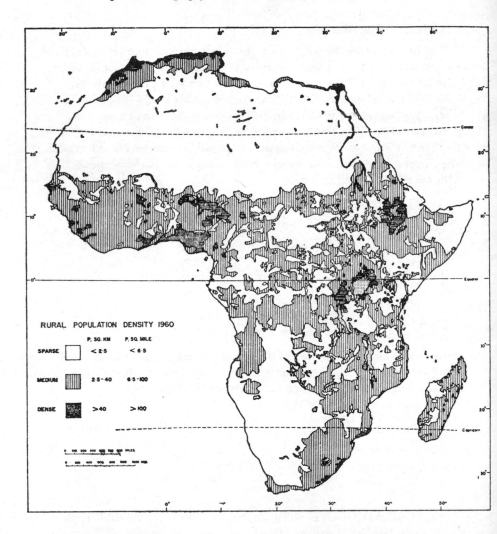

Fig. 3.3. Africa: rural population density, 1960 (after E. Schmidt and
P. Mattingly). Apart from the large negative areas, note the patchiness of
population distribution.

TABLE 3.3. RECENT ESTIMATED DENSITIES OF POPULATION OF SELECTED AFRICAN COUNTRIES

	Total pop. per km² of total area	Total pop. per km² of arable land	Rural pop. per km² of arable land
North			
Morocco (1966)	30	175	127
Algeria (1968)	5	194	140
Tunisia (1965)	27	102	79
Libya (1968)	1	70	54
Egypt (1968)	32	1144	688
Sudan (1968)	6	209	194
West			
Gambia (1967)	30	172	156
Ghana (1968)	35	300	280
Togo (1965)	30	76	71
Nigeria (1965)	63	264	221
Central			
Cameroon (1968)	12	129	120
Zaire (1965)	7	92	20
East			
Uganda (1967)	34	163	155
Kenya (1965)	17	552	516
Tanzania (1965)	13	97	93
Madagascar (1968)	11	230	206
Mozambique (1965)	9	263	—
Réunion (1966)	163	660	518
South			
South Africa (1965)	15	148	92
Angola (1965)	4	573	538
Zambia (1965)	5	193	160
South-west Africa (1965)	1	87	83
Botswana (1968)	1	139	111

Source: U.N., *Demographic Handbook for Africa*, 1971.

dense human populations, despite recent idealistic claims by St. Barbe Baker that by reclamation 2 million square miles of the Sahara could be covered by "homes and gardens for 3850 million people". Without massive schemes for discovery of new water supplies and desalinization of sea-water, settled agriculture is only possible in deserts where there is perennial river flow, as along the Nile, or where considerable quantities of underground water are available (e.g. Saharan oases). Sometimes such groundwater attracts seasonal movements of nomadic population at a local level.

No other vegetational or climatic zone of Africa presents such uniform conditions of population distribution as the deserts, although the northern and southern zones of Mediterranean climate are generally well peopled, and, in contrast, the Guinea savanna zone of West Africa, with poor soils and prevalent tsetse fly, has relatively low densities of population. The zones of moist tropical forest and grass steppe present much less uniform patterns of population distribution, and sometimes savanna belts, with longer rainy seasons than steppes, have lower population densities—because other physical and human factors exert an influence.

High altitude has attracted population in both the tropical and temperate zones of Africa, not only because of climatic amelioration but also because mountains have been refuges from marauding tribes and attackers. Consequently, mountains in many parts of Africa (e.g. Kabylie in Algeria, Nuba mountains in Sudan, Bandiagara escarpment in Mali, Mandara mountains in Cameroon, Ethiopian highlands and Drakensberg escarpment of Lesotho) have been densely settled by sedentary or semi-nomadic peoples, sometimes more than their physical environment would normally give reason to expect.

In some localities good soils permit much more intensive agriculture than would be otherwise possible; the volcanic soils of West Cameroon, Fernando Po, Rwanda and Burundi are examples, as are the brown soils of the Kano close-settled zone. In East Africa, moreover, the soil catena has been shown to be closely linked with agricultural utilization and population distribution. On the other hand, soil fertility is not intrinsically attractive to population; much depends upon what people want to grow. In contrast, diseases in Africa generally have a more repellent effect upon patterns of population distribution, as in the tsetse-infected areas of the Congo watershed, and in the valleys of northern Ghana where river blindness repels settlement. In the past the tsetse-fly has particularly infested areas depopulated by tribal contraction, making resettlement very difficult.

Although population density does not always diminish from coast to interior, the remote continental interior is lightly peopled. In contrast, islands seem to encourage high population concentration both around the African coastline (e.g. Djerba in Tunisia, Canary Islands, Cape Verde Islands, Fernando Po, São Tomé, Príncipe, Annobon, Zanzibar, Comoros, Seychelles, Mauritius, Réunion) and on lakes within the continent (e.g. islands on Lake Victoria and on Lake Zwai in Ethiopia).

An essential point concerning environmental influence upon population distribution is that no physical factor works in isolation, and therefore never has a uniform effect. Some sandy coasts are uninhabited (e.g. South-west Africa), some are populous (e.g. Dahomey). Rivers of deserts and steppes, like the Senegal, middle Niger and Webbe Shibeli, are attractive to man, but many in forested areas are not. Many African mountains are densely peopled, but we can find many in the Sahara which are not. The same qualification can be applied to plains, plateaux and other landforms. Although physical factors are an important influence upon population distribution in Africa, they are not individually pre-eminent, nor can they be dissociated from a wide variety of human factors past and present.

Social and economic factors have also had a profound influence upon population distribution in Africa, particularly such factors as traditional modes of life, organization of societies and the effects of modern economy upon migrations. In pre-colonial Africa there were immense areas, especially in Central and South Africa, which had not seen fixed human habitation, while, in contrast, the Nile Valley, the Maghreb and parts of West Africa had known sedentary civilization for thousands of years. Generally speaking, although this is a matter of dispute among anthropologists, rural densities are highest where well-established and organized societies have prevailed for a long time and where some form of economic diversification occurred, enabling people to engage in commerce. Consequently, the persistence of these past patterns of population distribution helps to explain some of the present contrasts in population density, as for example, between Central and West Africa.

The existence of nomadic societies has precluded dense concentrations of population in many regions of Africa, because the extensive economies practised by hunting and collecting groups, like Pygmies and Bushmen, or pastoral tribes, like the camel-herders of the Sahara or the Baggara cattle-herders of Sudan, permit only sparse populations. The rotating system of bush-fallowing practised in the tropical forests is also associated with low densities of population, although the periods under cultivation and fallow may vary greatly under the influence of soil fertility, land tenure systems, traditional customs and population pressure. The types and yields of staple foods may have a considerable effect upon population density, and so may export crops which are grown in most of the major densely peopled agricultural areas. There is in fact a two-way relationship between population size and crops, each influencing the other, and this relationship exists between population pressure and agricultural systems as a whole. Boserup has developed the idea of agricultural systems evolving in accordance with the demands made upon them by population growth, that population growth incites changes in such systems. Certainly, difficulties arise where there is a slow response of agricultural systems and settlement patterns to population growth, as Prothero has shown for north-western Nigeria, but nowadays a common answer to population pressure is migration.

Institutional structures also have this two-way intimate relationship with population density, and Hunter has indicated in his studies of northern Ghana how even aspects of kinship, such as the rule of descent and the rule of residence, may affect population densities. Warfare and civil strife were undoubtedly crucial factors in pre-colonial times, and their influence can still be seen. Mountain refuges have been mentioned already, and there can be no doubt that in the days of inter-tribal warfare and "protection" of weaker tribes, defence was an important criterion in the siting of any settlement, and nowhere more than in Ethiopia. Harrison Church states for West Africa that inter-tribal warfare (along with the tsetse-fly) has depopulated "former battlefields or frontiers such as those between Kano and Bornu, Katsina and Sokoto, the Mossi and old Mali settlements near the Niger River, the Yoruba and Dahomey, Dahomey and Ashanti". And in many other regions the core areas of tribes are still more populous than the peripheries. But in general, the influence of insecurity upon population distribution has diminished, and in many parts of Africa there is a downhill movement from mountain refuges, as in the Fouta Djallon in Guinea and the Jos plateau in Nigeria.

The population map of Africa also still bears the marks of the depredations of slavery, although it is always difficult to attribute the present population density of any particular area to this one cause. Nevertheless, slavery has been commonly mentioned as a principal reason for the sparse populations of East Africa, Western Central Africa and the "middle belt" of West Africa. In Western Central Africa today, some of the more populated localities are often remote and suffer from infertile soils, no effort having been made to recolonize, areas more fertile areas formerly devastated by slave-raiding; but the true picture of demographic loss and redistribution resulting from the European and Arab slave-trades may never be known.

So far, aspects of the modern economy have not accounted for enormous transformations in the population distribution map of Africa, although we shall see, when we come to discuss migrations, the transformations are increasing. At the moment, the proportion of the active population engaged in manufacturing in African countries is less than 10 per cent, and manufacturing is responsible for high population densities only in a few regions, such as lower Egypt and South Africa. Mining is still a more important employer in South Africa, and also accounts for the concentration of population in the Copperbelt and in a growing number of other mining centres and regions in Africa.

State Populations

There is a growing tendency for the populations of the many political units of Africa to evolve as distinct demographic units behind their political boundaries. Contrasts in the economic, political and social policies of European powers and subsequently of independent African states have engendered demographic differentials on a political basis formerly unknown in a continent largely cocooned from external influences. Now it begins to matter more that a man is an Algerian than an Arab, a Nigerian than a Negro, a Kenyan than a Kikuyu. Politicians play down tribalism in favour of nationalism—not always with success, as we see in Sudan and Nigeria, where ethnic and religious contrasts are blatant and frictional. Nevertheless, it is becoming apparent that the widespread fragmentation of ethnic and tribal groups by political boundaries is generally a matter of diminishing significance. Many tribes are losing or have lost their political functions, and as traditional groups are suffering in the process of nation-building. It is also noteworthy that with a few serious exceptions, such as among the Somali of East Africa and the Ewe of West Africa, there have been few tribal troubles over boundaries in Africa considering the great length and intricate sinuosit:es of these boundaries.

One only has to compare the populations of Egypt and Libya, Morocco and Mauritania, Nigeria and Niger, Ethiopia and Djibouti, Congo and Cabinda, South Africa and Lesotho to see some of the great demographic disparities between African states. These disparities, not only of numbers (Fig. 3.4) and densities but of population composition and dynamics, will augment as African states begin to introduce population policies. This is not to minimize the diversity of ethnic and social groups; only to emphasize that the political boundaries of Africa are gaining in demographic significance.

Som arranged the fifty-five countries of Africa in order of population size and classified them into five groups (Table 3.4). The obvious

TABLE 3.4. CLASSIFICATION OF AFRICAN COUNTRIES ACCORDING TO POPULATION SIZE, 1964

Population size (millions)	Number of countries	Total population (millions)	Percentage of African population
Less than 0.4	11	2.1	0.7
0.4–1.6	11	9.2	2.0
1.6–3.6	10	27.4	9.1
3.6–7.3	11	52.4	17.3
7.3 and over	12	211.7	69.9
	55	302.8	100.0

SOURCE: R. K. Som, Some demographic indicators for Africa, in J. C. Caldwell and C. Okonjo (Eds.), *The Population of Tropical Africa*, 1968, p. 190.

fact is that most African political units have only small populations. In 1964, forty-three countries had less than 7.3 million inhabitants (i.e. were smaller than Austria), thirty-two less than 3.6 million (i.e. were smaller than Norway), and twenty-two less than 1.6 million (i.e. were

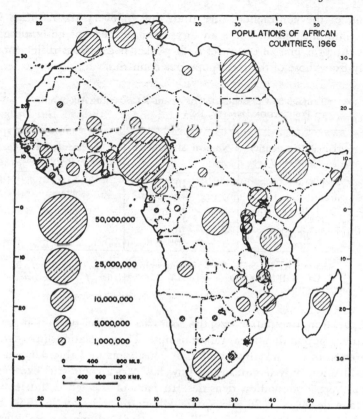

FIG. 3.4. Populations of African countries. Africa is so politically fragmented that it contains a large number of states with small populations.

smaller than Nicaragua or Jamaica) with a combined population of only 11.3 million people, 3.7 per cent of the total population of Africa. Moreover, many of these countries are independent—Libya, Liberia, Mauritania, Gambia, Central African Republic, Congo (Brazzaville), Gabon, Botswana and Lesotho—while Gambia and Gabon and some of the colonial territories had less than 500,000 inhabitants. At the other end of the scale, despite the fact that Africa has no giant states like Asia, twelve countries contained over two-thirds of the total population of the continent. More than one in every six Africans is a Nigerian, and one in ten is an Egyptian. It need not be emphasized that the problems of countries with pocket populations differ enormously from those of the most populous countries.

TABLE 3.5. CLASSIFICATION OF AFRICAN COUNTRIES ACCORDING TO POPULATION DENSITY, 1964

Population density (per km²)	Number of countries	Percentage of African population
1–3	10	4.3
4–10	12	22.9
11–18	12	20.6
19–35	11	29.7
36 and above	10	22.5

SOURCE: R. K. Som, Some demographic indicators for Africa, in J. C. Caldwell and C. Okonjo (Eds.), *The Population of Tropical Africa*, 1968, p. 192.

Apart from population size, the countries of Africa also differ greatly in their population–area relationships. These relationships can be expressed in one way by population density, as in Table 3.5, but this classification only demonstrates how few African countries experience high overall population densities. In fact, of the ten countries with average densities of 36 per square kilometre and over in 1964, only Nigeria had more than 5 million people, and most were islands: Mauritius (353 per square kilometre), Réunion (153), Rwanda (116), Seychelles (115), Burundi (99), Comoros (96), Nigeria (61), São Tomé and Príncipe (56), Cape Verde Islands (55) and Tunisia (37).

If on the other hand, we consider population size in relation to areal dimensions (Table 3.6), we may establish a different classification, which although arbitrary, helps us to understand some of the remarkable differences between states. Groups 1 and 2 in Table 3.6 include the micro-states or pocket states, the only difference being that group 1 contains countries with less than one million inhabitants, while those countries in group 2 are rather more populous. These micro-states arose from the multiplicity of European footholds in Africa, and the perpetuation of colonial boundaries. Many of those in group 1, particularly the islands, such as Réunion, Seychelles, Comoros and Cape Verde Islands, are still under colonial rule. Micro-states have severe economic problems owing to limited resources, lack of investment, high expenditures

TABLE 3.6. CLASSIFICATION OF AFRICAN COUNTRIES ACCORDING TO POPULATION SIZE AND AREA, 1972

Area (km²)	Population (millions)	Number of countries	Examples
1. Under 200,000	Under 1	13	Port. Guinea, Lesotho, Gambia, Djibouti, Swaziland, and many islands
2. Under 200,000	1–10	9	Liberia, Senegal, Dahomey, Sierra Leone, Rwanda, Burundi, Malawi, Togo, Tunisia
3. 200,000–1 million	Under 1	5	South-West Africa, Botswana, Congo (Brazzaville), Gabon, Spanish North Africa
4. 200,00–1 million	1–10	12	Rhodesia, Guinea, Somalia, Zambia, Central African Republic, Mozambique, Madagascar, Cameroon, Ivory Coast, Ghana, Uganda, Upper Volta
5. Over 1 million	Under 10	6	Libya, Chad, Niger, Mauritania, Mali, Angola
6. Over 200,000	Over 10	10	Sudan, Algeria, Zaire, South Africa, Ethiopia, Nigeria, Kenya, Morocco, Tanzania, Egypt

on administration and difficulties in marketing products, and they may experience rapid demographic change owing to sudden mortality decline or external migrations.

Group 3 includes a number of medium-size territories with small populations. Some of them, like the countries of group 5 those with large areas and medium-size populations, contain considerable areas of desert. In fact, many result from the division of the Sahara into ten different states, six of which are relics of French colonial rule. Egypt and Sudan are saved by the Nile from joining group 5, which includes countries with scattered populations, major transportation problems and some with tiny budgets dependent upon one or two exports, such as the groundnut states of interior West Africa.

The countries in group 6 are the major states of Africa, those with medium–large areas and relatively large populations. Most are in peripheral positions, and most are concerned with the integration of diverse human elements within their territories. Only Egypt and to a lesser extent Nigeria are faced with serious population pressures. The difficulty of Egypt, with 99.5 per cent of her 32 million people concentrated on only 3.5 per cent of her territory, is unique in the world, let alone Africa. As resources are developed, these major countries should play an increasing role in Africa, greater perhaps than the countries of group 4, which are those of medium-size in area and population. And yet many of the countries in group 4 have varied resources, none suffers from population pressure, and some are making energetic strides toward economic development.

Migrations

Migrations are not new to Africa (Fig. 3.5). Historical study of any part of the continent reveals complex patterns of migrations, particularly in those regions where pastoral nomadism has been the prevalent mode of life. Some of these traditional movements persist, such as the pilgrimage movement of "Westerners" through Central Sudan toward Mecca, involving the settlement of more than a million people on the way. Other migratory movements have been modified, particularly through the decline of pure nomadism and the spread of semi-nomadism, which is now prominent on the Saharan fringe. Moreover, Barbour has described rural–rural migrations of a traditional and spontaneous type, resulting from poverty at home or economic enterprise, in Uganda, Ghana and Nigeria. However, rural–rural migration has become relatively rare since the beginning of the colonial era, which brought the end of intertribal wars as well as in some parts of the continent, like Central Africa, a stabilization of population distribution previously unknown, so that the present population map is largely one

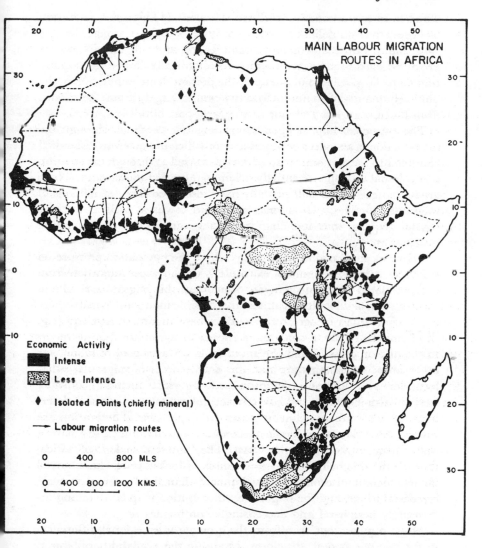

Fig. 3.5. Main labour migration routes in Africa (after R. Mansell Prothero). The "islands" of intense economic activity are the poles of attraction for migrant workers.

which is inherited from the pre-European period. This is the contention of Trewartha and Zelinsky in their study of the Belgian Congo. On the other hand, European conquest, colonization and rule have elsewhere provoked massive movements which have radically altered the population map. To give but one example, the present dense population in the Shire Highlands of southern Malawi results largely from the exodus from Portuguese Mozambique in the early part of this century.

The European impact upon migrations has persisted, through the introduction of a modern economic sector which has given an "islandic" character to the economic map of Africa, as well as through the creation of a colonial economy essentially orientated toward the exterior. These great changes, which still prevail, have instigated flows of millions of migrants to mines, plantations, ports and towns as well as towards coastal regions, thus inducing increasing unevenness of population distribution.

Migrants come mainly from areas where the population pressure on resources is high; a common example is the outward migration from overpopulated mountain refuges. Sometimes this migration results in the desertion of difficult and almost inaccessible mountain massifs where cultivation brings meagre returns. Elsewhere mountain-dwellers (e.g. the Bamileke of Cameroon) make successful agricultural adjustments to population growth, and the mountains act as a pool of labour for other areas. Mountains are not the only sources of migrants; other localities with adverse population pressure exist, including offshore islands (although Fernando Po attracts migrants), and areas of deteriorating soil conditions, but in general the patterns of migration are toward the "islands" of modern economic activity, which are particularly concentrated near the coast. The "internal sector" of Africa, now identifiable politically by fourteen land-locked states, has enjoyed far less social and economic development than the "external sector", or coastal fringe, and the population distribution map is becoming increasingly peripheral and decreasingly continental.

Modern migrations arise from the growing interregional differences in the rate of economic development and in the availability of labour, along with the growing pressure of population upon resources in rural areas. If data of the labour-force of any one mine or plantation are examined, it can be seen that workers come from a wide area, frequently from beyond international boundaries. In general, both push-and-pull factors are operative, although economic motives normally outweigh desires either to escape from tribal traditions and kinship obligations or to seek the freedom, entertainment and way of life associated with towns. Few African countries remain unaffected by labour migration, which takes on varied forms from long-distance international migrations, such as towards the mines of South Africa, to seasonal movements of harvesters. The vast majority of long-distance migrants are young men, although Mortimore has drawn attention to the importance of the migration of wives in northern Nigeria, and this is by no means an isolated example.

The problems of labour migrations are many. The seasonality and periodicity of most migrations are partly symptomatic of the seasonality of African agriculture with long periods when manpower is idle, and partly of the fact that neither the points of departure nor the points of arrival of migrants provide enough to sustain their families. Migratory harvesters in the Maghreb and Ghana, for example, are mostly migrating to subsist. As Spengler notes, some families can only survive by depending upon both subsistence farming and urban industry; but colonial governments and companies have sometimes encouraged seasonal rather than permanent migration, so that rural manpower would not be seriously reduced and that family housing need not be provided. The division of agricultural labour between the sexes in much of Central Africa enables men to leave women to carry on cultivation without reduction in productivity, but in some regions there is no choice, and men migrate to compete in large numbers for few jobs at low wages. This means that many men are unable to earn enough to bring their families to settle with them, and consequently disharmonious situations evolve with unbalanced sex-ratios in both towns and country. Detribalization, often desired by African governments, is therefore delayed. In any case, many migrants retain their tribal identities in towns, even when they have become permanent town-dwellers, and some African cities have well-defined tribal quarters. Another difficulty is that too few Africans are adequately trained to take on skilled and professional employment, although the number of places open to them is increasing annually, especially in administration and industries. In addition to these social and economic problems of migrations, Prothero has drawn attention to the fact that migrations in Africa are associated with the spread of diseases, notably malaria, and that these diseases cannot be controlled as long as migrants move unchecked. He has also pointed to the considerable volume of refugee movements, which, as in Zaire, have followed political independence. To these we may add the hundreds of thousands of war refugees in Algeria and, more recently in Egypt and Nigeria.

Future volumes of migration will depend on various factors, not only on population growth, but also on changing patterns of population pressure and on the relationship between agricultural development and industrialization. It is probably reasonable to suppose that migration will increase in future decades, and that it will assist both in the breakdown of tribalism and in the growth of nationalism. We shall have to wait to see what the real effects of African boundaries will be on long-distance migrations. African migrant labourers working outside their own countries may be numbered at present in their millions, but there is evidence in many parts of Africa that international migrations have been undertaken with greater difficulty since the wave of independence, and in some African countries there is fairly open hostility to other African nationals who have profitable occupations which might be taken by indigenous persons. Emigrant, skilful Ghanaian fishermen, for example, are less welcome than formerly in some other West African states. Congolese are unwelcome in Gabon, and Kikuyu in Tanzania. When jobs are short and prospects of economic advancement are small, this is perhaps an inevitable reaction. Some countries also dislike losing a considerable proportion of their manpower to other countries, even if only seasonally; the inland states of West Africa, notably Upper Volta, suffer particularly in this respect. Yet, in some parts of Africa where small nations are numerous the efficient use of manpower must involve international migrations.

Urbanization

The most important type of migration at the moment is towards the towns, and this is specially striking because in many parts of Africa, especially East, Central and South Africa, there were few towns before the arrival of Europeans. The main exceptions to this generalization were Arab cities of the Maghreb and the East African coast, Yoruba cities of Nigeria, Egyptian cities, and caravan centres in the Sudan zone of West Africa. Europeans, with their colonial economies and their coastally orientated transport systems, have encouraged particularly the growth of ports. It is highly significant that over two-thirds of the countries on the African mainland with direct access to the sea have coastal capitals, mostly ports. The growth of trade, industry and administration has attracted millions to coastal and other cities.

Yet Africa is still the least urbanized of all continents, and in 1960 only 13 per cent of its total population lived in localities with 20,000 inhabitants or more, in comparison with 17 per cent in Asia, and 32 per cent in Latin America (Table 3.7). However, lest we should think that this degree of urbanization is abnormally low, we should note that the proportions of the African population living in urban areas and in large cities with 100,000 inhabitants and over in 1950 were about the same as in the world as a whole at the beginning of this century. By 1960 there were about 310 towns with 20,000 inhabitants or more, and 71 with 100,000 inhabitants or more. About 30 million or one in nine Africans were living in large cities, and their numbers are growing rapidly. There are now six urban agglomerations in Africa with more than one million inhabitants: Cairo, Alexandria, Casablanca, Lagos, Kinshasa (formerly Leopoldville) and Johannesburg. The growth of some of these cities is little short of mercurial. The figures for Kinshasa in Zaire are particularly striking, as they rose from 110,300 in 1946 to about 1,400,000 in 1970. Casablanca was no more than a village when the French protectorate was established in 1912, but by 1971 had about 1,500,000 inhabitants. Johannesburg grew from 322,000 in 1938 to 1,970,000 in 1970, and Cairo from 1,300,000 in 1937 to 4,220,000 in 1966. And Egypt's urban population rose from 1.9 million in 1897 to 12.4 million in 1966, a growth which is twice as rapid as that of the total population of the country. In Cameroon, which is very much less urbanized, the two main cities of Douala (200,000) and Yaoundé (100,000) are growing at about 6 per cent per annum, and only 16 per cent of their inhabitants were born in these cities. This polarization of urban growth in a few large cities has produced very high rates of primacy, nowhere more than in Tunisia, where the agglomeration of Tunis is nearly ten times the size of the next largest city.

TABLE 3.7. ESTIMATED PERCENTAGE OF TOTAL POPULATION IN URBAN AREAS OF AFRICAN COUNTRIES

Countries	Year	Percentage of total population in localities of 20,000 and more inhabitants	Population in localities of 100,000 and more inhabitants as percentage of	
			Total population	Population in localities of 20,000 and more inhabitants
North				
UAR (Egypt)	1966	38.2	29.6	77.2
Morocco	1960	23.7	18.9	79.7
Tunisia	1966	22.9	10.4	45.4
Libya	1964		22.5	
Algeria	1966	26.5	13.4	50.6
Sudan	1962	3.9	1.7	44.6
West				
Senegal	1960-61	22.5	12.6	55.9
Ghana	1960	12.3	9.5	77.7
Nigeria	1963	19.2	8.8	45.9
Sierra Leone	1963	7.1	5.9	83.1
Gambia	1963	8.8		
Liberia	1962	7.9		
Ivory Coast	1960	7.0	5.6	79.3
Dahomey	1961	8.3		
Togo	1961	5.9		
Guinea	1960	6.6	5.7	86.6
Upper Volta	1960	3.1		
Mali	1962	4.7	2.3	70.5
Central				
Congo (Brazzaville)	1961–62		16.0	
Zaire	1959	9.1	5.9	65.1
Cameroon	1962–64	6.6	4.4	66.7
Central African Republic	1950	10.0	10.0	100.0
Burundi	1965	2.6		
Chad	1963	2.8		
East				
French Somaliland	1963	58.0		
Réunion	1954	45.0		
Mauritius	1962	30.1		
Madagascar	1962	9.0	5.2	57.6
Kenya	1962	5.9	5.2	87.9
Somalia	1962–63	7.7	5.7	75.0
Tanzania	1967	5.1	2.2	43.3

TABLE 3.7 (cont.)

Countries	Year	Percentage of total population in localities of 20,000 and more inhabitants	Population in localities of 100,000 and more inhabitants as percentage of	
			Total population	Population in localities of 20,000 and more inhabitants
Mozambique	1960	1.2	2.7	
Uganda	1969	5.1	4.0	78.3
Ethiopia	1965	4.7	3.4	73.5
South				
South Africa	1960	35.1	26.5	75.5
Zambia	1969[a]	25.3	16.3	64.4
Rhodesia	1960	15.0	12.4	79.2
Botswana	1964	18.0		
South-West Africa	1960	6.9		
Angola	1960	7.0	4.6	65.7

SOURCE: U.N.,*Demographic Handbook for Africa*, 1971.

[a] African population only.

Apart from the scattered capital cities, the large cities of Africa tend to form several distinct clusters (see Fig. 3.6). In the mid-1960s Egypt had seventeen cities with more than 100,000 inhabitants, South Africa eleven, Morocco ten and Nigeria twenty-four and these four countries had more large cities than were found in all the remainder of the continent. Large cities are rare in the continental interior, and so far only three of the fourteen land-locked states, namely Uganda, Zambia and Rhodesia, have a large city with more than 100,000 inhabitants. Such cities are few in East and Central Africa, where in some countries, like Mozambique and Burundi, the proportion of the total population living in localities of 20,000 and more inhabitants is below 5 per cent, in contrast with about 40 per cent in Egypt, 35 per cent in South Africa, and 25 per cent in Morocco and Tunisia.

Fig. 3.6. Africa: city size about 1960 (after E. Schmidt and P. Mattingly). Note the clustering of cities in the Maghreb, Egypt, Nigeria and South Africa, and the sporadic distribution elsewhere.

It would therefore be wrong to exaggerate the degree of urbanization in Africa. Whereas some countries, especially those with strong urban traditions, European contacts, modern mines or industries, have large cities and experience rapid urbanization, other countries have rarely any modern towns and know only African "small-town life". The large modern cities and the small traditional towns are poles apart in mode of life. The big cities are the main points of contact with the outside world, and the principal centres for the location of the modern sector of the economy. Their contrasts in modernity and tradition and in wealth and poverty, epitomize many of the disharmonies visible in developing countries. They have concentrated the bulk of the Europeans in the continent, the main social amenities (hospitals, schools, universities, entertainments), and a high proportion of the service sector, but most are unable to absorb the growing numbers of rural urban migrants. At the moment, they are extremely consumer-orientated, and urgently need industries.

African cities also exhibit the two common manifestations of urban overpopulation in developing countries, namely acute housing problems and excessive unemployment. Shanty-towns and slums are found in all large cities, sometimes peripherally located, sometimes within the heart of cities. Some are enormous; the number of inhabitants in the "bidonvilles" of Casablanca in 1960 was 180,000. And many of these shanty-town dwellers are unemployed, partially employed or inadequately employed. The degree of employment is, in fact, very difficult to determine in countries where so many are scratching a living in a desultory fashion, in a menial job or in crime. We think, for example, of the innumerable boot-blacks, petty street-traders, and street vagabonds, often living at a lower level than rural populations.

Mortality

The early impact of Europeans upon African population growth was undoubtedly disastrous, but in recent decades, medicine and public health programmes, introduced by Europeans and expanded by independent African states, have had a marked lowering effect upon mortality. Most African countries are benefiting from lower mortality than previously experienced, but the position is far from ideal. Unfortunately, mortality data are often less easily obtained than fertility data, owing to the usual lack of compulsory death registration and the inadequacy of much of the demographic data which have a bearing on mortality rates. Generally we are unable to measure accurately the mortality of the various countries, but it is clear that North Africa and South Africa enjoy lower mortality than tropical Africa (Table 3.8).

TABLE 3.8. AFRICA: ESTIMATED POPULATION GROWTH RATES BY REGION 1965–70

	Birth rate (per 1000)	Death rate (per 1000)	Annual increase rate (%)
AFRICA	46	20	2.6
North	48	17	3.1
West	46	20	2.5
Central	45	24	2.1
Southern	41	17	2.4
East	43	18	2.5

SOURCE: *UN Demographic Yearbook*, 1970, Table 1.

While crude death rates in North and South Africa are usually below 20 per thousand, corresponding to an expectation of life at birth in excess of 45 years, in tropical Africa death rates exceed 20 per thousand, expectation of life at birth being generally less than 37 years, and sometimes less than 30 years. Som noted that of the 28 infant mortality rates available for African countries only two were less than 100 per thousand, and many were over 200 per thousand (Mali, Guinea, Zambia, Gabon). Moreover, these are mere national averages; the situation is much worse in rural areas, where infant mortality rates of 350 per thousand births are not exceptional.

Really dramatic declines in mortality have occurred only in small countries, like Mauritius, Réunion, Rwanda, Tunisia and the Spanish Plazas de Soberanía. In Mauritius the average life expectancy increased from 33 to 51 in an 8-year period after the Second World War, progress which Sweden took 130 years to achieve. The progress was largely due to the eradication of malaria, which is one of the main causes of high infant and child mortality. Oil-rich Libya can expect a similar decline in mortality following the provision of free medical services to poor people and those in the public sector.

Colbourne estimated that in hyper-endemic malaria areas in Africa, malaria causes the death of about 5 per cent of children under the age of 5. Gastro-enteritis, measles and pneumonia are also great child killers. Because of the localization of medical facilities in towns, infant and child mortality rates are often lower in urban areas than in rural areas. Smith notes that the typical infant mortality rate in tropical African towns is about 100–150 per thousand live births, and that about one in every four children born fails to live until the age of 5. Indeed, he suggests that in African conditions total mortality over the first 3 or 5 years of life is probably a more useful demographic measure than infant mortality. Public health services are much fewer in rural areas, especially among nomadic groups, who have suffered not only from the suppression of raiding and protection, the imposition of political boundaries, the decline of caravan traffic, the loss of many favoured pasture areas and the general neglect or disapproval of the authorities, but also from less favourable demographic conditions. All these features can be seen among Saharan nomadic tribes. So the power and prosperity of many nomadic groups has been reduced, and their numerical significance has dwindled too.

It is unlikely that the whole of Africa will experience in the next few years dramatic mortality declines comparable with that in Mauritius. The health measures necessary would be numerous and costly, and as yet there is not enough money in most countries to implement large-scale public health schemes. However, the rates of mortality decline will largely determine the rates of population increase in the next few decades, because mortality decline seems more likely than fertility decline.

Fertility

African population fertility is high, and has been little influenced by European contact. Crude birth rates, which are subject to severe statistical limitations, usually range from about 35 to 60 per thousand, but there are exceptions, such as Ceuta and Melilla with rates below 20 per thousand. The highest rates seem to be in West Africa, especially in Mali and Guinea, although the difference from other African regions is not great, and this is confirmed by general fertility rates usually in excess of 200 (per thousand women aged 15–49) and an average gross reproduction rate of more than 3.0 (the maximum level possible is about 4.0).

The main influences upon high fertility are universal marriage, early marriage and the lack or limited amount of birth control. In general, earlier marriage means a shorter period between generations and quicker population growth. Most African women marry within a year or two of puberty, and marriage rates of women aged 15–19 are very high; in Guinea, for example, the proportion is over four-fifths. It is not surprising that the fertility rates of this age-group are sometimes over 200 per thousand.

We should not retain the impression that African fertility is everywhere high. Analysis of fertility within a particular country reveals the influence of a number of factors tending to lower fertility. There are many infertile unions in Africa, much one-child sterility and a very rapid progression of sterility with age of woman. This was specially noted in a survey made in 1959 of the Azande in the Congo, which revealed astonishingly low fertility, 35 per cent of women having had no children. Romaniuk and others have attributed much of this sterility to the widespread nature of venereal diseases, but he has also collected much evidence of induced abortion and contraception in the Congo. Polygamy is specified as an important factor by Dorjahn and some other anthropologists, who stress that monogamous African women produce more children than polygynous women, and evidence is available for various countries, including Congo, Guinea and Sierra Leone. On the other hand, this is a controversial subject, because various other factors are involved, such as the older average age of polygamous husbands and the higher proportion of sterile women in polygamous households. Another check on high fertility is the common custom prohibiting cohabitation of husband and wife until the baby is weaned (which is usually much later in Africa than in either western societies or Asia). This is not a general custom, but is very common in much of West Africa. Obviously, the practice of labour migration, which mostly involves males, is also a key influence upon fertility, although seasonal migrations have less significance than long-distance migrations. Urbanization will in the long run probably lower fertility, but there is some conflicting evidence on this; whereas most towns appear to have lower fertility than their surrounding rural areas, some, like Kinshasa and Lubumbashi (formerly Elisabethville), have higher fertility. Moreover, evidence from Egypt shows that while urban areas demonstrate inverse relationships between fertility and education and between fertility and occupational status, in rural areas it is the professional and administrative classes which have the highest fertility. Another factor sometimes mentioned in relation to occasional low fertility in Africa is the quality of the diet, but the evidence is limited.

Total fertility therefore varies considerably from region to region, from under 3.5 (children born per woman during child-bearing ages according to current fertility rates) in Gabon to over 8.0 in parts of Kenya, Uganda and south-eastern Sudan. In tropical Africa, Coale points to a ridge of high fertility in the interior regions of East Africa with a westward spur through southern Congo to northern Angola. He also notes a strip of very high fertility along the coast of West Africa from coastal Nigeria to Ivory Coast with a northward spur through the western part of Nigeria into parts of Niger and Upper Volta. Rather lower fertility is found along the East African coast and in much of western Central Africa. However, Coale emphasizes that these variations should not be allowed to convey any other impression than that the fertility of tropical Africa is very high, with an average birth rate of about 49 per thousand and a total fertility of about 6.5 children.

Natural Increase and Age Structures

The obvious result of the interplay of high fertility and declining mortality is high natural increase, and the UN estimate for Africa during the period 1965–70 is 2.6 per cent per annum, or 9 million more persons each year (equivalent to the total population of Uganda). We should recall, however, that all natural increase rates for Africa and its territories are subject to the same source limitations as the component birth and death rates. Of the 32 rates of natural increase available for African states, 28 lie within the range 15–36 per thousand, with North and South Africa generally experiencing higher rates than tropical Africa (Fig. 3.7). With reference to these high rates, the population of

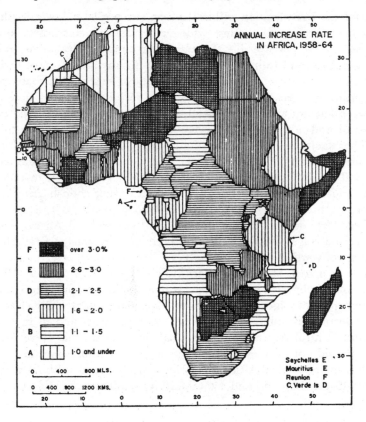

Fɪɢ. 3.7. Annual increase rate in Africa, 1958–64. Owing to the diverse influences of fertility, mortality and migration, no simple pattern emerges.

South Africa rose from 5.2 million in 1904 to 23.0 million in 1970, and that of Egypt from 9.7 million in 1897 to 30.9 million in 1967.

High natural increase rates are not universal in Africa. Algeria suffered high mortality during its recent war of independence, and consequently had a temporarily low natural increase. Moreover, the rates for countries conceal considerable regional variety. In Cameroon, for example, we can find ethnic groups with rates varying from 2.8 to 27.8 per thousand, and this evidence tends to support the contention that in Africa we can recognize separate economic and demographic systems with significant differences occurring over distances of a few miles.

In most of Africa rapid population growth has taken place only in the last decade or so. In the 1940s the average annual increase for Africa was 1.5 per cent, and in the 1950s 2.1 per cent, in comparison with the present 2.6 per cent. And as mortality continues to decline with no appreciable change in fertility levels, there is a prospect of further acceleration of the rate of growth in the near future. Indeed, United Nations estimates indicate that in the 1980s Africa may have the highest rate of population growth among the world regions.

With rising rates of natural increase, nearly all African countries have a so-called dependency burden, i.e. a high proportion of young and aged in relation to adults. Although most African age data must be

TABLE 3.9. PERCENTAGE AGE DISTRIBUTION OF SELECTED AFRICAN COUNTRIES

	Year	Under 15	15–59	60 and over
Morocco	1969	46.4	49.4	4.2
Algeria	1966	47.2	46.1	6.6
Tunisia	1966	46.3	48.1	5.6
Libya	1964	43.7	49.3	7.0
Egypt	1960	42.8	51.3	5.9
Sudan	1966	47.3	49.1	3.6
Dahomey	1961	45.0	49.0	6.0
Ivory Coast	1961	42.7	53.7	3.6
Ghana	1960	44.5	50.5	5.0
Niger	1962	45.5	50.3	4.2
Mali	1966	48.8	47.7	3.5
Upper Volta	1960–61	40.9	53.9	5.2
Central African Republic	1965–66	41.6	53.9	4.5
Mauritius	1968	42.7	51.6	5.7
Réunion	1964	45.3	49.4	5.3
Tanganyika	1957	42.4	54.1	3.5
Uganda	1959	41.4	54.8	3.8
Mozambique	1960	42.0	53.4	4.6
Madagascar	1966	46.5	50.4	5.8
Rhodesia (Africans)	1969	48.0	49.0	3.0
South Africa	1960	40.1	53.8	6.1
South-West Africa	1960	39.6	53.2	7.2

SOURCE: U.N., *Demographic Handbook for Africa*, 1971.

regarded with suspicion, Table 3.9 gives a general idea of age compositions in selected African countries. In North African countries, Ivory Coast, Dahomey, Ghana and Mauritius, persons in the working age groups support in theory about an equal or slightly larger number of dependents, but elsewhere the ratio is usually four dependents to five in the working age groups. High dependency ratios mean problems of education, housing, and employment, but the numerical effect of mortality decline upon the dependency ratio is to some extent compensated by an improvement in the health and age composition of the labour force.

Population and Economic Development

There is a real danger that population growth may become a major barrier to social and economic progress. Whereas demographic transition in European countries was slow and accompanied by gradual improvement of economic and social conditions, rise in *per capita* incomes and emigration, the recent mortality decline in Africa has taken place with no comparable changes in incomes and no important flow of emigrants. Moreover, the present rate of population growth in Africa is about double that of industrial Europe in the nineteenth century. Inevitably, immense strain is placed upon the economies of African countries, which require huge investments in new means of production and in social and economic infrastructures. None save South Africa and perhaps Libya (because of recent oil revenues) has a high enough level of educational attainment or of *per capita* income to enable production increase to adequately overcome population increase.

Per capita output in Africa has been estimated to be about one-eighth of that in industrial countries, and to reach the level of these countries *per capita* industrial output in Africa would have to be raised 25-fold and *per capita* agricultural output two-fold. These are daunting targets.

We should recall here the great differences between the modern and traditional sectors of the economy, despite the fact that these terms oversimplify a situation which is perhaps more of a continuum than two contrasting poles. The development of Africa has meant the development of the modern capitalist sector and the quasi-neglect of the traditional sector. Yet in most African countries the traditional sector is predominant and experiences most of the natural increase in population and the rise in population densities, in relation to capital as well as land. One of the main difficulties as far as the traditional sector is concerned is the inadequate supply of capital, not only in total but in type, for monetary capital is needed particularly for agricultural education and extension, for marketing and research.

One danger is that in some localities fast population growth in the traditional agricultural sector may cause permanent damage to the environment, through soil erosion and decline in soil fertility. As Gourou has said, the bush-fallowing system which prevails in the humid tropics is an extensive form of land-use incapable of satisfactory adaptation to the dynamics of rapid population growth. Moreover, communal ownership of land, so widespread in Africa, leads to dangerous reductions in the fallow period, without accompanying efforts to intensify production. In some areas shorter fallows, manuring and the introduction of new crops have enabled the survival of greater numbers, but critical levels of population density have sometimes been surpassed with drastic results, inspiring Allan to propose the concept of critical density of population (CDP). He defines it as "the human carrying capacity of an area in relation to a given land use system, expressed in terms of population per square mile; it is the maximum population density which a system is capable of supporting permanently in that environment without damage to the land". This is a conservationist approach, one which is concerned with the environment and its well-being, and it is particularly applicable to the varied subsistence economies found in Africa south of the Sahara. On the other hand, some may say that man's well-being is more important than that of his environment. The CDP involves the calculation of (a) the percentage of cultivable land according to traditional methods, (b) the land-use factor, or relationship between duration of cultivation and duration of fallow, and (c) the cultivation factor, or acreage planted *per capita* per annum. These are no easy calculations, and inaccuracies are inevitable, but it demonstrates that in some pockets of tropical Africa there is a dangerous lack of balance between land resources and population.

We must not exaggerate this danger for in large areas of Africa there is no overpopulation, and there are manifold ways in which farming can be improved, intensified and extended: better methods of cultivation, livestock farming, water supply, storage of crops and marketing as well as introduction of new crops and breeds of livestock. Such changes in agricultural techniques can greatly modify population pressures.

Mabogunje also emphasizes that the social and economic expectations of a community are a crucial factor in the understanding of population pressure upon resources, and explains how in West Africa the level of expectations decreases sharply as one goes inland from the coast. Increased expectations may have several results including fuller utilization of resources, out-migration, or changes in social and economic attitudes to land ownership, training and wealth.

Agricultural improvements and investments are vital, because although industrial expansion is rapid in many cities of Africa, industries and mining are often more capital-intensive than labour-intensive. They have had only localized and limited influences on raising levels of *per capita* income and on reducing volumes of unemployment. It is vital to develop industries and mining, but it is unlikely that in the near future they will solve the problem of providing new employment for fast-growing populations. Consequently, many countries will have to consider family planning as a means of increasing *per capita* incomes.

Family Planning

What are African governments doing about it? Caldwell has shown that family planning activities and government population policies in Africa exhibit a definite pattern, largely determined by the distribution of former colonial empires. In territories formerly under British rule birth control has been open, although little used by Africans, and family planning clinics are being established, particularly in Mauritius, where the birth rate is declining rapidly. In South Africa and Rhodesia, family planning services have long been available to Europeans, and have been recently extended to Africans, although their success may depend upon racial attitudes. The same is true in Kenya, but where the Luo suspect that the Kikuyu want to reduce their numbers. In contrast, in most former French, Spanish, Portuguese, Belgian and

Italian colonies of tropical Africa there is little use of contraceptives by the African populations because their import or sale is illegal, and there are no family planning clinics. Many francophone territories of tropical Africa have even inherited systems of family allowances for civil servants, a luxury which they can ill afford. Although these countries are aware that this is mostly a colonial heritage, they have not yet rejected it, nor have they concerned themselves with population policy. In muslim North Africa family planning programmes have been accepted as part of official policy in Tunisia and Egypt, both greatly affected by rapid population growth. Yet we find the ironical situation that these two countries are geographically separated by sparsely inhabited oil-rich Libya, which offers family allowances and encourages immigration of skilled workers from some other Arab countries.

Family planning in Africa is not on a large scale, and the majority of Africans probably know very little about birth control. The demand for it is mostly from urban, educated people, especially in Commonwealth territories and in the Arab north. In some of these countries there may be slight changes in fertility in the near future. Elsewhere, there is less chance of government support, and some governments, especially of Tanzania, Madagascar and Somalia, stress that population growth in their countries could not occur rapidly enough to jeopardize economic advance. In other words, it looks as if national boundaries are going to influence still further the patterns of population dynamics and distribution in Africa.

Select Bibliography

ABU-LUGHOD, J. L., Urbanization in Egypt: present state and future prospects, *Econ. Devel. Cult. Change* **3**, 313 (1965).

ALLAN, W., *The African Husbandman*, Edinburgh, 1965.

BARBOUR, K. M., *Population in Africa*, Ibadan, 1963.

BARBOUR, K. M., Rural–rural migrations in Africa—a geographical introduction, *Cahiers de l'ISEA*, 47 (1965).

BARBOUR, K. M. and PROTHERO, R. M. (Eds.), *Essays on African Population*, London, 1961.

BASCOM, W. R. and HERSKOVITS, M. J. (Eds.), *Continuity and Change in African Cultures*, Chicago, 1959.

BEAUJEU-GARNIER, J., *Géographic de la Population*, Paris, **2**, 9 (1958).

BLACKER, J. G. C., The demography of East Africa, in RUSSELL, E. W. (Ed.) *The Natural Resources of East Africa*, Nairobi, 1962.

BOSERUP, E., *The Conditions of Agricultural Growth*, London, 1965.
BOURGEOIS-PICHAT, J. in WOLSTENHOLME, G. & O'CONNOR, M., *Man and Africa*, London, 1965, chapter 3.
BOUTE, J., *La Démographie de la Branche Indo-Pakistanaise d'Afrique*, Louvain, 1965.
BRASS, W. *et al.*, *The Demography of Tropical Africa*, Princeton, 1968.
BROOKFIELD, H. C., Population distribution in Mauritius, *J. Trop. Geog.* **13**, 1 (1959).
CALDWELL, J. C., *Population Growth and Family Change in Africa; New Urban Elite in Ghana*, Canberra, 1967.
CALDWELL, J. C. and OKONJO, C. (Eds.), *The Population of Tropical Africa*, London, 1968.
CHEVALIER, L., *Le Problème Démographique Nord-Africain*, Paris, 1947.
CHURCH, R. J. H., *West Africa*, London, 5th ed., 1966.
CHURCH, R. J. H., CLARKE, J. I., CLARK, P. J. and HENDERSON, H. R. J., *Africa and the Islands*, London, 1964.
CLARKE, J. I. (Ed.), *Sierra Leone in Maps*, London, 1966.
DELF, G., *Asians in East Africa*, London, 1963.
DESPOIS, J., *L'Afrique du Nord*, Paris, 2nd ed., 1964.
ECONOMIC BULLETIN FOR AFRICA, Recent demographic levels and trends in Africa, **5**, 30 (1965).
ECONOMIC COMMISSION FOR AFRICA, *Report of the Seminar on Population Problems in Africa*, E/CN/14/186.
ELKAN, W., *Migrants and Proletarians*, London, 1960.
FAGE, J. D., *An Atlas of African History*, London, 1963.
FAIR, T. J. D. and SHAFFER, N. M., Population patterns and policies in South Africa, 1951–1960, *Econ. Geog.* **40**, 261 (1964).
GANN, L. H. and DUIGNAN, P., *White Settlers in Tropical Africa*, London, 1962.
GOUROU, P., *La Densité de la Population Rurale au Congo Belge*, Brussels, 1955.
GOUROU, P., *The Tropical World*, London, 3rd ed., 1961.
GREENBERG, J. H., *The Languages of Africa*, Bloomington, Indiana, 1963.
LORD HAILEY, *An African Survey*, London, 1957.
HANCE, W., *Population, Migration and Urbanization in Africa*, New York, 1970.
HERSKOVITS, M. J., *The Human Factor in Changing Africa*, New York, 1963.
HILTON, T. E., *Ghana Population Atlas*, Edinburgh, 1960.
HOUSTON, J. M., *Western Mediterranean World*, London, 1964.
HOWELL, F. C. and BOURLIERE, F. (Eds.), *African Ecology and Human Evolution*, London, 1964.
HUNTER, G., *The New Societies of Tropical Africa*, London, 1965.
HUNTER, J. M., Regional patterns of population growth in Ghana 1948–60, in J. B. WHITTOW and P. D. WOOD (Eds.), *Essays in Geography for Austin Miller*, Reading, 1965, pp. 272–90.
INTERNATIONAL AFRICAN INSTITUTE, *Social Implications of Industrialization and Urbanization South of the Sahara*, UNESCO, 1956.
INTERNATIONAL UNION FOR THE SCIENTIFIC STUDY OF POPULATION, *Problems in African Demography*, Paris, 1960.
KAY, G., The distribution of Africans in Southern Rhodesia, *Rhodes–Livingstone Institute*, no. 28, Lusaka, 1964.
KAY, G., *A Social Geography of Zambia*, London, 1966.
KAYSER, B., La démographie de l'Afrique occidentale et centrale, *Les Cahiers d'Outre Mer*. **18**, 73 (1965).

KIMBLE, G. H. T., The pattern of population, in *Tropical Africa*, vol. 1, Land and Livelihood, New York, 1962.
KROTKI, K. J., *21 Facts about the Sudanese*, Khartoum, 1958.
KUCZYNSKI, R. R., *Demographic Survey of the British Colonial Empire*, vols. 1 and 2, London, 1948–9.
KUPER, H. (Ed.), *Urbanization and Migration in West Africa*, Univ. of California, 1965.
LORIMER, F., *Demographic Information on Tropical Africa*, Boston, 1961.
LORIMER, F., BRASS, W. and VAN DE WALLE, E., Demography, in R. A. LYSTAD (Ed.), *The African World*, London, 1965, pp. 271–303
LORIMER, F. and KARP, M. (Eds.), *Population in Africa*, Boston, 1960.
MABOGUNJE, A. L., *Urbanization in Nigeria*, London, 1968.
MAY, J. M., *The Ecology of Malnutrition in Middle Africa*, New York, 1966.
MORGAN, W. T. W. and MANFRED SHAFFER, N., *Population of Kenya: Density and Distribution*, Nairobi, 1966.
MURDOCK, G. P., *Africa: Its Peoples and their Culture History*, New York, 1959.
NEL, A., Some problems in compiling a population map of Africa, *J. Geog.* **1**, 66 (1959).
OMINDE, S. H., *Land and Population Movements in Kenya*, London, 1968.
OMINDE, S. H. (Ed.), *Studies in the Population of Africa*, London, 1971.
PORTER, P. W., East Africa—Population Distribution, *Ann. Assoc. Am. Geog.* **56** (1966), Map supplement no. 6.
PRESCOTT, J. R. V., Population distribution in Southern Rhodesia, *Geog. Rev.* **52**, 559 (1962).
PROTHERO, R. M., Population patterns and migrations in Sokoto Province, Northern Nigeria, in *Natural Resources, Food and Population in Inter-Tropical Africa*, London, 1956.
PROTHERO, R. M., Continuity and change in African population mobility, in R. W. STEEL & R. MANSELL PROTHERO (Eds.), *Geographers and the Tropics*, London, 1964, pp. 189–213.
PROTHERO, R. M., *Migrants and Malaria*, London, 1965.
SAUVY, A., La République de Madagascar. Population, économies et perspectives de développement, *Population* **17**, 443 (1962).
SCHMIDT, E. A. and MATTINGLY, P., Das Bevölkerungsbild Afrikas um das Jahr 1960, *Geog. Rund.* **18**, 447 (1966).
SELIGMAN, C. G., *Races of Africa*, 4th edn., London, 1966.
SIMMS, R. P., *Urbanization in West Africa. A review of Current Literature*, Evanston, Illinois, 1965.
SMET, R. E. de, *Cartes de la Densité et de la Localisation de la Population de la Province Orientale (Congo)*, and *de l'Ancienne Province de Léopoldville (Republique Démocratique du Congo)*, Université Libre de Bruxelles, 1962 and 1966.
SMITH, T. E. and BLACKER, J. G. C., *Population Characteristics of the Commonwealth Countries of Tropical Africa*, Commonwealth Papers IX, University of London, Institute for Commonwealth Studies, 1963.
SOCIOLOGICAL REVIEW, Special Number on 'Urbanization in West Africa,' vol. 7, No. 1, 1959.
SPENGLER, J. J., Population Movements and Problems in Sub-Saharan Africa, in E. A. G. ROBINSON (Ed.), *Economic Development in Africa South of the Sahara*, London, 1965.
STEEL, R. W., Land and Population in British Tropical Africa, *Geography* **40**, 1 (1955).
STEEL, R. W., An inventory of Land and people, *J. African Admin.* **12**, 211 (1960).

STEPHENS, R. W., *Population Pressures in Africa South of the Sahara*, Washington, 1959.

STEPHENS, R. W., *Population Factors in the Development of North Africa*, Washington, 1960.

STEVENSON, R. F., *Population and Political Systems in Tropical Africa*, New York, 1968.

TITMUSS, R. and ABEL-SMITH, B., *Social policies and population growth in Mauritius*, London, 1960.

TREWARTHA, G. T., New population maps of Uganda, Kenya, Nyasaland and Gold Coast, *Ann. Assoc. Am. Geog.* **47,** 41 (1957).

TREWARTHA, G. T. and ZELINSKY, W., Population problems in Tropical Africa, *Ann. Assoc. Am. Geog.* **44,** 135 (1954).

TREWARTHA, G. T. and ZELINSKY, W., The population geography of Belgian Africa, *Ann. Assoc. Am. Geog.* **44,** 187 (1954).

UN POPULATION STUDIES, No. 2, *The Population of Tanganyika*, 1949.

UN POPULATION STUDIES, No. 14, *Additional Information on the Population of Tanganyika*, 1953.

UN POPULATION STUDIES, No. 15, *The Population of Ruanda-Urundi*, 1953.

VENNETIER, P., La population et l'économie du Congo, *Les Cahiers d'Outre-Mer* **15,** 360 (1962).

WELLINGTON, J., *Southern Africa*, London, 1955, vol. 2, pp. 212–70.

4

SOUTH-WEST ASIA

Size of Population

The highly distinctive shatterbelt region of South-west Asia lies on the crossroads between Europe, the USSR, the Indian subcontinent and Africa. Its limits may be variously defined. In this volume the definition of South-west Asia differs from that employed in recent *UN Demographic Yearbooks* by the addition of Iran and Afghanistan, because in terms of population geography these two countries are more properly considered as part of sparsely peopled South-west Asia rather than of populous South Asia, dominated by India and Pakistan. Two minor difficulties of definition are Turkey and Egypt, both of which span two continents, but recently Egypt's Asian territory has been seized by Israel, and Turkey is more appropriately treated as a whole rather than just the Asian part.

In 1970 South-west Asia contained nearly 122 million people, about as many as Indonesia in over four times its area. Indeed, the area of South-west Asia as defined above is larger than either the Indian subcontinent or Europe (excluding the USSR) where very much bigger populations reside. Its overall population density is therefore low, a fact which is not surprising in view of the pervasive influence of aridity, combined in parts with high altitude. Despite low population density, South-west Asia, like Middle America, Africa and South-east Asia, suffers from much political fragmentation, so that the 122 millions were divided among seventeen countries (Table 4.1). Two-thirds, however, are found in the three large northern countries of Turkey, Iran and

TABLE 4.1. POPULATIONS OF SOUTH-WEST ASIA, 1970

	1970 Estimate (thousands)	Annual increase 1963-70 (%)	Area (thousand km²)	Density (per km²)
Turkey	35,232	2.5	781	45
Iran	28,662	2.9	1,648	17
Afghanistan	17,125	2.4	647	26
Iraq	9,440	3.2	435	22
Saudi Arabia	7,740	2.7	2,150	4
Syria	6,098	3.0	185	33
Yemen	5,733	2.7	195	29
Israel	2,889	2.8	21	140
Lebanon	2,787	2.9	10	268
Jordan	2,317	3.7	98	24
Southern Yemen	1,281	2.7	288	4
Cyprus	633	1.0	9	68
Muscat and Oman	657	3.0	212	3
Kuwait	711	9.0	16	44
Bahrain	215	3.0	1	360
Trucial States	200	3.1	84	2
Qatar	79	5.3	22	4
	111,384		6,802	18

SOURCE: *UN Demographic Yearbook*, 1970.

Afghanistan, while the remaining fourteen countries shared only 40 million people. The northern tier of three non-Arab states, greatly influenced by the physical presence of fold mountains, contrasts strongly with the politically divided, Arab and more arid part of South-west Asia between the Mediterranean Sea and the Indian Ocean. Here geometric political boundaries are mostly products of the twentieth century, but they are gaining effectiveness as demographic divides. On the other hand, the state of Israel, an excellent example of political influence upon population numbers and dynamics, has demonstrated an expansionist policy which has completely transformed the population geography of the Levant.

Data

As in previous chapters it must be stated that the population data are unreliable. In fact, they are especially poor in South-west Asia, as some countries have never had a modern national census: Afghanistan, Lebanon, Qatar, Yemen, Southern Yemen, Muscat and Oman. For several of these countries estimated population totals are quite conjectural. A number of factors account for this shortage of census data. The social structure is particularly important, for census enumerations are very difficult among populations which are nomadic, illiterate or have fear or suspicion of the motives of enumerators. It follows that for many parts of the Arabian peninsula there are few population data. Saudi Arabia actually held a population census in 1962–63, but found the total enumerated unsatisfactorily small (3,297,000) and so for political reasons has neither accepted nor published the results. The UN estimate for 1967 (6,990,000), based on the Saudi Arabian official estimate, is twice as high. The reason for not taking a census in the Lebanon is a matter of social and political structure, for the relations between the Christian and Muslim communities, which have a delicate numerical balance, would probably be worsened by any attempt to determine more accurate numbers.

Vital registration is even more limited in South-west Asia, so much so that El Badry considers published data of little value in countries like Lebanon, Jordan, Syria and Iraq. Even for towns it is hard to calculate natural increase, owing to inadequacies in birth and/or death registration as well as poor age reporting.

The consequence is that only three small countries, Cyprus, Kuwait, and Israel, have reasonably reliable population data, although Greek–Turkish tension in Cyprus, immigration into Kuwait and Israeli expansion have greatly complicated their respective demographic situations. Other countries with fairly adequate data are Turkey, Iran, Syria and Jordan.

Population Distribution

In spite of the imperfections of population data, it is possible to ascertain the broad lines of population distribution. One basic fact is its unevenness. Like Latin America and Africa, South-west Asia has vast uninhabited and scantily populated areas. In individual countries a large proportion of the total population is usually concentrated on a

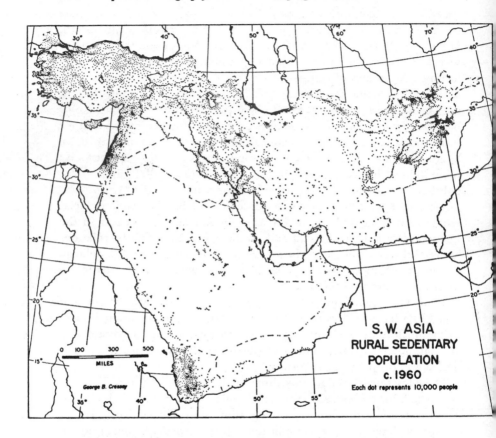

FIG. 4.1. South-west Asia: rural sedentary population *ca.* 1960 (from G. B. Cressey, *Crossroads*, 1960). The population density in the northern tier of countries, namely Turkey, Iran and Afghanistan, contrasts with that in the Arabian peninsula.

small proportion of the total area. In Israel three-fifths live on 11 per cent of the area, in Iraq over half live on 15 per cent of the area, and in Saudi Arabia population distribution must be even more uneven. In view of the existence of large uninhabited areas–much less evident in Turkey than in the rest of South-west Asia—crude population densities for countries differ substantially from densities per unit area of culti-

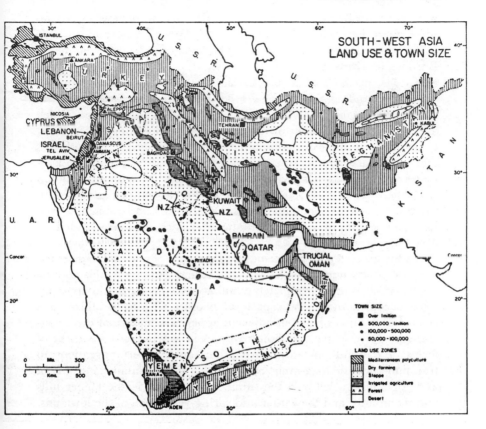

FIG. 4.2. South-west Asia: land use and town size. Again the contrasts between the northern and southern zones of South-west Asia are apparent.

vated land. For example, in Iraq about 1960 the two densities were 16 and 135 per square kilometre, and in Syria 25 and 131.

With about three-quarters of the active populations in South-west Asia employed in agriculture, it is not surprising that the broad pattern of population distribution corresponds with that of cultivated land (Figs. 4.1 and 4.2), which now covers only about 7 per cent of the total area. The cultivated land, however, is of variable value agriculturally and there are obvious differences in population density between regions of Mediterranean intensive agriculture, dry farming areas and irrigated areas. The main zones where a fairly high concentration of population is associated with normal cultivation or dry farming are the moister zones: the coastlands of the Black Sea, Caspian Sea and Mediterranean Sea, the uplands of Yemen, the Fertile Crescent, a number of valleys in western Turkey and the subhumid plains of Anatolia. Irrigation, which affects about 17 per cent of the cultivated land of South-west Asia, generally permits the densest populations, as along the Tigris, Euphrates and Orontes, where densities rise to over a hundred per square kilometre and in many lesser valleys and basins in the northern mountain tier. There the close settlement of irrigated areas contrasts vividly with the brown skeletal mountain chains. Desert oases, in Arabia and Iran for example, also have high population densities, with clearly identifiable boundaries.

Aridity exerts a strong imprint upon the map of population distribution. Deserts as desolate as the Rub al Khali in southern Arabia and the salt kavir of Iran are completely uninhabited, but semi-arid areas are often occupied by nomadic pastoral peoples who have utilized the ecological contrasts between adjacent zones. The nature of these contrasts in different parts of South-west Asia has induced a variety of forms of pastoral nomadism, from horizontal desert migrations to transhumance and long-range nomadism in the mountain zone of Iran and Afghanistan, between the summer vegetation in the higher hills and mountains, and the winter and spring vegetation of the lowlands.

Nomadic Imprint and Decline

Although nomadic peoples today survive mostly as minority groups, in the past they have greatly influenced the political instability of South-west Asia and have restricted population size. No analysis of population distribution in South-west Asia would be complete without some more explicit reference to nomadic influence. De Planhol has pointed out that the distribution of nomadic peoples in South-west Asia owes much to the medieval movements of Turkish and Arab nomads. Turkish bactrian camels were more suitable for mountain life than Arab dromedaries, a fact which has affected the distribution of

Turks, who were nomads of mountains, uplands and cold steppes, whereas Arabs were nomads of plains and hot deserts. He also contrasts the low densities of population in the Turkish mountains with the higher densities in the Zagros of Iran. When Turkish nomads occupied Anatolia in the Middle Ages they found a countryside already partly ruined by raids during the long struggle between Arabs and Byzantines, and subsequently sedentary life never recovered. On the other hand, in the mountains of Iran and Afghanistan medieval Arab and Turkish invasions did not everywhere extinguish the old rural civilization based on irrigated agriculture, and peoples reacted to external menace by developing their own large-scale mountain nomadism. The result has been a much denser human occupation of mountains than in Turkey.

One other type of mountain life common in South-west Asia is the mountain-refuge, where heretical and unorthodox peoples escaped from the Arab waves. Moister Lebanese mountains which were formerly forested offered shelter to Maronites and Druses, and the Jebel Ansariya in Syria fulfilled a similar function for Alawis and Ismailiya. Today mountain-refuges are experiencing more emigration than either those mountains which were inundated by nomads or those where sedentary peoples managed to survive nomadic invasions. Nevertheless, Maronites and Druses are still more numerous in Mount Lebanon than in Beirut.

In South-west Asia today less than 10 per cent of the population are nomadic and there is increasing sedentarization of nomadic peoples. One reason is the impact of technical modernity, such as vehicle transport and work opportunities in industries or oil installations. The political division of pastures and the prohibition of raiding have also curbed pastoral nomadism. Little by little nomadic tribes are losing their age-old struggle with central governments. At the beginning of this century tribes in Syria, Iraq and eastern Turkey were prominent in resisting governmental authority and foreign rule. But central governments, in Iraq and Iran for example, have strongly attacked the power of chiefs, although struggles persist with the Kurds and the Qashqai. Nomadic tribes pose too many difficulties for administrators, whose bureaucratic machinery is generally insufficiently flexible to deal with tribes. Law courts, police posts, schools and dispensaries are easier to establish as sedentary rather than mobile phenomena, and it is in the interest of central governments to encourage sedentarization of nomadic tribes in order to impose a bureaucratic system and to reduce their political danger to the state.

Not all sedentarization of nomads is under government stimulus; some is spontaneous. Barth has suggested that more favourable demographic conditions (particularly lower mortality) among nomadic tribes explain some of the past flow from nomadic to settled life in South-west Asia, a flow from areas of low population density to areas of high density. In recent years the greater decline of mortality among settled communities has altered the demographic balance between nomadic and sedentary populations, but the latter are usually more capable of extending their economy to cope with higher rates of natural increase. The surplus population of nomadic tribes finds its way into villages and towns but only at the lowest levels of sedentary society. Consequently, sedentarization, forced or otherwise, is frequently accompanied by impoverishment and discontent. It is therefore highly desirable for governments to regularize their relations with nomadic groups, many of whose lands need redevelopment with a view to improvements in livestock farming. This can often be accomplished without detriment to neighbouring sedentary agricultural populations, who have usually lived in close mutual interdependence with nomadic pastoralists.

Peoples

It has often been said that the physical geography of South-west Asia does not encourage cultural or political uniformity. In the northern tier of states physical fragmentation has impeded uniformity, the widely separated and sometimes isolated regions favouring particularism. Problems of unity are real in Turkey, Iran and Afghanistan, and Ankara and Tehran are to some extent compromises to offset provincialism and to centralize national administration. In the Levant physical diversity has induced similar problems in replica, particularly the conflicting interests of mountain-dwellers and plainsmen. And in Arabia the ecological hazards to travel, along with long distances between oases, have fostered separatism and some cultural distinctions.

While the component regions of South-west Asia are diverse and separate, there is a broader characteristic of the whole, that of linking Asia, Africa and Europe. South-west Asia has been a routeway for the migration of peoples. The easiest and most favoured route was the Fertile Crescent, a discontinuous, relatively fertile zone stretching from the Nile Valley and the Mediterranean to Mesopotamia and the Persian Gulf; an arcuate link between two great centres of early civilization. Along this ancient highway were the first transitions from nomadic to settled life and some of the earliest cities, like Ur and Jericho. Here nomads, peasants, and town-dwellers, the three basic elements of Middle Eastern society, lived in close juxtaposition, the nomads often holding sway because of their mobility and military ability.

The Fertile Crescent and other routeways in South-west Asia, like the Cicilian gates and the Khyber Pass, have witnessed the passage of peoples for millennia, movements which have resulted in great ethnic complexity, now difficult to unravel. In simple terms it may be said that the peoples of South-west Asia largely belong to one of three great strains: Semites from the Arabian deserts, Indo-Europeans from the north and Turkish peoples from Central Asia. The Semitic peoples, a linguistic rather than a racial group, are found generally in the southern half of South-west Asia, where they are most represented by two closely related peoples, the Arabs and the Jews, whose cultures are based on two of the three great monotheistic religions which arose among the Semites: Islam, Judaism and Christianity. The Arabic language, which was originally spoken in the districts of Mecca and Medina, was widely disseminated by the spread of Islam and came to be dominant in the lands south of the Taurus and Zagros ranges, and a unifying element in the Islamic world.

Indo-European or Aryan peoples, cattle raisers from the steppes of eastern Europe and central Asia, moved into Iran and Afghanistan during the first millennium BC, mixing with early inhabitants, but they also were later modified by invasions of Arabs and Mongols. Some of these modifications are evidenced by the Persian and Pushtu languages, the main languages of Iran and Afghanistan respectively, although both countries contain linguistic minorities, including Turkish speakers.

Turkish peoples originated from central Asia, their first invaders, the Hittites, coming into the region in the second millennium BC. Caucasian and Mongoloid in physical characteristics, Turkish peoples spoke a wide variety of Ural–Altaic languages of which Turkish, the language of the Osmanlis, came to be dominant in Asia Minor.

These three elements form the basic substratum of the present populations of South-west Asia, but there are lesser elements, like the Kurds, an Aryan people with their own language who have been established in their mountains for over 4000 years. Now numbering more than 3 million, the Kurds have found themselves dissected by the political boundaries of four states—Iraq, Iran, Turkey and Syria— their pleas and struggles for independence so far being fruitless.

Another people long enduring minority status are the Armenians, a Christian people speaking an Indo-European language, who were formerly concentrated in eastern Turkey. Following the massacres during the period 1880–1918 many fled to the Soviet Union, where the Armenian SSR is centred on Yerevan. Others went temporarily to Syria (where only a small proportion of a large influx remain), Iraq, Iran, Egypt or Europe.

Religions

Religion is perhaps the main distinction among people in South-west Asia, which has not only given birth to Christianity, Judaism and Islam but has also seen the rise of lesser religions, like those of the Zoroastrians, Yazidis, Mandaeans and Bahais, along with more than a score of sects. Among Muslims there is the important divide between Sunni and Shiah, the former experiencing a number of movements including the Wahhabi, Mahdiya and Sanusiya, while the latter contain a number of sects such as the Zaidiya, Imami, Ismailiya, Alawi and Druse. The Christian minority in South-west Asia who number only a few million adherents, particularly localized in the Lebanon and Cyprus, are split among a large number of denominations, the most numerous of which are the Maronites and Greek Orthodox. The Maronites are one of the many Uniate communities which have united with the Catholic Church; others are the Greek Catholic, Chaldean Catholic, Coptic Catholic, Armenian Catholic and Syrian Catholic churches. Sects of the Orthodox Church are the much persecuted Nestorians of the Eastern (or Assyrian) Church, the Armenians (or

Gregorians), and the Syrians (or Jacobites). To add further confusion, modern missionary activities have produced Protestant communities in various countries; an example is the Church of South Persia.

The diversity of religious communities in South-west Asia arises from the geographical fragmentation previously mentioned, the social isolation perpetuated by linguistic and cultural barriers, and the concomitant development of political division and religious schism. Some of the many religious minorities, like the Assyrians, Armenians and Jews, have suffered persecutions, but these lasted only for short periods. Islam has in the past been remarkably tolerant toward other monotheistic religions, so many religious communities have survived as social units, despite the recent overall weakening of the religious way of life. Sometimes they have been identified with certain economic activities but never exclusively, and it is clear that religious minorities, despite their geographical localization and their unequal status with the Muslim majority, have enjoyed a great measure of social and economic freedom in the heart of the Islamic world. Religious differences have unfortunately intensified with the upsurge of nationalism, as in Israel where the Jews aim at overwhelming preponderance, Lebanon where Christians are uneasy about Arab ideals of unity, Cyprus (Fig. 4.3) where Orthodox Greeks and Muslim Turks struggle for power, and Iraq where Sunni–Shiah hostility reflects numerical balance. Sectarian hostility is sometimes more bitter than that between different religions. It must be said that nationalism has had a disharmonious influence upon religious and other minority groups in South-west Asia, especially in Arab countries, where nationalism is associated with Islam. The status of minorities has deteriorated and social gulfs with the Muslim majorities have often widened.

Islam, the dominant religion, has provided a code of behaviour for all aspects of life, having originated as a community of believers existing for religious purposes. But under the pressure of Western influences, Islamic society, not without divided attitudes, has undergone considerable changes. Reformers have either ignored religious traditions and values or tried to interpret them liberally, and these traditions and values are either being swept away, as occurred in Turkey under Kemel Ataturk, or are being eroded less dramatically. Particularly significant in the context of this volume are the reduction in polygamy and the

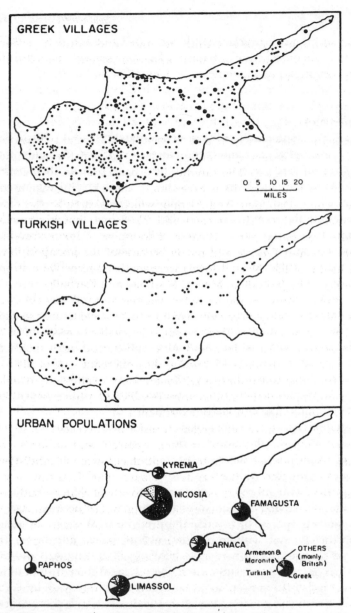

Greek Villages

Turkish Villages

Urban Populations

KYRENIA

NICOSIA

FAMAGUSTA

LARNACA

Armenian &
Maronite

Turkish

OTHERS
(mainly
British)

Greek

PAPHOS

LIMASSOL

0 5 10 15 20
MILES

FIG. 4.3. Communities of Cyprus, 1960. The Greek and Turkish communities do not have discrete geographical distributions.

changing attitudes towards veiling, seclusion and status of women. Inevitably, such changes are most apparent among the educated elements of urban centres.

Urbanization

Urbanization has greatly helped to liberalize the social structures of South-west Asia, inducing economic and educational ties other than those based on religion. The rapidity of urbanization is all the more remarkable in that town life is exceedingly ancient. This region contains two cities, Damascus and Aleppo, which claim to be the oldest continuously inhabited sites in the world. Trade was an early function of Middle East cities, partly because of transport of luxury products between Asia and Europe and partly because of the juxtaposition of diverse modes of life. Not all towns were markets; some were strongholds, others, like Jerusalem, Mecca, Mashhad and Karbala, were holy places. Many cities were the bases for religious and military conquest, their populations being more easily conquered, subjected, converted and taxed than nomadic tribes. Traditional cities evolved especially in the Fertile Crescent, western Iran and Asia Minor; elsewhere they were usually isolated. Surrounded by walls, they offered a way of life very different from that in rural areas, although many wealthy city-dwellers were parasitic upon their rural environs in which they have owned land but have made insufficient rural investment.

Traditional cities have been greatly transformed in recent decades by segmentation, the addition of modern quarters and suburbs with rectilinear layouts and hurtling traffic, and the growth of shanty-towns which have sprouted around capitals in particular. It is not easy to calculate the precise rate of population growth of many South-west Asian cities, because of inadequate census data, but it is evident that the populations of some cities have multiplied many times in recent decades; for example, in the 1930s Amman had only 30,000 inhabitants; but by 1966 it was more than ten times as large. In addition, there is the difficulty that a marked variation exists in the definition of urban status, in space and time, which considerably affects the percentages of population officially classed as urban. A purely administrative definition is often used, which is an inadequate index of urbanism; in Turkey

(1965), for instance, the definition includes chief towns of provinces and districts, in Syria (1960) cities, *mohafaza* centres and *mantika* centres, and in Iran (1966) all *shahrestan* centres and other places of 5000 inhabitants or more. Israel (1961) and Jordan (1961) are exceptional in having definitions of "urban" which include a functional element. In Israel urban settlements are those with more than 2000 inhabitants, except those where at least one-third of the heads of households participating in the civilian labour force earn their living from agriculture. In Jordan the definition includes district headquarters, localities of 10,000 or more inhabitants (excluding Palestinian refugee camps in rural areas) and those localities of 5000–9000 inhabitants and the suburbs of Amman and Jerusalem cities in which two-thirds or more of the economically active males are not engaged in agriculture. The Israeli definition is obviously more inclusive than that of Jordan, but if the United States definition were applied to Israel's population in 1961 then 90 per cent would be classed as urban, rather than 78 per cent.

It follows that international comparison of official levels of urban population is not very meaningful, as they give only a general picture, so in Table 4.2 locality size data have been used for purposes of comparison, in spite of the unsuitability of a size threshold as a true definition of urban status, and the lack of a comprehensive range of data.

One further problem of comparison arises from the fact that in some censuses data are provided for urban agglomerations as well as political cities, and in others only for political cities. It should be noted that the contrast in size of the two populations may be striking; the respective totals for Istanbul in 1965 were 1,751,000 and 2,052,000.

Most of the countries of South-west Asia are much more urbanized than the countries of South, South-east or East Asia or tropical Africa, and by their own definitions few are less than one-third urban (Table 4.2). On the other hand, Afghanistan, Yemen and Muscat and Oman are very feebly urbanized, and although accurate data are not to hand, it is probable that they are less than one-tenth urban.

For those countries which have had censuses the proportion living in localities of 10,000 inhabitants or more (and even 20,000 or more) exceeds one-quarter, in most it exceeds one-third, and in Israel and the small Gulf States the proportions range from one-half to nine-tenths.

The highest levels of urban population are found in micro-states such

TABLE 4.2. PERCENTAGE OF POPULATION BY LOCALITY SIZE, SOUTH-WEST ASIA, AT THE MOST RECENT CENSUS

	Total population (thousands)	1 million and over (%)	Percentage of population by locality size								Urban population (%)
			100,000–999,999		50,000–99,000		20,000–49,999		10,000–19,999		
			%	Cum. %	%	Cum. %	%	Cum. %	%	Cum. %	
Turkey (1965)	31,391	5.6	9.4	15.0	4.0	19.0	6.9	25.9	3.9	29.8	34.4
Iran (1966)	25,078	10.8	11.8	22.6	4.3	26.9	5.3	32.2	2.7	34.9	39.1
Iraq (1965)	8,261	21.1	10.3	31.4	6.4	37.8	4.0	41.8	3.2	45.0	44.1
Syria (1960)	4,565	—	23.9	23.9	3.6	27.5	2.4	29.9	4.3	34.2	36.9
Jordan (1961)	1,706	—	14.4	14.4	9.2	23.6	12.5	36.1	4.3	40.4	43.9
Israel (1961)	2,183	—	33.9	33.9	6.6	40.5	21.5	62.0	8.1	70.1	77.9
Cyprus (1960)	578	—	—	—	16.5	16.5	13.6	30.1	3.4	38.5	35.7
Saudi Arabia (1962–3)	3,302	—	15.3	15.3	5.4	20.7	4.5	25.2	4.5	29.7	?
Kuwait (1965)	467	—	63.9	63.9	—	63.9	13.9	77.8	12.6	90.4	94.0
Trucial States (1968)	180	—	—	—	31.9	31.5	23.6	55.5	—	55.5	65.4
Bahrain (1965)	182	—	—	—	43.4	43.4	22.6	66.0	—	66.0	82.3

NOTE: Unfortunately, incomplete data were available for Iraq 1957 and 1965. Afghanistan, Yemen, Southern Yemen, Muscat and Oman, Qatar and Lebanon are omitted through lack of censuses.

as Kuwait, Qatar, Bahrain, United Arab Emirates, Israel, Lebanon and Jordan, although Cyprus is a possible exception. Partly because of the influx of Palestinian refugees, Jordan has a higher proportion of urban-dwellers than Syria, which has a much longer history of urban life. Urban population growth in the small Gulf States, Saudi Arabia and Iraq has, of course, been greatly stimulated by the oil industry, whereas in Israel the level of urban population is largely attributable to the urban origins of Jewish immigrants, industrialization, influx of capital, tourism and the ubiquitous growth of the tertiary sector. Of the two most populous countries of Turkey and Iran, the more urbanized is Iran which in 1966 had 8,700,000 people (34.9 per cent) living in localities of 10,000 inhabitants or more. In Turkey the level of urban population is much lower, and is perhaps surprisingly comparable with that of Saudi Arabia, a country where nomads were formerly preponderant but are increasingly outnumbered by town-dwellers.

It therefore appears that traditions of urbanism are not a good guide to present levels of urban population, which seem more closely related (inversely) to the size of state and (directly) to the predominance of the modern sector (especially the oil industry) in the economy.

Obviously levels of urban population are not a true index of the importance or quality of urban life. Most of the town-dwellers of South-west Asia as well as most of the large cities are found in the more populous countries, namely Turkey, Iran and Iraq, all of which now contain urban agglomerations with more than 1 million inhabitants. Baghdad alone comprises over 21 per cent of the total population of Iraq, refuting Cressey's statement (1960) that "to develop a city with a population of over a million it appears necessary to have a country of 20 million people". All "millionaire cities" in South-west Asia are growing more rapidly than the urban populations of their respective countries, but Baghdad grew from 785,000 inhabitants in 1957 to 1,745,000 in 1965, an extraordinary rate of growth even among "millionaire cities". Tehran, however, added 1,200,000 inhabitants between 1956 and 1966.

The number of large cities with 100,000 inhabitants or more is increasing rapidly in South-west Asia, and by the mid-1960s there were over 50, nearly two-thirds of which were located in Iran (fourteen), Turkey (fourteen), and Iraq (six). In Iraq and Israel such large cities

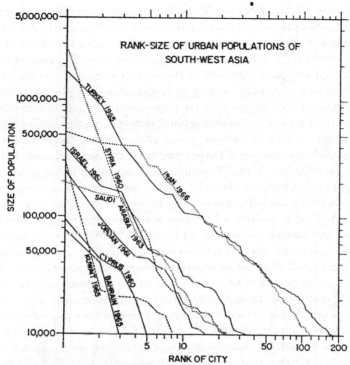

FIG. 4.4. Rank-size of urban populations of South-west Asia. The smooth curve of Turkey contrasts with most of the others, and the marked urban primacy of Iran contrasts with the duality in Syria and the triplicity in Saudi Arabia.

accounted for over 30 per cent of the population and in Iran and Syria between 20 and 30 per cent. Kuwait may even be regarded as a city state, as in 1965 64 per cent of its population lived in Kuwait city and 85 per cent in the agglomeration.

Table 4.3 and Fig. 4.4 reveal that urban primacy is most evident in Kuwait, Iran, Lebanon and Iraq, but in addition it occurs in Qatar and Southern Yemen, countries for which there are no census statistics. Apart from their primate cities being political capitals, these countries have little in common in size of area, size of population, location of primate city, or level/type of economic development.

TABLE 4.3. Urban Primacy in South-west Asia, at the Most Recent Census or Estimate

	Population of largest city (thousands)	Percentage of total population in largest city	Percentage of total population in two largest cities	P_1/P_2	$\dfrac{P_1}{P_2 + P_3 + P_4}$
Turkey (1965)C	1,751	5.6	8.5	1.94	1.09
Iran (1966)C	2,720	10.8	12.5	6.42	2.20
Iraq (1965)C	1,745	21.1	24.9	5.54	2.17
Syria (1970)C	835	13.3	20.9	1.31	0.84
Jordan (1970)E	500	21.6	20.1	3.68	?
Israel (1961)C	384	12.8	26.2	1.32	0.62
Cyprus (1970)E	115	18.1	24.1	2.23	1.00
Saudi Arabia (1965)E	225	3.3	10.8	1.16	?
Kuwait (1965)C	299	63.9	69.0	12.65	4.60
Bahrain (1971)E	89	41.1	62.3	2.35	1.49
Labanon (1970)E	939	33.6	39.3	5.97	4.16

NOTE: (a) P_1/P_2 is a simple measure of urban primacy in which the population of the largest city is divided by that of the second largest.

(b) $\dfrac{P_1}{P_2 + P_3 + P_4}$ the population of the largest city divided by the next three, is known as the Four City Index and probably gives a better indication of urban primacy, because primacy is affected by the number of urban centres.

(c) C = Census   E = Estimate

In countries where urban primacy is prevalent there is a tendency for it to increase; such growing centralization is especially evident in Tehran and Baghdad. There is no clear trend towards primacy, however, in countries like Turkey and Syria, where duality is more obvious than primacy, or Saudi Arabia, where triplicity may be noted. Indeed, in Turkey primacy is diminishing because Ankara, the capital and second largest city, is growing more quickly than Istanbul, the largest city.

The smoothness of rank-size curves is evidently influenced by the number of towns, and the curves of the two more populous countries Turkey and Iran are remarkably similar except for the larger cities. The countries with smaller populations have more dissimilar curves. Among the micro-states the size differences between the larger and smaller towns are very great, so rank-size curves plunge steeply In the case of Kuwait, the curve would be steeper if the agglomeration were plotted as one unit, but many large cities in this part of the world comprise socially and functionally segregated urban units which may be separated on the rank-size curve.

Although many of the countries of South-west Asia have larger networks of traditional cities than are found in tropical Africa or Latin America, there is a similar general tendency in each country for concentration of population in one or two large cities, sometimes at the expense of other cities. This phenomenon is particularly manifest in some of the more populated countries (e.g. Iran and Iraq) where cities of 100,000–250,000 inhabitants often experience modest growth. Owing to insufficient industrialization to meet the demands for employment, there is a case for suggesting that there is sometimes over-concentration of population in primate and other major cities, causing imbalance in population distribution; Baghdad may be cited as an example. On the other hand, there is less evidence to suggest that overurbanization is the rule, although in countries such as Iraq the "push" from the countryside has been strong, and in Syria and Iran there also seems to be relative overurbanization. This is certainly not the case in Kuwait and Saudi Arabia where cities are magnets of the modern sector, whose attraction exceeds the repulsion of rural areas. It may also be suggested that Cyprus is relatively underurbanized.

The present rapid growth rates of most cities in South-west Asia are due more to high natural increase, resulting from high fertility and low mortality, than to migration. The concentration of medical, public health and pharmaceutical facilities in urban centres means that natural increase alone may account for 3–4 per cent annual growth. Only in rare cases (e.g. Kuwait) is the migration component greater than that of natural increase, and the likelihood of this diminishes with city size. Moreover, natural increase of population in rural areas has also caused out-migration from areas with high rural population pressures, as in parts of Lebanon and western Turkey.

Pull factors include the attraction of the oil industry; the growths of Kuwait City, Dubai, Manama-Muharraq, Abadan and Kirkuk exemplify this influence. Industrialization also offers employment but in many countries it tends to be highly localized in the large cities. Ports are much less prominent in the pattern of city sizes than in Africa, South-east Asia or Latin America because South-west Asia has been less affected by European control and impact, and less externally orientated. Nevertheless, ports like Latakia, Jedda, Aden and Basra have great significance on a population map. Administrative status, especially as capitals, has contributed substantially to urban growth; cities like Ankara, Amman and Riyadh, small and humble towns a few decades ago, owe their present size to the growing bureaucracies and plethora of tertiary activities which evolve in capitals. Provincial cities, so notable in Iran, have also experienced rapid growth, especially where improvements in roads have enabled closer links with their environs, rural and urban. In this way the movement into cities has been facilitated.

In the early stages of migration streams into cities, there is normally an excess of males (Table 4.4), and as many of the migrants are young adults there is also a tendency for cities to have a more youthful population than in rural areas. Neither tendency is as clearly marked as in tropical Africa or South Asia, except in Kuwait City which in 1965 had only 632 females per 1000 males. In cities like Baghdad, Tehran and Ankara the sex imbalance is much less blatant.

Poverty and Wealth

Cities are vivid demonstrations of the discrepancies between wealth

TABLE 4.4. SEX-RATIOS ACCORDING TO SIZE–CLASS OF LOCALITIES IN JORDAN, 1961

Size–Class of localities	No. of males	No. of females	Males per 1000 females
100,000 and over	130,688	115,787	1129
50,000–99,999	85,102	71,466	1191
20,000–49,999	100,074	105,941	1020
10,000–19,999	64,180	64,585	994
5,000–9,999	44,911	41,712	1077
2,000–4,999	118,089	125,950	938
1,000–1,999	99,377	109,386	908
500–999	72,767	74,182	981
200–499	71,054	70,052	1014
Less than 200 + tent dwellers	73,355	59,568	1231
TOTAL	867,597	838,629	1035

and poverty in South-west Asia. The landlords, the big merchants, the property owners, the rulers, the oil-rich sheikhs, the higher civil servants live in utterly different conditions and may have different demographic habits from the mass of the population. Some spend more in a day than most earn in a year. Food, clothing and shelter for the few are ostentatiously magnificent, although a partial explanation may be found in the fact that a seat in the saddle in South-west Asia is never very secure. But beggars are more common than Cadillacs in most countries, and the luxury and amenities of cities like Beirut are counterbalanced by the inadequate facilities of innumerable small villages, many of which have poor housing, water supply and sanitation.

The oil industry has contributed to the exorbitant wealth of a minority, and this is seen at national level. While the *per capita* national income in Kuwait is more than $3000 per annum, the highest in the world, and Israel's exceeds $1000, those of Yemen and Afghanistan are less than $100. Moreover, until recently financial poverty was matched by educational poverty. Illiteracy rates are still 85–95 per cent in Saudi Arabia, Yemen, Afghanistan and a few other countries, but they are under 25 per cent in Israel and Cyprus and diminishing rapidly in Turkey, Lebanon, Kuwait and Iran. Nevertheless, the disparity between the illiterate and the literate (who are mostly localized in cities) is still wide, and comparable with the gap between rich and poor. Gradually this latter gap is being bridged, especially in the more advanced countries like Israel, Turkey and Lebanon, and the ranks of the "middle class" are swelling.

Fertility

Apart from Cyprus, Lebanon and Israel, where non-Muslim communities are preponderant or large, South-west Asian countries have uniformly high fertility. Birth rates are of the order of 43–50 per thousand and gross reproduction rates 2.8–3.4, with little sign of fertility decline. As in Africa, South Asia and South-east Asia, Muslim natality is higher than that of neighbouring peoples of other major religions. Arabs and Jews in Israel and Arabs and Christians in Lebanon exemplify this. In his analysis of Muslim fertility, Kirk notes that apart from the general pro-natalist social forces which exist in peasant and pastoral societies, Islamic resistance to efforts to control family size is very great, but attitudes and practices are more significant than religious doctrine. It is a strongly conservative society in which marriage of women is nearly universal, age of marriage for women is low, sexuality is emphasized and subordination of women is general. In addition, Kirk considers polygamy a pro-natalist factor in Muslim societies, by promoting marriage opportunities for women, including widowed and divorced women who are common in Muslim countries. There are contrary views, however, and in any case polygamy is on the wane in the more advanced countries of South-west Asia.

Urban fertility differs little from rural fertility among Muslim populations, except where urban life (e.g. Tehran) brings higher incomes and more education, for family planning is only practised by an educated minority. So far it has had little effect upon birth rates of Muslim populations. On the other hand, high birth rates and mortality decline, with an annual increase of 3–3.2 per cent, encouraged Turkey to repeal the law prohibiting the import, sale or use of contraceptives and to adopt a family planning programme in 1965—in marked contrast to its earlier policies designed to increase the population size. Despite evident conservatism, it is feasible that more Muslim countries will follow suit during the next decade. Much will depend upon the spread of education, the prohibition of child labour and the emancipation of women.

The countries of South-west Asia with low–medium fertility are non-Muslim. Cyprus and Israel both have birth rates of 24–26 per thousand, well below even Lebanon, where the rate is probably 32–36 per thousand. At this stage it is obviously not in the best interests of Israel to foster family planning when it is surrounded by much larger numbers of Arabs.

Mortality

Mortality has been traditionally high in South-west Asia. Natural disasters, like earthquakes and droughts, have taken a toll, and so incidentally does the heat of the summer and the scorch of *khamsin* winds. In the past, man's inhumanity to man was severe. Many parts of South-west Asia have an appalling history of bloodshed. Most Afghan and Persian cities have known sackings and sieges, and on some occasions most of the inhabitants have been put to the sword. In 1387, for example, Tamerlane slaughtered 70,000 Isfahanis and piled their skulls into pyramids, a favourite architectural device of the time. Even in the late nineteenth and early twentieth centuries Armenians, Kurds and Nestorians were massacred in tens of thousands. Life has been cheap. Epidemics of plague, cholera, smallpox, malaria and typhoid fever, partly spread by migrant nomads and by pilgrims to the holy places (especially Mecca), have ravaged populations, although nowadays epidemics are more rare save in Afghanistan, Iraq and Saudi Arabia. Endemic diseases, however, are very common in South-west Asia. Malaria is widespread and especially severe in Iraq, Syria, Saudi Arabia and Yemen. Tuberculosis and the eye disease trachoma are also prevalent in a number of these countries; and in the irrigated areas of Iraq, as in Egypt, bilharziasis and ankylostomiasis are frequent afflictions. Addiction to hashish and opium in some countries, poor housing conditions, inadequate sewerage facilities and much malnutrition all contribute to high death rates, sometimes (e.g. Afghanistan, Yemen) in excess of 20 per thousand.

On the other hand, provision of good medical facilities in some small countries with youthful populations has led to very low death rates:

Aden, Cyprus, Israel and Kuwait all have death rates below 7 per thousand. Saudi Arabia, Kuwait, Qatar and Bahrain have such large oil royalties that they can now afford free medical care, health services and social services; the effect upon population growth is enormous.

Although cities in South-west Asia were at one time great centres of disease, as documented by Elgood for Iran, they are very much healthier owing to the localization of general medical facilities and improved sanitation. Consequently, urban mortality tends to be lower than mortality in rural areas, where medical provisions are generally poor, except in the small countries mentioned above. Two interesting features of infant mortality in areas of Lebanon are mentioned by El-Noss: (a) infant mortality of females is higher than that for males, quite the reverse of the situation in advanced countries of western Europe and North America, and (b) infant mortality tends to decrease with improvement in the quality of the motor-road leading to a village.

Natural Increase

Mortality is the main variable in determining differences in rates of natural increase of South-west Asian countries. These rates range from about 18 to 46 per thousand, the highest rate being that of Kuwait (45.9 per thousand in 1966) which has lower mortality than any other Muslim country, and the lowest being those of Israel (Jewish population) and Cyprus (19.2 and 18.8 per thousand respectively in 1966) where fertility is lower than elsewhere in South-west Asia. Among the other countries, Turkey, Syria and Jordan have high rates of natural increase; less advanced countries where mortality is higher, like Afghanistan, Yemen and Southern Yemen, have lower rates. In view of social limitations upon the spread of birth control and the present trend of declining mortality, it would seem that natural increase will almost certainly rise in most countries of South-west Asia in the near future (Table 4.5).

In several countries natural increase is far from being the only determinant of population growth: Syria, Lebanon, Cyprus, Yemen and Southern Yemen have all experienced much emigration, while Israel, the Gulf States and Jordan are all countries with substantial immigration.

TABLE 4.5. PROJECTED POPULATIONS OF SOUTH-WEST ASIAN COUNTRIES

	Projected population 1980 (millions)	Number of years to double population	Population under 15 (%)
Turkey	48.5	28	44
Iran	3˙.0	23	16
Afghanistan	22.1	31	—
Iraq	13.8	28	45
Saudi Arabia	9.4	39	—
Syria	9.2	24	46
Yemen	6.9	—	—
Israel	—	24	33
Lebanon	3.6	28	—
Jordan	3.3	17	46
Southern Yemen	1.6	32	—
Cyprus	0.7	39	35
Kuwait	—	19	38

SOURCE: Population Reference Bureau, World Population Data Sheet, 1969.

Emigrant Countries

Emigration has been a relief to population pressure in several countries of South-west Asia. Syrians and Lebanese (especially Christians) have provided the largest emigration stream. They began migrating in strength after European intervention in 1860. At first they went to Egypt, then to North America, particularly in the early years of this century, and since the First World War they have gone mainly to South America and to Africa. The migration stream has fluctuated in volume:

    1860–1900:   3000 emigrants per annum
    1901–1914: 15,000
    1919–1930:   6000
    1931–1939:   1800

and there has been an important counter-stream of migrants returning home, but emigration has increased again after a lull during the 1930s and 1940s and is of the order of 1000–4500 each year. By 1953 there were over 810,000 Syrians and Lebanese in the Americas, of whom 650,000 were living in Brazil and Argentina alone. The total number of Syrians and Lebanese living abroad must now exceed 1,500,000, many of whom are traders. There are more men than women, but women emigrants are becoming more numerous. Substantial remittances by emigrants help the Lebanon, in particular, to enjoy a higher *per capita* income than most of the countries of South-west Asia, although tourism, international finance and trade also play an important role in its economy.

Yemenis also emigrate from their mountainous country. With about 5 million people, Yemen has probably half of the total population of the Arabian peninsula. Like Lebanon, it has well developed terraced agriculture but has sustained this by emigration, which has been further encouraged by political struggles, exacerbated by external pressures.

More remarkable is the emigration from the oasis cities of the Hadhramaut in Southern Yemen. Here emigration is a veritable industry, Hadrumis going to Java, Singapore, Zanzibar, India, Egypt and Sudan. It is said that there are 70,000 in Java alone. Mostly they go as traders, but some are military personnel, sending remittances or bringing back their wealth, and introducing surprising modernity into some of the oasis cities.

Cyprus is not a populous island, although the total population has grown rapidly during this century; there were 210,000 inhabitants in 1891, 311,000 in 1921 and 633,000 by 1970. Owing to declining fertility and emigration the present annual increase is only one per cent. Emigration has been mostly to Britain, of which Cyprus was a colony until 1960, and by the mid-1960s the Cypriot population of England and Wales was in excess of 60,000.

In recent years a large number of men have migrated temporarily from Turkey to work in the European Common Market countries. At any one time they number at least 250,000.

Immigrant Countries

While immigration into Kuwait and the other Gulf states is mainly for economic motives, that into Israel is primarily for religious–cultural reasons. The oil-rich Gulf states were formerly only sparsely peopled but they are now a great magnet for migrants from Palestine, Pakistan, Iran and many other Middle Eastern and European countries. Immigrants into Kuwait now outnumber Kuwaitis, raising the total population from 206,000 in 1957 to 733,000 in 1970, an annual increase of more than 10 per cent. Immigrants have quite different demographic habits from Kuwaitis, partly because male immigrants greatly outnumber females (Table 4.6). As other Gulf states become scenes of oil

TABLE 4.6. KUWAITI AND NON KUWAITI POPULATIONS OF KUWAIT, 1965

	Kuwaiti	Non-Kuwaiti	Total
Numbers: 1957	113,622	92,851	206,473
1961	161,909	159,712	321,621
1965	220,059	247,280	467,339
Birth rate	51.3	39.5	45.0
Fertility rate	196.6	232.2	211.3
Death rate	7.3	3.4	5.2
Infant mortality rate	49.5	30.4	40.2
Natural increase rate	44.0	36.1	39.8
Females per 1000 males	955	423	632

exploitation, so they attract migrants. The population of Qatar has probably doubled during the 1960s, and there has been rapid growth of the small populations of Bahrain and the United Arab Emirates.

Immigration has been vital to the creation and survival of the Jewish state of Israel. In the mid-nineteenth century there were less than 12,000 Jews in Palestine. Until the First World War their numbers were augmented by immigrants mostly from Russia. Between 1918 and 1948 about 450,000 Jews immigrated into Palestine including large numbers from Poland, who settled mainly in the urban centres. British restrictions on Jewish immigration in 1939 caused much tension, for by that time Jews numbered 450,000 of a total population of 1,500,000. The declaration of Israel as a nation in May 1948 completely altered the situation, because in the ensuing Arab–Israeli war nearly 1 million Arabs fled, abandoning their property, and by August 1948 only about 150,000 remained. Immediately Jewish immigration stepped up, not only from Europe but also from Muslim countries of Asia and North Africa, which sent an increasing proportion of the immigrants. During the years 1948–51 alone, 666,000 came into Israel, more than the total

TABLE 4.7. INCREASE OF POPULATION OF ISRAEL, 1948–64

	Population at start of period	Population at end of period	Natural increase	Migration balance	Total increase
JEWS					
1948–51	649,600	1,404,400	88,400	+666,400	754,800
1952–54	1,404,400	1,526,000	101,400	+ 20,200	121,600
1955–57	1,526,000	1,762,800	100,700	+136,100	236,800
1958–60	1,762,800	1,911,200	101,500	+ 46,900	148,400
1961–64	1,911,200	2,239,200	134,000	+194,000	328,000
NON-JEWS (including Muslims, Christians and Druses)					
1950–51	160,000	173,400	11,400	+2,000	13,400
1952–54	173,400	191,800	18,200	+200	18,400
1955–57	191,800	213,200	21,200	+200	21,400
1958–60	213,200	243,300	26,100	−100	26,000
1961–64	243,300	286,400	44,000	−900	43,100

SOURCE: Central Bureau of Statistics, *Statistical Abstract of Israel 1966.*

number of Jews at the beginning of the period (Table 4.7). Fears of economic decline then led to selection of immigrants, but the Hungarian uprising (1956) and Algerian independence (1962) caused temporary peaks, and in the period 1948–65 two-thirds of the increase in the Jewish population resulted from immigration.

In 1967, the demographic situation of Israel was once again totally transformed by Israeli advances to the River Jordan and the Suez Canal. Again there have been refugees, but a larger number of Arabs are now living in Israeli occupied territory. In view of the fact that in 1965 the Jewish birth rate was only 22.6 per thousand in comparison with 50.7 for the non-Jewish population, their death rates being 6.4 and 6.1 respectively, a continuing flow of Jewish immigrants (and of capital) is required to sustain this tiny state which is so much a thorn in the flesh of the Arab world. As there are about 13 million Jews in the world, this migration stream is possible.

One of the major consequences of Israeli immigration has been the exodus of Palestinian refugees. Of those who fled in 1948 about 500,000 went to Jordan, over 200,000 to the Gaza Strip, over 100,000 to Lebanon and just under 100,000 to Syria. By June 1964 their numbers

TABLE 4.8. PALESTINE REFUGEES REGISTERED WITH
UNRWA, APRIL 1st 1972

Country	In Camps	Not in Camps	Total
East Jordan	175,549	371,179	546,738
West Bank	70,560	206,302	276,862
Gaza	204,737	118,070	322,807
Lebanon	93,979	88,072	182,941
Syria	41,133	126,364	167,497
Total	585,958	910,887	1,496,845

SOURCE: Europa Handbook of the Middle East and North Africa, 1972–73.

had swollen by about one-quarter, largely through high fertility About one-third were living in camps, the remainder living with relatives or in rented accommodation. UNRWA has provided relief services and has assisted refugees to become self-supporting, but many remain unassimilated by the recipient states owing to a general Arab desire that the refugees should return one day to their former homes in Palestine. Jordan, the main recipient, has become a divided nation with the entry of so many refugees. Until the 1967 Arab–Israeli war they were most numerous in West Jordan, where their numbers nearly matched those of the indigenous population. The war, however, caused many of them to flee to the east bank of the Jordan. At the end of 1967 the total number of persons displaced by Arab–Israel conflict is estimated by UNRWA to have reached about 1,600,000, including about 1,400,000 Palestinians, 100,000 Syrians from the Golan heights and 60,000 Egyptians from Sinai. They constitute a human problem of enormous dimensions, which in Arab eyes cannot be resolved without repatriation and compensation (Table 4.8).

South-west Asia in Flux

The existence of the state of Israel is the major source of political and population instability in South-west Asia, and its aggrandisement within the Arab world has provoked a highly charged situation which may explode again with further demographic effects. Another area where population geography is at the mercy of political conditions is Yemen, a country with ill-defined boundaries. Colonial rule has almost disappeared now in South-west Asia, especially since the independence of the Republic of South Yemen, and behind political boundaries mostly conceived and created in the present century fervent nationalism has emerged as the strongest political force. An ambivalent reaction to European impact—ambivalent because it has been compounded of opposition and imitation—nationalism disguises a large number of actual or potential differences, so that the creation of strong homogeneous nation-states lies mostly in the future. At present there is a see-saw struggle between the forces of tradition and modernity, the precise strength of the forces varying from country to country.

The single most important catalytic agent in the economic growth of South-west Asia has been the development of the oil industry. Not all countries have benefited from the oil boom. Indeed, it is one of the great ironies of the region that several of the more populous and advanced countries, like Turkey and Lebanon, have little or no oil, while some small desert countries are almost entirely dependent upon oil royalties, enabling them to purchase technical modernization or transform their demographic situations. Developments in the agricultural sector have been much less dramatic, and although a number of large irrigation schemes and land reform programmes have attracted great attention their impact upon the population geography of South-west Asia as a whole has been only of minor significance. Inequalities of land-holding will probably persist as a prime cause of political instability, and future reforms will certainly affect population patterns in detail.

In most South-west Asian countries (Turkey and Israel are notable exceptions) industrialization has been insufficient to transform national economies, and is so highly localized that it impinges only indirectly upon the realities of rural life. It adds, however, to the attractions of cities, which are now receiving migrants from the most remote corners of the Middle East. Centres of economic, social and political flux, cities are also the main foci of population change.

Select Bibliography

ADAMS, D. G., *Iraq's People and Resources*, University of California, Berkeley, 1958.

AWAD, M., Nomadism in the Arab lands of the Middle East, in UNESCO, *The Problems of the Arid Zone*, 325 (1962).

BAER, G., *Population and Society in the Arab East*, 1964.

BARTH, F., Nomadism in the mountain and plateau areas of South West Asia, in UNESCO, *The Problems of the Arid Zone,* 341 (1962).
BERGER, M., *The Arab World Today,* 1962.
BERGER, M., *The New Metropolis in the Arab World,* New Delhi, 1963.
BRICE, W. C., The Population of Turkey in 1950, *Geog. J.* **120,** 347 (1954).
BRICE, W. C., *South-West Asia,* 1966.
CLARKE, J. I. and FISHER, W. B. (Eds.), *Populations of the Middle East and North Africa,* 1971.
CRESSEY, G. B., *Crossroads: Land and Life in South-west Asia,* 1960.
EL BADRY, M. A., Trends in the components of population growth in the Arab countries of the Middle East: A survey of present information, *Demography* **2,** 140 (1965).
ELGOOD, C., *A Medical History of Persia and the Eastern Caliphate from the Earliest Times until the Year A.D. 1932,* Cambridge, 1951.
EL-NOSS, E., *Population Conditions in the Arab World,* Cairo, 1955.
FISHER, W. B., *The Middle East,* 7th edn., 1966.
HILL, A., The population of Kuwait, *Geography* **54,** 84 (1969).
HOLLER, J. E., *Population Growth and Change in the Middle East,* George Washington University, Washington D C , 1964.
HUMLUM, J., *La Géographie de l'Afghanistan,* Copenhagen, 1959.
ISSAWI, C. and DABEZIES, C., Population movements and population pressure in Jordan, Lebanon and Syria, *Milbank Memorial Fund Quarterly* **29,** 385 (1951).
JONES, L. W., Accroissement rapide de la population de Bagdad et d'Amman, *Population* **23,** 150 (1968).
KIRK, D., Factors affecting Moslem natality, in BERELSON, B. and others (Eds.), *Family Planning and Population Programs,* Chicago, 1966, pp. 561–579.
LEBON, J. H. G., Population distribution and the agricultural regions of Iraq, *Geog. Rev.* **43,** 223 (1953).
MASHAKEYHI, M. B., MEAD, P. A. and HAYES, G. S., Some demographic aspects of a rural area in Iran, *Milbank Memorial Fund Quarterly* 149 (1953).
MELAMID, A., The geographical distribution of communities in Cyprus, *Geog. Rev.* **46,** 335 (1956).
PHILLIPS, D. G., Rural to urban migration in Iraq, *Econ. Devel. Cult. Change* **7,** 405, (1959).
PLANHOL, X. DE., Caractères généraux de la vie montagnarde dans le Proche-Orient et dans l'Afrique du Nord, *Ann. Géog.* **71,** 113 (1962).
TAEUBER, I. B., Cyprus: the demography of a strategic island, *Pop. Index* **21,** 4 (1954).
TASMA, R., Changes in the Jewish population pattern of Israel, 1948–1957, *Tijdschr. Econ. Soc. Geog.* **50,** 170 (1959).
TUMERTEKIN, E., The distribution of sex ratios with special reference to internal migration in Turkey, *Univ. Istanbul Geog. Inst. Rev.* **4,** 9 (1958).
VAUMAS, E. DE., La répartition de la population au Liban; introduction à la géographie humaine de la Republique Libanaise, *Bull. Soc. Géog. Egypte* **26,** 5 (1953).
VAUMAS, E. DE., La population de la Syrie, *Ann. Géog.* **64,** 74 (1955).
VAUMAS, E. DE., La répartition de la population à Chypre et le nouvel état chypriote, *Rev. Géog. Alpine* **47,** 457 (1959).
YAUKEY, D., *Fertility Differences in a Modernizing Country,* Princeton, 1961.

5

SOUTH ASIA

Volume of Population

The area under consideration in this chapter is the Indian subcontinent, a clearly definable part of the world isolated by high
mountains and seas. Apart from its physical identity, South Asia is
distinctive economically, being an inwardly orientated region in which
agriculture plays a dominant role. Moreover, it is also a region with
remarkable demographic and cultural distinctiveness, because it contains one of the great nodes of mankind with great diversity of races,
languages and religions.

With over 748 million people (1972 estimate), South Asia has about
19.8 per cent of the world's population on only 3.2 per cent of the
world's land area. Indeed, with less than half the area of China and
only a little more than half the area of the United States or Canada,
South Asia has a higher overall population density than any other
major world region. In this way South Asia differentiates itself strongly
from regions previously considered in this volume. Population density
levels which have been termed high for Latin America, Africa or
South-west Asia are sometimes only moderate or low by South Asian
standards, where tens of millions live at densities exceeding 1000 per
square mile; in fact, the average density of population in Bangladesh
now exceeds 500 per square km. So it is not merely a matter of large
numbers, but also of high densities.

In comparison with Latin America, Africa, South-west Asia or
South-east Asia, the region of South Asia exhibits little political frag-

170

mentation. It comprises only seven countries of contrasting population size, ranging from India with the second largest population in the world, to the tiny Himalayan state of Sikkim with just over 200,000 inhabitants. The vast majority of South Asians live in India and Pakistan, which were divided in 1947 when Pakistan emerged as a dual state with its two parts separated by some 1500 miles of Indian territory. This dual state lasted 24 years until the independence of Bangladesh. India has more people than there are in either Europe or the Americas, more than twice as many as in the USSR and nearly as many as there are in all the three southern continents. In contrast with the huge populations of India and Bangladesh, the second and eighth largest in the world, those of Sri Lanka (Ceylon) and Nepal appear rather small, but it may be noted that there are slightly more people living on the 66,000 square kms. of Sri Lanka than on the 7,687,000 square kms. of Australia, and that the population of little-known Nepal is larger than the populations of countries like Greece, Portugal, Hungary, Belgium, Venezuela, Chile and Ghana. At the bottom end of the scale, the two buffer states of Bhutan and Sikkim are micro-states by anyone's reckoning (Table 5.1).

TABLE 5.1. SOUTH ASIA: SIZES OF STATES

		Population (Millions)		Area
		Last census	1972 estimate	(thousand square kms.)
India	(1971)	547.4	—	3268
Bangladesh	(1961)	50.8	79.6	143
Pakistan	(1961)	42.9	66.9	804
Sri Lanka	(1971)	12.7	—	66
Nepal	(1971)	11.3	—	141
Bhutan		—	0.8	47
Sikkim	(1971)	0.2	—	7

Evolution

In contrast with South-west Asia, there is a mass of statistical material available for population study in South Asia (except for Bhutan, which at the time of writing has not had a census); decennial censuses have been held in India, Pakistan and Ceylon since 1871, but Nepal's first census was in 1952–54. In their major studies of the Indian population, Davis and then Coale and Hoover questioned the reliability of census data, and Sarkar has done the same for Ceylon. In general, there is much inaccuracy in age statistics, underenumeration of women and a tendency toward general underenumeration; for example, Krotki calculated that the population of Pakistan in 1961 was 102.2 million rather than 93.8 million as recorded by the census. Vital registration data are also very incomplete and thus growth rates may be only estimated in broad terms. So the usual reminder about statistical unreliability must be reiterated.

It has generally been assumed that the population of the Indian sub-continent was more or less stationary for some 2000 years preceding the colonial era, and that such fluctuations as occurred were generally caused by epidemics, famines and warfare. In 1600, at the height of the Mogul Empire, the total population was assumed to be 100–140 million. However Datta has shown that under the rule of Moguls the population increased during the sixteenth and seventeenth centuries, at least in the northern regions, but this increase was arrested during the second quarter of the eighteenth century with the dissolution of the Mogul Empire and also during the subsequent Afghan invasions, the struggles with the British and the Bengal famine of 1771. Datta therefore estimated the population of India in 1801 at 162–76 million. On the other hand, Durand has assumed that 160 million is a "low variant" for the Indian population in 1800, and has calculated a "high variant" of 214 million and a "medium variant" of 195 million. The "high variant" was calculated from Davis's corrected 1871 census total of 255 million, assuming an annual growth rate of 0.25 per cent.

It appears likely that population growth in India was slow during most of the nineteenth and early twentieth centuries. Between 1871 and 1921 the total population increase was only about 20 per cent, partly because of the famines of 1876 and 1878 and again at the end of the century, as well as the influenza epidemic of 1918–19 when there may have been as many as 15 million deaths. So by 1921 the population total of India had reached 306 million (Table 5.2), less than half the present combined total. After 1921 the rate of population growth greatly accelerated, mainly because of a decline in the number of demographic catastrophes. Between 1921 and 1951 the increase was 43 per cent, in spite of the disastrous Bengal famine of 1943–44, and in the decade 1951–61 the combined populations of India and Pakistan increased by at least 94 million or over 21 per cent. Since 1961 the rate has continued to accelerate so that another 150 million were added to the India-Pakistan total in the years 1961–71. In 1971 the rate of annual population growth in India was 2.5 per cent and in Pakistan it was 3.3 per cent; formidable rates for such huge populations, and a major influence upon the total world population growth.

In Sri Lanka, the trend of population growth has been somewhat different. In the period since 1871, growth has been more steady than in India–Pakistan, partly because of the lower incidence of decimating famines and partly because during the last quarter of the nineteenth century when natural increase was not high Sri Lanka received many Indian immigrant plantation labourers. Consequently, since 1881 the decennial rate of population growth of Sri Lanka has not fallen below 10 per cent (see Table 5.2), not even in the 1930s when there was a net emigration of Indian labourers and a severe malaria epidemic in 1935. Following the successful anti-malaria campaigns of the post-war years, mortality fell sharply and the rate of population growth soared, a 34 per cent increase being recorded in the decade 1951–61. The present rate of annual growth is about 2.3 per cent, reflecting a considerable decline in the birth rate.

Before we analyse population growth and its various influences in more detail, it is perhaps better to look at the ethnic structure and distribution of population in the Indian subcontinent.

Peoples

Many commentators on the Indian cultural scene have remarked about the incredible diversity of races, religions and languages, as well as the rather paradoxical fact of fundamental cultural unity, a unity according to Spate "more recognizable than definable, which except in the far western borderland had influenced even the Muslims". Indeed, Spate has stressed that the main mass of Muslims is "shot through with strands of Indianism (to avoid the word Hinduism)". Such unity undoubtedly arises partly from the shape and definition of

TABLE 5.2. POPULATION GROWTH IN INDIA (UNDIVIDED) and SRI LANKA, 1750–1971

	Undivided India total population (millions)	Percentage growth in preceding decade	Sri Lanka total population (millions)	Percentage growth in preceding decade
1750	190			
1800	195		1.6	
1850	233		2.2	
1871	255		2.8	
1881	257	1	3.0	7
1891	282	9	3.3	10
1901	285	1	4.0	21
1911	303	6	4.7	18
1921	306	1	5.3	13
1931	338	11	6.1	15
1941	389	15	6.8	11
1951	438	12	7.8	15
1961	532	21	10.6	34
1971	682	23	12.5	18

SOURCE: G. Myrdal, *Asian Drama*, vol. 2, Table 27.1 and J. D. Durand, The modern expansion of world population, *Proc. Am. Phil. Soc.* **111**, 137 (1967).

the Indian subcontinent and the barrier nature of the northern mountain arcs. However, neither the mountains nor the seas have prevented the entry of intruders, colonizers and conquerors of diverse origins and types, who have contributed to the evolution of a distinctive cultural complex. It is important to emphasize this cultural complex (rather than a melting pot), because original ethnic distinctions have been perpetuated by the great size of the country (India and Pakistan together are about the size of Europe excluding Russia), and the existence of internal barriers such as (a) the Vindhya and Satpura ranges which with the densely forested uplands to the east separate the northern lowlands from the Deccan, and (b) the region of the Aravallis stretching from the Gulf of Cambay toward Delhi-Agra, which acts as a climatic divide and is now occupied by the Sikh community. In addition to these physical influences upon ethnic distinctions, Tayyeb also points to the effect of the slow and late development of transport routes, encouraging provincialism, as well as the Hindu concept of social segregation, by which castes retained cultural and ethnic identity, particularly as conquerors differentiated themselves from the conquered in different castes.

So although the Indian subcontinent demonstrates a basic cultural unity, a bewildering array of peoples have persisted, the diversity of which is further intensified by the fact that ethnic, linguistic and religious patterns do not coincide, and this poses difficulties for census enumeration of peoples. Consequently in Indian censuses the terms "community", "tribe" and "scheduled caste" have been used; but perhaps there can never be a wholly acceptable nomenclature or terminology for classifications of the many peoples of South Asia.

The ethnic stock of South Asians is of no great concern to us here, partly because race is not a politically divisive force in this part of the world, except where it is associated with language and/or religion, as in the case of the Untouchables of southern India. In fact, religions have a considerable influence upon ethnic distinctiveness, although racial mixing is greater among Muslims and Christians than among Hindus. The great majority of the subcontinent's population are Caucasoids (with Mediterranean traits predominating) who entered from the north-west. The Alpines were the first to arrive, and they contributed to the early Indus valley civilization about 3000 BC. However, in the second milennium BC they were driven south into peninsular India by Mediterranean and Nordic peoples identified as Aryans who introduced an Indo-European language from which Urdu and Hindi and other languages are derived.

The Caucasoid peoples disseminated throughout the subcontinent and mixed with the aboriginal Negroid, Proto-Australoid and Mongoloid peoples, although some of these peoples remained isolated, retaining their cultures and languages, and many today are tribal. The Andaman islanders are the main example of Negroid or Negrito peoples, although the Kadars of Cochin have some Negroid characteristics. The Proto-Australoids, speaking Austro-Asiatic languages, are mostly found in the tribal hill regions of central and southern India, and the Veddas of Sri Lanka are related to this type. Proto-Australoids, often known as pre-Dravidians, are, however, a basic strain of much of the Hindu population. Mongoloids are also found in small isolated groups, mainly along the fringes of the Himalayas, and isolation is so marked that they include more than 50 ethnic groups and languages, of the Sino-Tibetan family.

It will be evident that the social pluralism so common in South Asia is largely derived from the early history of the subcontinent, rather than from the impact of colonialism. Farmer has emphasized for Sri Lanka that the roots of the plural society are pre-colonial, the hostility between the Sinhalese and Ceylon Tamil communities being of long standing, to which the colonial period merely added fresh elements of plurality exacerbating inter-communal tensions. This is also true for south India, where colonialism brought Christianity but few other elements of social pluralism.

Languages

Language is a much more significant divisive force in South Asia than ethnic origins, probably because people know what languages they speak whereas they do not know their ethnic origins. Moreover there is great linguistic heterogeneity. Broadly speaking, apart from the many languages spoken by the tribal minorities already mentioned there is a fundamental dichotomy between the preponderant northerners who speak Indo-European languages and the less numerous southerners who speak Dravidian languages; in essence while the Indo-European languages are often mutually intelligible, the Dravidian languages are not.

The subcontinent contains a huge variety of languages and dialects. In 1951 the census of India recorded 844 languages and dialects, including (a) 14 major languages each spoken by 5 million or more and in total by 98 per cent of the population, (b) 47 more important tribal languages and dialects, (c) 63 foreign languages, and (d) 720 languages spoken by less than 100,000 persons each. The number of languages counted is probably in excess of reality, but the real number is undoubtedly extremely high. The problem of languages in India, however, is not so much a matter of the profusion of minor languages at local level, because multi-lingualism is common even among the poor and illiterate, as of the considerable number of major languages spoken by many millions of people in regional blocs. The areal limits of these linguistic regions often roughly coincide with the political boundaries of states, a fact which was encouraged by the Indian National Congress and has subsequently strengthened centrifugal tendencies toward particularism. Language problems have arisen in zones of contact between languages, in cities where minority communities are often numerous, and also in the sphere of education where knowledge of English and Hindi has been an advantage.

In India, language has become a national problem. The constitution of 1950 stated that Hindi in the Devangari script should be the official language of the Union, that English should be used for official purposes until 1965, that Parliament might by law provide for the subsequent use of English, and that English should be the official language for communication between one state and another and between a state and the Union. The sole use of Hindi as official language obviously presents grave problems, as it is less developed than some other languages like Bengali or Marathi, and is becoming a rather more "pure" or "classical" language, but it is also resented as the official language by Dravidian language speakers and by people of West Bengal. Riots in 1965, when Hindi was declared the official language of India, resulted in English being retained as an associate language; and in addition a trilingual basis for education was accepted in which Hindi states have to teach a southern language while Hindi is taught in non-Hindi speaking states. The language problem of India is still not solved.

Nor is it solved in Sri Lanka (Fig. 5.1), where there have been clashes between linguistic groups, especially in 1958 when Singhala—a language related to Bengali and spoken by the Buddhist Sinhalese who constitute 70 per cent of the total population—became the official language. This was deeply resented by the Hindu Tamils, who form about one-fifth of the total population, and whose language is of the Dravidian family. The Tamils fall into two groups: (a) the Ceylon Tamils who live mainly in the north and east (the Dry Zone) and are descendants of peoples who came to the island in waves from the second century BC onward, and (b) the Indian Tamils who mostly live in the south-west of Sri Lanka and are descendants of labourers brought from south India in the late nineteenth century to work on the tea and rubber plantations. The conflict between the Sinhalese and Tamils is not solely linguistic, but language is certainly a key factor.

Again, in former Pakistan the linguistic situation was also

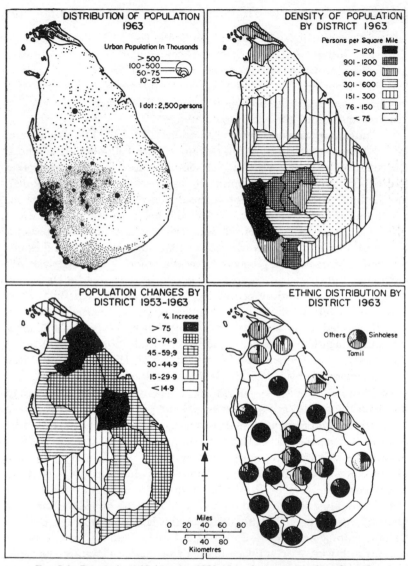

FIG. 5.1. Population of Sri Lanka, 1963. Note the concentration of population and towns in the wet zone of the south-west, the more rapid population growth in the dry zone of the north-east, and the contrasting population distributions of Sinhalese and Tamils (With thanks to P. Balasundarampillai).

problematic, and a cause of the independence of Bangladesh. Nearly all East Pakistanis spoke Bengali, while in West Pakistan Urdu was the main language (although there are other important languages like Punjabi). After Partition, it was decided that the national language would be Urdu, a language with similar origins to Hindi and, like that language, with many Arabic, Persian and Turkish words, although unlike Hindi written in the Arabic script. In East Pakistan there was so much resentment that it was decided to accept Bengali as another national language; Bengali is now the national language of Bangladesh, and this new country is extremely uniform linguistically.

Religions

The Indian subcontinent contains diverse religions which have also acted as a powerful divisive force encouraging partition. The two religions with the most numerous adherents, Hinduism and Islam, are the most sharply opposed and incompatible. Islam is a relatively recent religion in South Asia, being brought by invaders in the twelfth century, but it was a religion of conquerors and the Muslim rulers only lost their political power when the British arrived. In 1947, after much friction, the Muslims were to achieve a separate political state, Pakistan, which by 1961 was 88 per cent Muslim, the percentage being 97 in West Pakistan and 80 in East Pakistan. However, Pakistan and Bangladesh do not contain all the Muslims in the Indian subcontinent, and there must be at least 50 million in India alone.

Hinduism is the dominant religion of India, the religion of more than four-fifths of its people—however, the minority of non-adherents must number about 100 million—and it is also the religion of the majority in Nepal. Separatism has been prominent in the past: Buddhism and Jainism were early revolts against Hinduism, and in the early sixteenth century the Sikh movement began as a protest against various aspects of both Hinduism and Islam, stressing the need for a cultural compromise; but the Sikhs have now evolved as an exclusive and separatist movement.

Perhaps the most controversial feature of Hinduism has been the caste system, which arose when the victorious Aryans conquered the northern plains and formed two groups, the Brahmins and Kshatriyas, controlling the church and army. Native peoples who had mixed with the Aryans performing lesser occupations were known as Vaisyas. Menial services were performed by darker, non-cooperative Dravidians called Sudras, and those who resisted or escaped to the south were called Untouchables. Although Hinduism spread throughout the Indian subcontinent, the general pattern of castes remains, with the upper castes being concentrated in the Indus valley, middle Ganges valley and central India, while the lower castes are preponderant in the marginal east and south. Inevitably, many of the resentful lower caste peoples have deserted Hinduism and have joined other religious communities. Christian communities, for example, form a considerable minority in south India, especially in the south-west, in Travancore-Cochin.

Conflict between religious groups, with or without association with linguistic, cultural and economic matters, is still apparent in South Asia, especially in Sri Lanka and Kashmir. In the state of Kashmir as a whole about 77 per cent of the population are Muslims, but Kashmir is a zone of religious convergence; in the Indian administered Frontier District of Ladakh Buddhists are preponderant whereas Jammu Province is predominantly Hindu.

As we shall see later, religion plays a very important part in demographic matters in South Asia, although as in many other parts of the developing world there is a constant struggle between the traditionalists and the modernists.

Distribution and Density of Population

Overall population densities in South Asia are high. Estimated 1970 densities were India 168 per square km., Pakistan (West) 77, Sri Lanka 191, Nepal 77, Sikkim 27, Bangladesh 517, Bhutan 18. The overall density of Bangladesh is the highest of the world's major states and is only exceeded by micro-states such as Hong Kong, Singapore, Malta and Gibraltar. Of course, the densities per square km. of crop land are much higher; in Bangladesh over 800 per square km., and even in Pakistan more than 400.

In South Asia population distribution is not nearly as irregular as in South-west Asia, South-east Asia or East Asia. In India, however, half the population live on a quarter of the land area, and one-third live on only 6 per cent of the area. Until independence Bangladesh had four-sevenths of the population of Pakistan, but only one-seventh of the area. The Wet Zone of south-west Sri Lanka contains four-fifths of the island's population, but only one-third of its area. And Nepal's population is mainly found in the Katmandu valley and the Himalayan foothills rather than in the high Himalayan country to the north or the densely wooded and malaria-ridden Terai along the southern margins.

The main concentrations of population in South Asia (Fig. 5.2) are on (a) the alluvial lowlands of the Indo-Gangetic Plains, in states like Uttar Pradesh, Bihar and West Bengal as well as Bangladesh, and (b) the eastern and western littorals of Peninsular India, especially the deltas and plains such as those of Gujarat between Surat and Ahmedabad and of Kerala, where the population density in 1961 was 1127 per square mile.

The principal areas of low population density (by South Asian standards, although many of these areas have 30–50 per square mile, high densities by African and South American standards) are the Thar desert where some districts had only 9 per square mile in 1961, the semi-arid areas further west toward Baluchistan, the Dry Zone of north-east Sri Lanka, the high Himalayas where Ladakh has only two persons per square mile, the Western Ghats of Mysore, the swampy Kutch region of Gujarat and parts of Assam. It will be observed that many of these lower population densities are located in arid or mountainous areas, or areas which combine both these conditions.

In contrast, most of the plateau area of India is notable for its average densities of 350–500 per square mile, except for Hyderabad where the densities rise to over 1000 per square mile.

In India the overall pattern of population density has not changed greatly in recent decades. According to Bhat, the period 1951–61 was characterized only by infilling and by the extension of areas of very high density to the areas of high density (Fig. 5.3). The areas of dense population (500 per square mile and over) generally showed a low growth rate during 1951–61, except the very densely peopled areas of the Kerala coast and Hooghlyside, while areas of low density generally

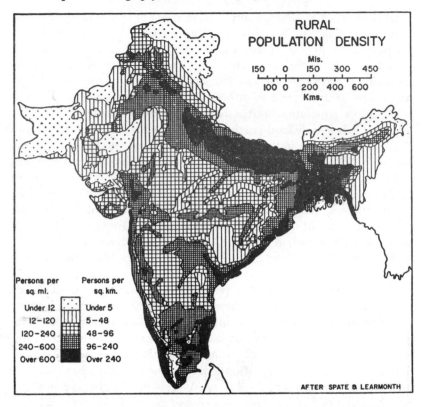

Fig. 5.2. Rural population density, India and Pakistan, 1961 (after O. H. K. Spate and A. T. Learmonth). In this simplified version of the original map by Spate and Learmonth, the shading contrasts should not delude the reader into assuming that the rural population density is low anywhere except in the areas marked with the lightest shade.

had a high growth rate. The result was that the curve of population concentration did not change very much during that decade (Fig. 5.4)

In Pakistan until 1971, the smaller, poorer eastern province was more populous and crowded than West Pakistan, although it lacked many of the minerals and other resources found in that province as well as its share of the development projects. In former East Pakistan population was almost entirely rural and crowded along the narrow stretches

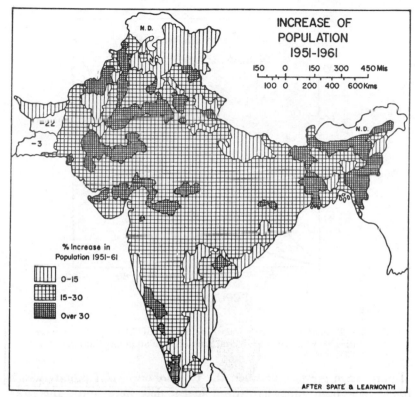

Fig. 5.3. Increase of population, 1951–61, India and Pakistan (after O. H. K. Spate and A. T. Learmonth). Areas of high and low population increase are often adjacent, because of the influence of short-range migration.

of land along the delta distributaries. Where soil and water conditions are favourable, as in the Districts of Dacca and Mymensingh, densities may exceed 1000 per square km. In West Pakistan the population distribution is much more diffused, and the number of old and new urban centres is much higher. Moreover, the possibilities of agricultural expansion are greater and the problems of population pressure are much less severe than in former East Pakistan, although during the decade 1951–61 the population of the west wing increased by 27.1 per cent while the east increased by 21.2 per cent. Unfortunately the imbalance

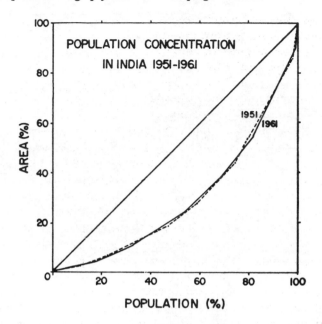

Fig. 5.4. Population concentration in India, 1951–61. The two Lorenz curves show little change in the overall character of population distribution.

of population pressure between the two provinces of Pakistan, which might have been somewhat attenuated if they were contiguous, was supplemented by profoundly different cultural and economic characteristics, and they separated definitively in 1971.

Rural Populations

An essential feature of the population of South Asia is that it is primarily rural. At the last censuses the rural population amounted to 80 per cent in India, 70 per cent in Pakistan, 95 per cent in Bangladesh, 81 per cent in Sri Lanka and 97 per cent in Nepal. In other words, there are now well over 500 million rural-dwellers in South Asia. Naturally, this fact is closely related to the high proportion of the active population employed in agriculture: 68 per cent in India, 70 per cent in former Pakistan, 53 per cent in Sri Lanka, and 92 per cent in Nepal. This dependence on the soil for a livelihood means that agriculture has a great influence upon patterns of population distribution in South Asia. Four basic types of agriculture have a particular influence: sedentary dry farming, paddy cultivation, plantation agriculture and shifting cultivation. Sedentary dry farming is the main type of agriculture practised over large parts of South Asia, and its prevalence accounts for many of the economic problems and much of the poverty of South Asia, especially in those regions experiencing a weak and unreliable monsoon such as West Pakistan and north and central India. Fortunately, in some of those areas paddy cultivation is particularly prominent in river valleys, deltas and coastal plains. It is the main form of agriculture, for example, in Bangladesh, where more than four-fifths of the cropped area is devoted to rice. However, although paddy cultivation is very important in some regions, on the whole it plays a smaller role in South Asia than in South-east Asia. This is also true for plantation agriculture, which is only locally important, notably in south-west Sri Lanka, Kerala, southern Mysore, Assam and West Bengal. Both paddy and plantation agriculture are, of course, associated with dense rural populations. In contrast, shifting cultivation, common in east and central India, in the Himalayas and in Sri Lanka, is normally accompanied by much lower densities of population.

In general, the Indian subcontinent is a land of villages. Except in a few areas, in the Himalayas and in the Bengal Delta, where small hamlets prevail, the typical settlement pattern is of compact villages. Official statistics of India group homesteads into villages so that "rural population" and "village population" are virtually synonymous. In 1961, India had 565,000 villages most of which had less than 500 inhabitants. These small villages contained about one-fifth of the rural population, while about half lived in villages of 500–2000 inhabitants, about one-fifth in villages of 2000–5000 and one-tenth in villages of more than 5000 inhabitants.

Urbanization

Although the level of urbanization in South Asia is still low by world standards (especially in the small Himalayan kingdoms)—only about one in six of the total population live in towns—it is rising rapidly, and now more than 100 million people may be classed as urban. The growth of the urban population was fairly steady until the Second World War; in 1881 it comprised 9.3 per cent of the total population of India–Pakistan, and by 1941 it had risen to 12.8 per cent (Table 5.3). This moderate growth may be associated with the slow economic development and lack of industrialization, and consequently larger cities grew more rapidly than small towns. Most urban growth prior to the Second World War resulted from rural–urban migration, because urban mortality was high and natural increase low. After the Second World War urban growth gained momentum through the decline in urban mortality, the expansion of trade and the development of modern industries, transport facilities and services. In addition, many refugees moved into towns; in all some 2 million Pakistanis moved to Indian urban centres following partition. At the moment, however, the various countries exhibit rather different trends in urban population growth.

In India during the period 1951–61 there was a deceleration in the rate of urbanization; the urban population grew by 26.4 per cent compared with an increase of 20.6 per cent in the rural population, and its proportion of the total population only rose from 17.3 to 17.8 per cent (Fig. 5.5). This slower rate of urban growth may be partly attributable to a modification in the definition of urban status at the 1961 census. In addition to areas under municipal government, the 1961 census considered areas as urban if they contained at least 5000 persons, the population density exceeded 1000 persons per square mile, and three-quarters of the population were employed in non-agricultural production. This meant that some settlements with more than 5000 persons previously classified as urban lost this status, while others not considered as urban in 1951 qualified in 1961; but in sum the numbers of towns and cities diminished. Naturally, the majority of localities affected by reclassification were small, with less than 10,000 inhabitants.

Another factor influencing the decelerating rate of urbanization in India during 1951–61 was a marked drop in rural–urban migration. Of the net urban population growth of 16.5 million, only 4 million were migrants. This has been a disappointment to some, because urbanization has been looked upon as the main hope for reducing population pressure in rural areas, but India's Registrar-General has found contributory causes in rural development, the increased profitability of agriculture and the lack of pronounced urban–rural demographic differentials.

TABLE 5.3. SOUTH ASIA: PERCENTAGE RURAL AND URBAN POPULATIONS

	India		Pakistan		Sri Lanka	
	Rural	Urban	Rural	Urban	Rural	Urban
1901	89.0	11.0	94.0	5.1		
1911	90.0	10.0	95.1	4.9		
1921	89.0	11.0	94.6	5.4	85.8	14.2
1931	88.0	12.0	93.5	6.5	86.8	13.2
1941	86.0	14.0	92.1	7.9	(1946)84.6	15.4
1951	82.7	17.3	89.6	10.4	(1953)84.7	15.3
1961	82.2	17.8	86.9	13.1	(1963)81.1	18.9
1971	80.1	19.9	82.5	17.5		

SOURCE : S. Chandrasekhar (Ed.), *Asia's Population Problems*, London 1967, pp. 78 and 151 and *Statistical Abstract, Ceylon*, 1965.

Large cities (class I cities) accounted for two-thirds of India's urban population growth during the decade and by 1961 there were 107 (each with more than 100,000 inhabitants) incorporating some 38 million people, just under half of the total urban population of 79 million (Fig. 5.6 and Table 5.4). This is in spite of the fact that the class I cities grew by only 45 per cent during the decade, whereas in the two previous decades they had grown by 58 and 65 per cent. By 1966 eight of the large cities had populations in excess of 1 million, compared with only two in 1911: Bombay, Calcutta, Delhi, Madras, Bangalore, Ahmedabad, Hyderabad and Kanpur. Of these cities, the capital Delhi, the port and industrial city of Bombay and the industrial centres of Bangalore and Ahmedabad are growing most rapidly.

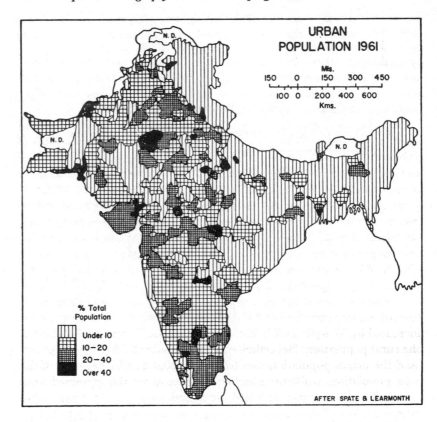

Fig. 5.5. Urban population, 1961, India and Pakistan (after O. H. K. Spate and A. T. Learmonth). The western part of the Indian peninsula is distinctly more urbanized than the eastern part.

Except for these very large cities, the regional patterns of growth in number and population of cities conform substantially to the general pattern of population distribution. Learmonth has noted that the feebly urbanized areas are in the northern mountains (with exceptions, like the Vale of Kashmir and the Darjeeling area), Assam and most of the north-east of India, the eastern Terai, the Eastern Ghats and the edges of the Mahanadi delta. In contrast, many other parts of India are highly urbanized: southern Kerala, Mysore, the Krishna delta, the Coimbatore and Madurai areas, Hooghlyside, parts of the Punjab plains and western Uttar Pradesh, Rajasthan, around Ahmedabad, Kathiawad and between Bombay and Baroda.

Between 1961 and 1971 the urban population of India increased more rapidly—by 38 per cent or 30 million inhabitants to a total of 109 million, one-fifth of the whole Indian population. The number of towns increased by 459, but these extra towns included only 2,500,000 urban-dwellers; over nine-tenths of the increase in the urban population resulted from the growth of towns existing in 1961. The main growth has been in the large cities with 100,000 inhabitants or more, which accounted for less than 5 per cent of the number of towns in 1971 but 52 per cent of the urban population. The growth of small towns (10–50,000 inhabitants) is much more modest, and they contain a diminishing proportion of the urban population.

In contrast to India, former Pakistan showed an accelerating trend toward urbanization between 1951 and 1961 when the urban population increased by 57.4 per cent in comparison with a 20 per cent increase in the rural population. Nevertheless, Pakistan was still feebly urbanized, and the urban population rose from only 10.4 to 13.1 per cent of the total population, while the number of towns and cities increased from 282 to 393. With old-established cities and more family rural–urban migration, West Pakistan was much more urbanized than East Pakistan, and in 1961 their urban populations amounted to 22.5 and 5.2 per cent of their respective total populations. In West Pakistan there were twelve large cities including two with more than 1 million inhabitants (Karachi and Lahore), while there were only four large cities in East Pakistan (see Fig. 5.6). Indeed, East Pakistan, now Bangladesh, must be the least urbanized of the large populations of the world.

However, the much smaller population of Nepal is even less urbanized; in 1961 it had merely one large city, Katmandu, with 122,000 inhabitants, and five other towns with more than 10,000 inhabitants, so that the urban population amounted to only 3.6 per cent of the total.

TABLE 5.4. GROWTH OF INDIA'S URBAN POPULATION, 1901-71

	Urban population (thousands)	% Change in decade	Number of towns and cities					
			Class I 100,000+	Class II 50-100,000	Class III 20-50,000	Class IV 10-20,000	Class V 5-10,000	Class VI <5000
1901	25,852	—	27	45	148	422	768	500
1911	25,942	0.25	25	38	157	390	756	547
1921	28,086	8.27	28	49	172	398	780	623
1931	33,456	19.12	32	56	224	484	856	609
1941	44,153	31.97	49	87	272	553	988	478
1951	62,444	41.43	74	111	375	670	1189	638
1961	78,937	26.41	107	141	515	817	844	266
1971	108,787	37.81	142	198	617	931		

SOURCE: S. Chandrasekhar (Ed.), *Asia's Population Problems*, 1967, p. 78 and J. E. Brush, Some dimensions of urban population pressure in India, (paper presented at the symposium of the International Geographic Union's Commission on Cartography and Geography of World Population held at The Pennsylvania State University, September 1967.)

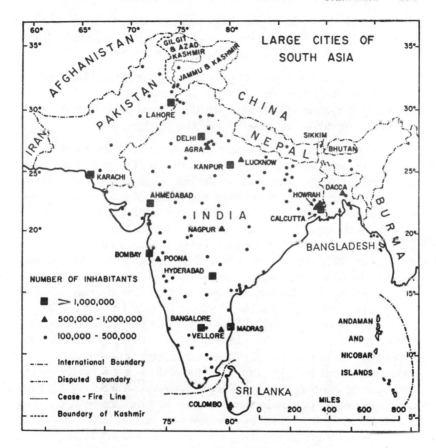

FIG. 5.6. Large cities of South Asia. Large cities are more evenly spread than in most other major regions of the developing world.

The slightly more populous country of Sri Lanka is much more urbanized, but the percentage of 18.9 urban population in 1963 is inflated by the addition of town council areas to urban areas at that census. As in Nepal, there is marked urban primacy, because Colombo is outdistancing all rivals; in 1963 its conurbation contained 768,000 people.

Although the levels of urbanization in South Asia are still low, the picture of urban growth is not a happy one. Urban population densities are extremely high: Delhi 22,000 per square mile, Greater Bombay 24,000, Madras 28,000 and Greater Calcutta 36,000. Studies by Brush in Indian cities indicate the persistence of two trends:

—maximum concentration of population in the central bazaars and old compact settlement areas;
—sharp density gradients between the central areas and the peripheral or suburban areas.

This compact urban growth pattern has meant that in some sectors and wards population densities may attain half a million per square mile. Brush refers to this situation as "urban implosion", where town-dwellers stay as near as possible to the centre of the city, near their work and the market. Inevitably, housing conditions deteriorate and are frequently appalling. Shanty-towns or *bustees* mushroom; they contain about one-quarter of the population of Calcutta, and the proportions are only slightly lower in cities like Delhi, Ahmedabad and Kanpur. In Indian cities the average family lives in a one-room tenement or a temporary shelter, in shocking conditions of congestion and squalor. In 1961, Calcutta Metropolitan Region had an average of 3 persons per room and only 1.55 rooms per dwelling unit. The problem of housing is fearful, and thousands have no other home than the city pavements. India needs 1,700,000 new dwellings per annum, but only about 200,000 are being constructed. One of the many difficulties in the development of urban housing is that many of the urban immigrants are too poor to purchase houses and have to save money in order to send it home to their relatives. Moreover, caste and family ties cause excessive social segregation, and there is also a lack of satisfactory urban transport facilities and public utilities which would assist suburban growth. Consequently, urban expansion appears to lack zonation. This depressing picture is not true for the whole of South Asia. New towns exist like Faridabad near New Delhi, and other cities like Jamshedpur-Tatanagar have grown rapidly during this century on an industrial basis; Jamshedpur had 5672 inhabitants in 1911 and 450,000 in 1968. Nevertheless, it is certain that South Asian cities are generally deteriorating as places for working and living. Urban unemployment and underemployment are constant problems, and exceed one in ten of the active population in much of South Asia. The problem is aggravated by male preponderance in cities, especially in north India and Pakistan where young male migrants prevail. In Bangladesh, for example, the urban population in 1961 comprised 1422 males per thousand females, in comparison with the rural sex-ratio of 1059; and some towns (e.g. Chittagong and Khulna) had twice as many males as females. In south India rural–urban migrants often move as families, so urban sex-ratios are less unbalanced, but poverty-stricken conditions are still common

Present trends seem to indicate little improvement in the conditions of urbanization, and the situation will probably get worse. In 1960, Davis made projections for the growth of the major cities of India, in which Calcutta would have 35.6–66 million inhabitants by AD 2000, Delhi 17.8–33.0 million and Bombay 11.9–22.0 million. It is possible that these astronomical estimates are too high, for they were made prior to the 1961 census, but they are not unreasonable. In these circumstances, the need for industrialisation is urgent; but at present many of the cities lack economic dynamism and give little hope for relieving the under-utilization of the active population.

Internal Migration

In South Asia rural stagnation has been spatial as well as social, partly because of the influence of the complex social structure and partly because of ignorance and lack of opportunities. In this connection, it is noteworthy that only 13.6 per cent of the rural population of Pakistan (9.1 per cent of West Pakistan) were literate at the time of the 1961 census. Immobility of population is a general phenomenon; in India only about 10 per cent live outside their district of birth and only 3–4 per cent outside their state–territory of birth. However, recent analysis by Bose of yearly migration figures indicates that the population is not nearly as immobile as previously imagined. Improved transport and communications, increased education and employment opportunities all play a part, but so do "push" factors, which result in a high rate of turnover migration (people moving from one area to another without settling down). Both rural–rural and urban–urban turnover migrations have assumed significant proportions, so that floating populations occur, most noteworthy in big cities like Bombay, Madras, Calcutta and Hyderabad, where too many are in search of employment or better employment. And not all are poor and illiterate; many unemployed migrants are well educated. It is also apparent that short-range migrations are more intense than long-range migrations, and while the former are mainly rural–rural the latter are mostly rural–urban. Indeed, the most common form of life-time migration is short-range rural–rural migration, especially of women for marriage, as village exogamy occurs in several parts of India.

In India there is a very positive relationship between the level of economic development of a district and its intra-state and inter-state migration, and states with most industrialization attract more migrants than other states. Immobility is particularly prevalent in the densely peopled rural areas of the Gangetic plain and delta and the coastal plains, as well as in the sparsely peopled hill areas. On the other hand, there has been marked migration into Assam since about the turn of the century, into West Bengal where the Damodar coalfield and Hooghly-side are the areas of attraction, into Maharashtra state where Greater Bombay is the main magnet, into south and south-west Mysore where plantations and Bangalore draw immigrants, and into the Union Territory of Delhi. The main sources of Indian migrants in the north are the states of Punjab, Uttar Pradesh and Bihar, and in the south the states of Kerala and Madras, although within these states there are large internal movements to areas favoured by irrigation or industry. However, Gosal has pointed out that despite out-migration the southern states have fairly balanced sex-ratios, because women enjoy a reasonable social status; in contrast, the northern states, especially those in the north-west where a patriarchal society prevails, have a low proportion of females. This is also the case in most of Pakistan, and in Bangladesh.

In the future, migration must be encouraged from regions of high population pressure to regions of low pressure, although some of the social restraints on long-distance migration could be seen in Pakistan where transmigration from East to West offered little hope for relief of population pressure in the East. In the case of India, Miss Sen Gupta calculated regional imbalance of population pressure (Fig. 5.7) by use of the formula $I = \dfrac{P_1 - P}{A}$ where I is the index of population pressure per square kilometre of rural area, P_1 is "the districtwise derived rural

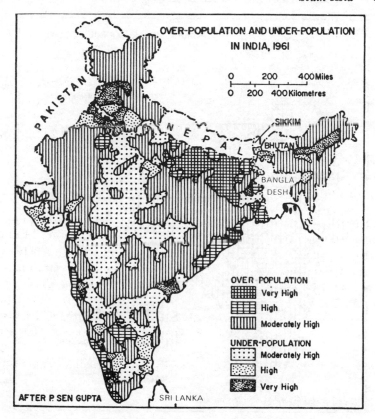

Fig. 5.7. Overpopulation and underpopulation in India, 1961 (after P. Sen Gupta). For method of calculation see text. The range of population pressures obviously varies markedly from one part of India to another.

population capable of being supported by the utilized land resources by assuming a constant income per person," P is the actual rural population for each district, and A is the total rural area in square kilometres. Miss Gupta revealed that (a) the areas of very high density (with more than 200 per km²) are not always overpopulated, (b) areas with good irrigation facilities and conditions for commercial agriculture are often underpopulated, (c) areas of low density (less than 50 per km²) are invariably overpopulated, and (d) population pressure is very

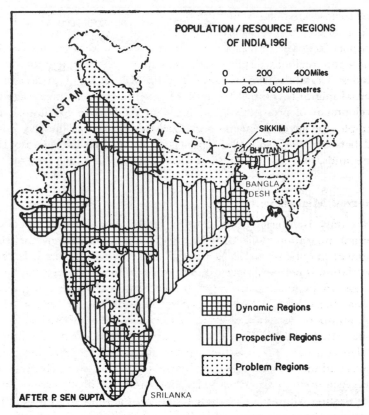

FIG. 5.8. Population–resource regions of India, 1961 (after P. Sen Gupta). The dynamic and problem regions are widely scattered.

high in non-irrigated rice-growing areas, especially the middle and east Ganga Plain, the Bhagirathi delta and the Kerala coast. She was also able to divide the country into three types of population–resource regions (dynamic, prospective and problem regions) according to the combined impact of the demographic structure, resource potentiality and levels of socio-economic development upon the supporting capacity of non-agricultural population (Fig. 5.8). Dynamic regions support advanced industrial areas and mainly urban population. Prospective regions have large resource potentials but deficient technology and some socio-economic obstacles to development. Problem regions show little promise, owing to overpopulation, limited resources, lack of transport facilities or other factors. Such a division throws considerable light upon regional disparities, which may well augment in future decades. Certainly, the dynamic regions will be most attractive to internal migrants. One of the tasks of government is to encourage the development of prospective and problem regions. In Sri Lanka, for example, the government has organized colonization of the Dry Zone, and between 1945 and 1955 about 100,000 people moved into Dry Zone lands, but full utilization of these lands is still a long way off.

External Migration

Not only is internal migration in South Asia limited, but so is external migration, and consequently the populations of the subcontinent may be regarded to a considerable extent as closed. In fact, repatriation is perhaps more likely than expatriation. There can be no solution to population pressure in South Asia through emigration, because there is nowhere to go where migrants can be welcomed in large numbers. As nationalism has evolved in Asia and Africa, South Asians can find little prospect of settling abroad. Fear of minority problems dissuade potential immigrant countries from receiving South Asians, and the latter are deterred by fears of ill treatment. Even within South Asia itself, international migration cannot radically ease population pressure. Migration between India and Pakistan is a continuation of a process begun at partition in 1947, but during the period 1951–61 it was mostly from Pakistan to India, of whose total population growth it accounted for about 2.2 per cent. Migration to Sri Lanka had largely ceased by independence in 1948.

Indian external migration demonstrates the problems. Between 1834 and 1934 some 30 million persons left India. Most went as indentured labourers for plantation agriculture in European overseas possessions, notably to the Caribbean, Fiji and South Africa. From Uttar Pradesh, Bihar and Madras, they provided cheap labour for plantation owners after the abolition of slavery; and many broke all ties with their homeland—even the caste system died. Later migrations were of a periodic type to Sri Lanka and Malaya; mostly from South India, migrants went for a few years under the organization of headmen or *kangani*. A third type of migrant, mainly from the northern districts of Bombay province, Gujarat and Sind, went freely to East Africa as traders, and like those migrants under *kangani* they kept closer ties with their homelands, and adhered to the caste system.

Four-fifths of the Indian emigrants returned home, and the descendants of Indians who remained abroad now number about five million. Table 5.5 reveals that the largest groups are in Sri Lanka, Burma and Malaya, although Indians form larger proportions of the total populations of Mauritius, Fiji, Guyana, Trinidad and Surinam.

TABLE 5.5. INDIANS OVERSEAS

	Number of Indians	% of total population
Sri Lanka (1953)	1,132,000	10.6
Burma (1956)	800,000	4.1
Malaya (1960)	850,000	12.1
South Africa (1961)	404,000	2.5
Mauritius (1957)	400,000	67.0
East Africa (1963)	352,000	1.3
Trinidad (1960)	302,000	36.5
Guyana (1960)	268,000	48.2
England and Wales (1966)	224,000	0.5
Fiji (1960)	198,000	49.3
Surinam (1959)	94,000	35.4

SOURCE: Mostly from C. Jayawardena, Migration and social change: a survey of Indian communities overseas, *Geog. Review* **58,** 429 (1968).

Population Growth

Accelerating rates of population growth in South Asia result from a decline in mortality which was slow and irregular until 1945, when there was an unprecedented and unforeseen decline. Subsequent development plans have thus seriously underestimated population growth. India's First and Second Five-year Plans assumed population growth rates of 12.5 per cent a decade, but before they had ended it became obvious that the assumptions were too low; in fact, the 1961 census showed that the growth between 1951 and 1961 was 21.5 per cent, 70 per cent higher than assumed by the plans. The Third Five-year Plan (1961–66) assumed a population growth of 2.2 per cent per annum but this was still too low, so in the Fourth Five-year Plan (1966–71) the assumed growth rate is 2.5 per cent.

In Pakistan, population growth has again been unexpectedly high. It was assumed that during the First Plan period (1955–60) population would increase by 7.5 per cent, but this was much too low. In the Second Plan (1960–65) the estimated population growth was 9 per cent, but the reality was over 12 per cent. In fact, the Second Plan used figures of 88.9 and 96.9 million for 1960 and 1965, but the 1961 census enumerated 93.8 million and there may have been more than 100 million at that time. The situation was not remedied in the Third Plan (1965–70), for it was based on 2.6 per cent as the current annual growth rate when the real growth rate exceeded 3 per cent.

The planners are not the only ones to blame, for the demographers have invariably been inaccurate in their forecasts of future growth. In 1949, Kingsley Davis estimated the future populations of India and Pakistan by fitting past data to a logistic curve, and also by projecting from the recently experienced rate of natural increase. By the former method he obtained a total of 525 million for 1970, a number which was actually attained by 1960, and by the latter method he obtained two estimates of 550 and 465 million. In 1956 Coale and Hoover used assumptions of declining mortality, stable or rising fertility and little influence of international migration in their population projections, but even in their "high" projection they underestimated mortality decline, a fact revealed by the 1961 census. An Expert Committee of the Planning Commission prepared in 1961 projections of India's population until 1976, but it assumed a substantial decline in fertility between 1971 and 1976 which may not be achieved. It is possible, therefore, that Shrinivasan's projected total of 639 million for 1976 may be nearer reality (Table 5.6).

Most population projections of Pakistan made during the 1950s also badly underrated growth. The 1961 census of Pakistan revealed in particular a striking increase in the proportion of children. By 1961 the under 15 age group comprised 44.5 per cent of the total population (cf. 41.1 per cent in India and 40.7 per cent in Sri Lanka), and between 1951 and 1961 the percentage of children under 5 rose from 14.2 to

TABLE 5.6. SOME POPULATION PROJECTIONS OF SOUTH ASIA

	Actual population 1961 (millions)	Projected population (millions)					Average annual growth rate	
		1961	1966	1971	1976	1981	actual 1956–61	projected 1961–81
INDIA								
Coale and Hoover, 1956 "high"	438	424	473	532	601	682	2.0	2.4
Agarwala, 1959	—	423	472	526	574	626	—	—
Expert Committee for Planning Commission, 1961	438	438	492	555	625	—	2.0	2.4
Shrinivasan, 1961	438	438	491	558	639	—	2.0	—
PAKISTAN								
UN 1958 "moderate"	94.5	92.5	103.5	116.7	132.5	151.7	2.1	2.5
UN 1958 "modified"	94.5	95.4	109.0	125.7	154.6	169.9	2.1	3.1
SRI LANKA								
UN 1958	9.9	9.9	11.4	13.8	15.5	18.3	2.4	3.1
S. Salvaratnam, 1958 "high"	—	—	—	—	15+	20	—	—

SOURCE: Mostly from G. Myrdal, *Asian Drama*, 1968, vol. 2, Table 27.8, pp. 1452–53.

17.4 per cent (14.6 to 18.2 in Bangladesh) while those aged 5–9 rose from 14.1 to 17.7 per cent (14.9 to 18.7 in Bangladesh), a very high proportion of the total population. Fortunately, the United Nations 1958 population projections of Sri Lanka have proved much more realistic, although most other projections have overestimated the population.

Whatever the accuracy of population projections, the age structures of South Asian countries indicate a high growth potential for at least a generation, as the number in the reproductive age groups could only begin to decline a generation after fertility began to fall. In other words, even if fertility declines immediately, a high rate of population growth is assured in the short term.

Mortality

Fluctuations in mortality have been the main determinant of population growth in the history of the Indian subcontinent, for calamities such as famines, epidemics and wars have greatly checked growth.

Apart from the influence of calamities, the crude death rate in India–Pakistan before 1920 was just over 40 per thousand, but during the inter-war years it declined steadily until the early fifties (Table 5.7).

TABLE 5.7. INDIA'S BIRTH AND DEATH RATES, 1901–70

	Birth rate		Death rate	
	Registered	Estimated	Registered	Estimated
1901–10	40.20	52.4	35.10	46.8
1911–20	36.94	48.1	34.14	47.2
1921–30	34.55	46.4	26.29	36.3
1931–40	34.17	45.2	22.99	31.2
1941–50	27.32	43.0	20.10	30.0
1951–60	29.81	40.0	19.13	22.0
1961–70		40.0		18.0

SOURCE: S. Chandrasekhar (Ed.), *Asia's Population Problems*, 1967, p. 80.

This decline was associated with the elimination or reduction of famines and epidemics, as well as the control of three major killers—

smallpox, plague and cholera. Since the early fifties, when the death rate was about 30 per thousand, mortality has declined rapidly, largely owing to a reduction in death rates from all causes (except maternal mortality and tuberculosis), but especially from typhoid and malaria. In the mid-sixties the death rate of India was about 18 per thousand and that of Pakistan about 19 per thousand. Future reductions in death rates will depend on (a) the success of campaigns against malaria, tuberculosis and typhoid, (b) reduction in excessive child-bearing, (c) improved nutrition and standards of living, and (d) better sanitation and water supply.

In Sri Lanka the situation has been rather different, for the death rate began to decline from about 27–28 per thousand in the mid-twenties and descended to a little over 20 per thousand by the end of the Second World War. Then following the successful campaigns against malaria, using DDT spraying (Table 5.8), the crude death

TABLE 5.8. MORBIDITY AND MORTALITY FROM
MALARIA IN SRI LANKA

	Rate per 100,000 perons	
	Morbidity	Mortality
1937–45 (average)	44,300	112.8
1946	41,200	187.3
1947	19,600	66.1
1949	9,900	32.8
1951	5,800	20.6
1953	1,300	9.1
1955	220	3.1
1957	380	1.9
1960	5	—

SOURCE: G. Myrdal, *Asian Drama*, 1968, vol. 3, p. 1569.

rate plunged to less than 10 per thousand by 1960; by the mid-sixties it was about 8 per thousand. It is unlikely that India, Pakistan or Bangladesh will achieve such a low rate in the immediate future.

Despite reductions in mortality, age-specific mortality rates are still high, so there is still room for considerable improvement. In particular, there is a great contrast with advanced countries in that female mortality exceeds male mortality, and this is most striking in the 15–40 age group. High maternal mortality is one cause, and child marriage is another, but women also suffer from much indifference as to their welfare. The situation is much better in Sri Lanka; but there the rate of improvement in mortality conditions has not been as rapid among infants and old people as among the adult age-groups, whereas the opposite situation has occurred in India and Pakistan.

Generally speaking, there is better health and lower mortality among groups with high social and economic status, in cities and in rural areas, and infant mortality rates are especially sensitive to living conditions. In the immediate future population growth in South Asia will depend considerably upon the effectiveness of health policies and the emphasis put on them by governments. This is certainly not the only factor, for in addition education, economic development, overseas aid and other criteria will be influential. Nevertheless, health policies will be crucial.

India has many more difficult health problems than either Pakistan or Sri Lanka, partly because medical facilities are insufficient, and partly because of the vast size and great poverty of many of its population. Certainly there were remarkable achievements during the 1950s, when the average expectation of life at birth rose from 32 years to 45, progress due mainly to increased control of malaria. However, health was given low status in the first three five-year plans, and consequently facilities improved little; the doctor–population ratio (about 17 per 100,000 inhabitants), hardly rose at all during the 1950s. The Fourth Five-year Plan (1966–71) aims at a supply of doctors and auxiliary medical personnel similar to that in Sri Lanka about 1960, but there is a real danger that the country's health expenditures will soon suffer from diminishing returns in terms of increasing the expectation of life. It is improbable, therefore, that by 1980 the death rate will go below 13 per thousand, or that average life expectancy will extend beyond 52 years.

Despite a rapid increase in the number of doctors from 4.2 per 100,000 inhabitants in 1950–52 to 12.5 in 1964, public health improvements in Pakistan have been even slower than in India, and the present mortality situation is worse. In fact, by 1970 Pakistan hoped to achieve India's 1960 level of doctors, nurses and hospital beds. In view of its progress against major diseases, it is possible that Pakistan may lower its death rate to 15 per thousand by 1980, with a life expectancy of 50 years.

Sri Lanka's health services and medical facilities are clearly larger and better than elsewhere in South Asia, but they are still quite inadequate. Myrdal has stated that raising the supply of medical personnel and facilities by 1975 to the level prevailing in Portugal in 1955 would require a five-fold increase in output of trained personnel. Although Sri Lanka has a low death rate, much is attributable to the youthfulness of its population. In some ways it has reached a threshold as far as mortality is concerned, for further reductions cannot be achieved without substantial economic progress and higher standards of living as well as better nutrition, housing and sanitation. These are not easily achieved, and it would be unreasonable to expect more than very gradual decline in the death rate over the next decade to about 7 per thousand by 1980.

Fertility

Registration of births in South Asia is often more defective than that of deaths, and birth data are only rarely classifiable by age of mother or duration of marriage. Recorded figures are thus of limited value.

In contrast to mortality, the fertility of the peoples of South Asia has not altered greatly for many decades, although some reduction is discernible in India and particularly Sri Lanka (Table 5.9). In the past

TABLE 5.9. VITAL RATES IN SOUTH ASIA, EARLY 1970's

	Birth rate	Death rate	Infant mortality rate	Current rate of population growth
India	42	17	139	2.5
Pakistan	51	18	142	3.3
Sri Lanka	31	8	48	2.3
Nepal	45	23	—	2.2

SOURCE: Population Reference Bureau, 1972 World Population Data sheet.

high mortality necessitated high fertility in order to achieve a stationary population.

What, then, are the causes of high fertility? Marriage is certainly influential, because illegitimate births and pre-marital conceptions are rare. Marriage is almost universal among women in South Asia; factors affecting this are the shortage of adult females (although women are probably under-enumerated) and the ban on remarriage of widows by high-caste Hindus. It may be argued that this Hindu ban has a lowering effect upon fertility, but it is probably not substantial. In India and Pakistan marriage is early, and about 70 per cent of all girls aged 15–19 are married, compared with less than 25 per cent in Sri Lanka. Expressed otherwise, the modal age of marriage for women is about 18 in India and Pakistan and about 22 in Sri Lanka. In all countries the decline in mortality has reduced the frequency of widows and widowers, raised fertility and reduced the demand for young wives. Child marriages, however, are still numerous in India, although several years may elapse before cohabitation, and reduction of child marriage, necessary morally and physically (it sometimes causes death), would have little effect upon fertility. On the other hand, postponement of marriage to a much later age, as in Sri Lanka, causes a marked decline in fertility. Another factor affecting universal marriage and high fertility in South Asia is the extended family system, which cares for young couples in their early years of married life, and consequently marriages are not notably less numerous in years of poor harvests or financial conditions.

It has been commonly believed that fecundity (ability to conceive) is higher in South Asia than in the West, but this is doubtful. There are many Hindu restrictions upon sexual intercourse, and abstinence is common during religious festivals as well as among grandparents; but in the long run such religious influences may weaken. Muslims do not attach so much importance to these customs, and their marital fertility, like that of Buddhists, is generally higher than that of Hindus (and Christians); this may well account for Pakistan's higher birth rate. Malnutrition and disease, especially malaria, cholera, venereal diseases and relapsing fever, have caused a high proportion of stillbirths. Learmonth has emphasized that malaria has a very lowering effect upon birth rates, and has shown that variability of birth rates is also due to some extent to famines. Poor health certainly causes high mortality among the reproductive age groups, and consequently many women lose their husbands and become "socially sterile". Therefore improved health will tend to increase the duration of marriage and increase fertility and thus will probably be the key influence upon fertility in the immediate future.

Various authors have indicated that fertility differentials are almost absent in India and Pakistan. Fertility seems to be little affected by literacy, education, income, occupation or caste except at the very highest levels where family planning is practised. In Pakistan no rural–urban fertility gap could be discerned in the period of the late 1950s and early 1960s; fertility was uniformly high. In some Indian cities fertility appears to be higher than in rural areas, but this may be due to defective data. Robinson stressed that in Pakistan urbanization has not been accompanied by a general urbanism, and this must be true for much of the Indian subcontinent, but not in Sri Lanka, where urban fertility is lower than rural fertility.

Population Policies

In these conditions of limited differential fertility there seems little possibility of widespread spontaneous family planning in the immediate future. Consequently, governments must produce effective population policies if they want to lower fertility; especially as there is strong evidence to suggest that population growth is impeding economic advance. Lower fertility would have a positive influence upon *per capita* incomes and levels of living as well as on the productivity of labour, but its achievement is no simple task, for the conservative traditionalism of the population and their "survival mentality" have acted as obstacles to population policies.

Family planning is no new concept in India, as neo-Malthusianism dates back to the inter-war period, when it was widely considered that the country was "overpopulated". India has long had a declared policy of spreading birth control among the masses, and has constantly increased budget appropriations for this purpose:

    First Five-year Plan (1951–56) 1.5 million rupees
    Second Five-year Plan (1956–61) 21.6 million rupees
    Third Five-year Plan (1961–66) 261.0 million rupees
    Fourth Five-year Plan (1966–71) 950.0 million rupees

Reliance on family planning clinics and on the rhythm method of birth control led to early lack of success, but increased emphasis on sterilization and IUDs has been more effective. The aim of the Fourth Plan is to reduce the birth rate from about 40 per thousand to about 25 per thousand as soon as possible, especially by the mid-1970's, but present trends give little reason to be confident. On the other hand, it is a measure of determination that India's current health minister is a distinguished demographer and advocate of family planning.

In Pakistan a later start was made with family planning. Only after the military takeover in 1958 and the introduction of a more authoritarian form of government was the population problem taken seriously. Although Pakistan was able to learn from the Indian example, the achievements of the Second Plan (1960–65) fell short of expectations, partly because the programme was aimed primarily at urban populations. In the Third Plan (1965–70) annual expenditure on family planning was raised from 1 cent per person to 12 cents, aiming at a decline of the birth rate from 55 to 35 per thousand over 20 years, half of the decline to take place during the first 5 years. Pakistan's aims are therefore less ambitious than those of India, but its present natural increase is much higher.

The decline in the birth rate of Sri Lanka to 32 per thousand in 1967 was mostly the result of changes in the age structure and the marital status of women in the reproductive age groups, and latterly of a decline in marital fertility. The National Family Planning Programme began only in 1966, and its effects are awaited. The goal is a crude birth rate of 25 per thousand in 1975, and with a better public health system than other South Asian countries Sri Lanka has a real chance of success, despite a slow beginning, in particular because of the varied influence of the educational upsurge upon fertility: delaying marriage and the effective reproductive period, encouraging female employment and stimulating social mobility.

Select Bibliography
AGARWALA, S. N. (Ed.), *India's Population: Some Problems in Perspective and Planning*, Bombay, 1961.
AHMAD, N., *An Economic Geography of East Pakistan*, 2nd edn., 1968.
AHMAD, Q., *Indian Cities: Characteristics and Correlates*, Chicago, 1965.

AHMAD, Q., Distribution pattern of urban centres in Pakistan, *Pakistan Geog. Rev.* **22,** 1 (1967).

AHMAD, Q., Distribution of city sizes in Pakistan, *Pakistan Geog. Rev.* **22,** 77 (1967).

BHAT, L. S., Regional contrasts in population density and growth in India, 1951–61, *Geography* **48,** 313 (1963).

BOSE, A. (Ed.), *Patterns of Population Change in India, 1951–61,* Bombay, 1967.

BREESE, G., Urban development problems in India, *Ann. Assoc. Am. Geog.* **53,** 253 (1963).

BRUSH, J. E., Spatial patterns of population in Indian cities, *Geog. Rev.* **58,** 362 (1968).

BULSARA, J. F., *Problems of Rapid Urbanization in India,* Bombay, 1964.

CHANDRASEKHAR, S., *Population and Planned Parenthood in India,* 2nd edn. 1961.

CHANDRASEKHAR, S. (Ed.), *Asia's Population Problems,* 1967.

CHATTERJEE, S. P., Regional patterns of the density and distribution of population in India, *Geog. Rev. India* **24,** 1 (1962).

COALE, A. J. and HOOVER, E. M., *Population Growth and Economic Development in Low-Income Countries: A Case Study of India's Prospects,* Princeton, 1958.

DATTA, J. M., A re-examination of Moreland's estimate of population of India at the death of Akbar, *Indian Pop. Bull.* **1,** 166 (1960).

DAVIS, K., *The Population of India and Pakistan,* Princeton, 1951.

DRIVER, E. D., *Differential Fertility in Central India,* Princeton, 1963.

GEDDES, A., Half a century of population trends in India: a regional study of net change and variability, 1881–1931, *Geog. J.* **98,** 228 (1941).

GEDDES, A., The population of India: variability of change as a regional demographic index, *Georg. Rev.* **32,** 562 (1942).

GOSAL, G. S., The regionalism of sex composition of India's population, *Rural Sociol.* **26,** 122 (1961).

GOSAL, G. S., Internal migration in India—a regional analysis, *Indian Geog. J.* **36,** 106 (1961).

GOSAL, G. S., Literacy in India: an interpretative study, *Rural Sociol.* **29,** 261 (1964).

GUPTA, Sen, *Some Characteristics of Internal Migration in India,* Office of Registrar General, India, New Delhi, 1967.

GUPTA, Sen, Population and resource development in India, in PROTHERO, R. M. et al. (Eds.), *Geography and a Crowding World,* New York, 1970.

INTERNATIONAL UNION FOR THE SCIENTIFIC STUDY OF POPULATION, Sydney Conference, Australia, 1967 (several papers of value by Bose, Mitra, Narain, etc.).

JAYAWARDENA, D., Migration and social change: a survey of India communities overseas, *Geog. Rev.* **58,** 426 (1968).

JOHNSON, B. L. C., Rural population densities in East Pakistan, *Pacific Viewpoint* **3,** 51 (1962).

JOHNSON, B. L. C., *South Asia,* 1969.

KARAN, P. P. and JENKINS, W. M., *Nepal: A Cultural and Physical Geography,* Lexington, Kentucky, 1960.

KARAN, P. P. and JENKINS, W. M., *The Himalayan Kingdoms: Bhutan, Sikkim and Nepal,* Princeton, 1963.

LALL, A., Patterns of in-migration in India's cities, *Geog. Rev. India* **23,** 16 (1961).

LALL, A., Age and sex structures of cities of India, *Geog. Rev. India* **24,** 7 (1962).

LALL, A. and TIRTHA, R., India's urbanization, *Focus* **19,** No. 1. (Sept. 1968).

LEARMONTH, A. T. A., Selected aspects of India's population geography. *Australian J. Polit. Hist.* **12,** 146 (1966).

MAJUMDAR, D. N., *Races and Cultures of India*, Bombay, 1958.
MEMORIA, C. B., Growth of population in India, *Geog. Rev. India* **19**, 13 (1957).
MYRDAL, G., *Asian Drama, An Inquiry into the Poverty of Nations*. 3 vols., 1968.
OBAIDULLAH, M., Internal migration in East Pakistan, *Orient. Geog.* **11**, 23 (1967).
PANT, Y. P., Nepal's population growth, *Far Eastern Econ. Rev.* **37**, 499 (1962).
PAULUS, C. R., *The Impact of Urbanization on Fertility in India*, Mysore, 1966.
QURESHI, M. L. (Ed.), *Population Growth and Economic Development*, Karachi, 1959.
RASHID, H., *East Pakistan: A Systematic Regional Geography and its Development Planning Aspects*, Lahore, 1965.
ROBINSON, W C, Urban rural differences in Indian fertility, *Pop. Studies* **14**, 218 (1961).
ROBINSON, W. C. (Ed.), *Studies in the Demography of Pakistan*, Karachi, 1967.
SARKAR, N. K., *The Demography of Ceylon*, Colombo, 1957.
SCHWARTZBERG, J. E., Agricultural labour in India: a regional analysis with particular reference to population growth, *Econ. Devel. Cult. Change* **11**, 337 (1963).
SEN, J. C., The sex composition of India's towns from 20,000 to 50,000, according to the 1961 census, *Indian Geog. J.* **37**, 90 (1963).
SINHA, R. P., *Food in India*, Bombay, 1961.
SOUANI, N. V., *Urbanization and Urban India*, India, 1966.
SPATE, O H. K. and LEARMONTH, A. T. A., *India and Pakistan*, London, 3rd edn. 1967.
TAYYEB, A., *Pakistan: A Political Geography*, London, 1966.
THOMPSON, W. S., *Population and Progress in the Far East*, Chicago, 1959.
TREWARTHA, G. T. and GOSAL, G S, The regionalism of population change in India, *Cold Spring Harbour Symposia on Quantitative Biology* **22**, 71 (1957).
TURNER, R. (Ed.), *India's Urban Future*, Berkeley, 1962.
UN, *The Mysore Population Study*, Population Studies No. 34, 1961.
VISARIA, P. M., Migration between India and Pakistan, 1951–61, *Demography* **6**, 323 (1969).

6

EAST ASIA

EAST ASIA contains the largest concentration of mankind, and even without Japan (excluded from this volume because it is a developed country) it has more than 855 million people (1972 estimate). Most of these people, however, are living in Mainland China, which has between one-quarter and one-fifth of the total world population, about as many as the combined populations of Latin America, Africa and South-west Asia, and more than the combined populations of Europe and the USSR. Consequently, the population of this one country will be the almost exclusive concern of this chapter, with only passing references to the much smaller populations of other countries of East Asia: North Korea, South Korea, Taiwan, Hong Kong and Mongolia (Table 6.1).

TABLE 6.1. EAST ASIA: DEMOGRAPHIC DATA

	Estimated population mid 1972 (millions)	Birth rate ‰	Death rate ‰	Current rate of population growth %	Projected population, 1985 (millions)
China (Mainland)	786.1	30	13	1.7	964.6
China (Taiwan)	14.7	28	5	2.3	19.4
Hong Kong	4.4	20	5	2.4	6.0
North Korea	14.7	39	11	2.8	20.7
South Korea	33.7	31	11	2.0	45.9
Mongolia	1.4	42	11	3.1	2.0

SOURCE: 1972 World Population Data Sheet—Population Reference Bureau.

This volume has never attempted a state-by-state treatment of the population geography of developing countries, but China obviously merits individual consideration, not only because of the magnitude of its population and its preponderance in East Asia, but also because of its highly distinctive cultural, political and demographic conditions, which make it difficult to treat simultaneously with other countries of East Asia, some of which have more demographic affinities with South east Asia. Part of this distinctiveness, but only part, arises from the long environmental isolation from the pervasive culture of Europe, caused by the enormous mountain barriers to the west and the vast Pacific Ocean to the east. In recent years political isolation has added to this distinctiveness, making China one of the most fascinating and problematic populations.

Evolution of Population

Unfortunately, although China has the biggest population in the world, it is also, as Aird suggests, the largest demographic question mark: "Few statements can be made about China's population which are simple, safe and significant". Although it is said that a census was taken in the twenty-third century BC, and records remain of censuses in 814 and 589 BC, AD 2, 140, 730, 1491 and 1710, there has been only one modern census, made as long ago as 1953. Moreover, statistics of any sort are difficult to obtain and often inaccurate, owing to the past prevalence of illiteracy and the inefficiency of statistical services as well as to the present tendencies to be secretive about data and to release only those which cast a favourable light on the communist regime. At the same time, it must be said that the sheer size of the country and its population causes difficulties of communication and administration, which impede a complete and accurate count.

The size of China's population has long been an enigma. Although the country has the longest records of population, maintained for purposes of taxation, military conscription and police registers, their interpretation has been a matter of some contention among scholars, who have proposed different totals for the intermittent growth of the Chinese population over the centuries. For much of Chinese history, most authors, including Ta Chen and Ping-Ti Ho, have subscribed to the idea of population cycles, in which periods of peace and growth were followed by periods of misery and decline, all associated with dynasties (Fig. 6.1). Population peaks occurred during the Han (206 BC–AD 214) T'ang (AD 618–907), Sung (960–1279) and Ming (1368–1644) dynasties and were separated by troughs or plateaux caused by invasions, revolutions, disorders, floods or famines. From the late seventeenth century there was a period of rapid population growth, but most authors agree that after the last decade of the eighteenth century growth slowed

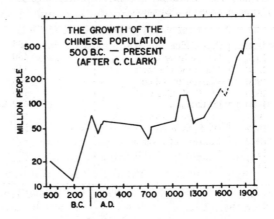

Fig. 6.1. The growth of the Chinese population, 500 BC—present (after Colin Clark). China has experienced many cycles of growth and temporary decline.

down. During the nineteenth century the main check to growth was the Taiping Rebellion of 1848–64, which had a devastating effect in central China and caused stability of population numbers between 1850 and 1900. However, there is some disagreement over the value and interpretation of the population records of the *pao-chia* system, which lasted from 1714 into the latter half of the nineteenth century and was devised to transmit civil control from the lowest level of magistrates down to heads of households.

During the first half of the twentieth century unsuccessful attempts were made to hold complete censuses in 1909–11, 1912–13 and 1928–29, although partial enumerations collected a variety of demographic information, including data on age, sex, births, deaths, family size, marital status, literacy, education, ethnic status and occupation. Unfortunately, these enumerations gave no reliable population totals, and so a wide-ranging variety of contemporary estimates were made, based on postal, fiscal and other records (Table 6.2), although before the communist take-over in 1949 it was generally assumed that the total population was of the order of 450 million.

TABLE 6.2. PRE-CENSAL ESTIMATES OF THE POPULATION OF CHINA (IN MILLIONS)

1926	Post Office	486
1930	Chang-heng Chen	480
1930	Maritime Customs	444
1930	Warren H. Chen	445
1930	M. T. Z. Tyau	463
1930	D. K. Lieu	470–80
1931	Ministry of Interior	474
1937	W. F. Willcox	350
1940	Ministry of Interior	450
1946	Directorate of Statistics	449
1953	Census	583

SOURCE: W. S. Thompson, *Population and Progress in the Far East*, 1959, p. 203.

In these circumstances of uncertainty it is perhaps inevitable that considerable credence has been placed upon the data of 1953 census, published on 1 November 1954, "the first scientific census" of China. In fact, the census schedule was restricted to four questions on habitual residence, ethnic identity, age and sex, and it was largely based on reports of heads of households who had to register at specific localities. Moreover, the enumeration was held in connection with national elections to the All-China People's Congress and with development planning, and this might have affected its impartiality, but the administrative controls were effective enough at the time to ensure a reasonably efficient census. The reported total of 582.6 million, which included an allowance for an estimated 8.4 million people who lived in frontier areas and were not enumerated, was received at first with some incredulity by many experts, as it exceeded most previous estimates by over 100 million. Many felt that the total was much too high, but there are proponents of the opposite view, and recent studies by Aird suggest that the reported population total in 1953 might have been understated by 5–15 per cent.

After the 1953 census, the census records were used to extend population registration, but the system met with great difficulties, and the last total published (in 1959) was 647 million for the end of 1957. For subsequent information about the total population, observers have either hung on the occasional utterances of communist leaders, who have referred to figures between 600 and 700 million, or have derived estimates from models. The *UN Demographic Yearbook* compromises by adding 10 million people each year to the 1953 total, arriving at 786 million for 1972 —a mammoth total, but which may understate reality.

In other words, little more is available on the population numbers of China in the 1960s than reasoned guesses, and this makes it virtually impossible to determine *per capita* rates. Expert observers have been able to make many deductions from chance offerings by Chinese newspapers and political leaders, but there is pitifully little precise information on the world's largest population, which offers so much intrinsic interest because of the continuity of its great concentrations of population, and because of the effects of the communist regime upon patterns and growth of population. Although there can be little doubt that the Chinese government possesses much population data of certain sectors of the population, such as the urban-dwellers, it is not easy to imagine how the state manages to plan satisfactorily its economy in default of reliable population data concerning the state as a whole. The lack of such data, which may be a temporary political expedient to avoid accepting wholeheartedly the practical need but philosophical anathema of family planning, is certainly a deterrent to rational projections of the country's social and economic future.

Ethnic Composition

China has much greater ethnic uniformity than its nearest demographic rival, India, and there is greater homogeneity of traditions and culture as well as fewer religious divisions and antagonisms. At the 1953 census 94 per cent of the population were enumerated as Han,

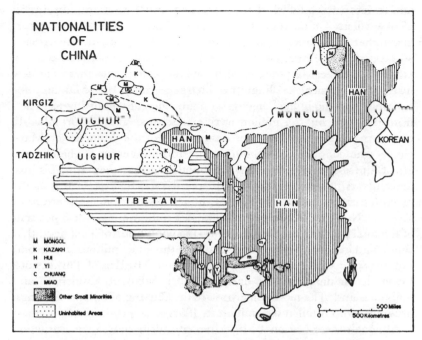

Fig. 6.2. Nationalities of China. Although the overwhelming majority of the population of China are Han, there are many other nationalities in the west and frontier regions.

descendants of a civilization which evolved 5000 years ago in the loessial middle valley of the Hwang Ho, or Yellow River. From this cradle area the Han migrated to the valleys and lowlands of the south, leaving the less fertile uplands to minority peoples. In recent decades they have also spread to the north-east in Manchuria, so today the Han people are mostly found in the lowland areas of eastern China (Fig. 6.2). In the north and north-east they are almost solidly Northern Mandarin in speech, but in the south a complexity of dialects of the Chinese Group are spoken: South-western Mandarin, Southern Mandarin, Wu Group, Foochow Group, Amoy-Swatow Group, Cantonese, etc.

Enduring a cyclical pattern of historical evolution in which famine and invasion were followed by adjustment, expansion and absorption of new rulers, China retains about fifty religious or tribal minorities, known as nationalities. In their efforts to stress the equality of status of all peoples, the communists have tried to differentiate between as many ethnic minorities as possible, although in some cases there are few distinctive physical or linguistic characteristics; the Manchu, for example, have no living language and are "virtually indistinguishable" from the Han, but 2.4 million were enumerated in 1953, presumably people regarding themselves as descendants of the Manchu of Manchuria who conquered China in the seventeenth century. The Hui are also Chinese-speaking, but their distinction is that they are Muslims, descendants of peoples who began to enter north-west China in the seventh century, and today they have their own autonomous areas. In 1953 the National Minorities totalled 35.3 million people or 6 per cent of the total population (but four times the population of Taiwan at that time), and included ten peoples with more than one million (Table 6.3) ranging from white skinned Uighur, who are Muslims of Turkic stock living in Sinkiang, to the darker slender Miao of Kweichow and Hainan island. The most numerous are the Chuang of western Kwangsi province, who totalled 6.6 million in 1953.

Although these National Minorities constitute only a small fraction

TABLE 6.3. THE MAIN NATIONAL MINORITIES OF CHINA, 1953

Minority	Region	Population (1953) (millions)
Chuang	West Kwangsi region	6.6
Uighur	Sinkiang Uighur autonomous region	3.6
Hui (Muslims)	Kansu and Chinghai	3.6
Yi	Szechwan-Yunnan borders	3.3
Tibetan	Tibet, Chamdo and Chinghai	2.8
Miao	Kweichow and West Hunan	2.5
Manchu	Widely distributed	2.4
Mongolian	Inner Mongolian autonomous region	1.5
Puyi	South-west Kweichow	1.2
Korean	Yenpien Korean autonomous *chou* in Kirin	1.1

SOURCE: T. R. Tregear, *A Geography of China*, 1965, p. 103.

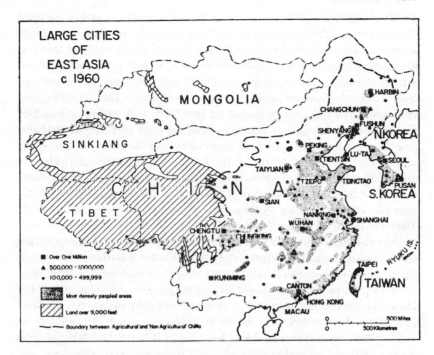

FIG. 6.3. Large cities of East Asia, *ca.* 1960. Most of the many large cities are concentrated in the agricultural regions of eastern China.

of the total population, their significance is great partly because they occupy between one-half and two-thirds of the land area of the country, especially in the peripheral, strategically important and less densely peopled regions of the south-west and north-west which could assimilate more than people. So China is very conscious of the fact that she is a multi-national state.

Distribution and Density

In strong contrast with India and Pakistan, the great bulk of China's population is highly localized, some two-thirds to three-quarters living on one-seventh of the territory (Fig. 6.3). This concentration of population largely results from the existence of an important geographical division within the Chinese territory, between (a) Inner or Agricultural China, where rainfall is adequate for cultivation and there are fertile alluvial lowlands, loessial plateaux and easily terraced slopes, and (b) Outer or non-agricultural China, characterized by high mountains and interior basins, aridity and poor soils. The Indian subcontinent possesses no areas comparable in size with the high plateaux of Tibet and the mountains and desert basins of the Gobi and central Asia. The result of the geographical contrast between east and west is that if a line is drawn from Yunnan province in the south-west to Heilungkiang province in the north-east (in Manchuria) it is found that about 96 per cent of the population of China live on the 58 per cent of the land to the east of the line. The only areas of moderately dense population to the west are where irrigation and lines of communication exist, as along the Kansu corridor or upper Hwang Ho.

Over thousands of years Chinese civilization evolved in Inner China on deltaic plains and lowland valleys suitable for intensive cultivation. They became the scenes of clustered settlements and dense population, whereas the upland areas with less fertile lateritic soils were much less attractive except for firewood and timber. Repellent to the lowland cultivators they became the home of minority peoples, specialists in shifting farming at low densities of population. The relationship between the population map and landform map is therefore extremely close, and is particularly striking in South China where, as Trewartha has emphasized, a dendritic pattern of population concentration occurs. Mediocre soils are frequently neglected in order that greater effort can be given to soils of high quality, so the pattern of soil fertility has a marked relationship to the pattern of population distribution.

The vast majority of the population live on the one-tenth of the land which is cultivated, because China is essentially an agricultural civilization. In 1953, 86.7 per cent of the population lived in places with "2000 persons and less and in places where the population was more than 2000 but 50 per cent of the total were peasants or otherwise engaged in agriculture." The patterns of population distribution are largely influenced by the patterns of rural settlement, especially nucleated settlement, for China is a country of villages and hamlets. In the past the essential needs of this great peasant civilization were met from high yielding food crops and plants produced by traditional techniques.

Rice, in particular, was basic to this civilization, and is of great demographic significance. Because of multiple cropping and its high production of protein per acre, rice enables a very intensive occupation of land, rarely experienced, for instance, in tropical Africa. Rice is also a food which permits human survival despite small quantities consumed, and because it is an excellent food for weaning babies it has a lowering effect upon child mortality in monsoon Asia

The longevity of agricultural systems in China has meant great continuity and persistence in population distribution, so that, as Buchanan mentions, the regions of major concentration of population are "the key areas of early Chinese history". Four regions contain three-quarters of the population of China. First is the cradle area of the North China Plain, the lower alluvial plain of the Hwang Ho, about 150,000 square miles (25 per cent bigger than the British Isles) of level, yellow loessial soils supporting a thick cover of more than 100 million people. Four-fifths of these are dependent upon agriculture in this winter wheat–kaoliang (giant millet) area, and densities in many rural districts exceed 1000 per square mile of cultivated land.

The lowlands of the central Yangtse basin and the Yangtse delta constitute the second region of high population, and again contain over 100 million people, many of whom are rice and wheat growers. This great region is separated from the icy blasts of Inner Asia by the Tsinling-Tapan Shan, which acts as a sharp climatic barrier between the cold winters, hot summers, semi-aridity and dusty brown landscapes of North China and the milder winters, hot moist summers and abundant rainfall of sub-tropical South China, where rice and tea are prominent crops and the landscape is green in all seasons. As many textbook geographers have testified, the contrasts between North and South China go much further, but suffice it to note here that these environmental differences mean that the lowlands of South China generally have higher population densities than those of the north, with less likelihood of famines.

High up the Yangtse Kiang the mountain-bound Red Basin of Szechwan, with its equable climate, 11-month growing season and startling variety of agricultural production, is the third great concentration of population, and like the lowlands of the middle and lower Yangtse it was occupied from the North China cradle area. Despite the decimation of its population in a great uprising four centuries ago, the province of Szechwan has grown to be the most populous in China; in 1953 it contained 62.3 million people, more than any country in Africa or Europe except the USSR and more than all but seven other countries in the world. And its irrigated rice-growing Chengtu Plain, which is a gently sloping alluvial fan, is now one of the most densely peopled agricultural regions in the world.

The fourth major population concentration is the scattered coastal plains and deltas of South-east China (especially the Canton delta) where intensive rice and tea growing and other crops are associated with population densities in excess of 1000 per square mile and sometimes 2000 per square mile. Population pressure has long been high enough to stimulate emigration, particularly among the independent people of Fukien province, for whose remittances special investment facilities have been provided by the People's Government.

Of course, these are not the only densely peopled areas, but they have been stressed because they may be counted among the major concentrations of world population. But many other regions, especially peripheral or adjacent to these, support densities of 250–650 per square mile.

Internal Migratory Movements

Faced with such marked unevenness of population distribution and the vital need to increase food supply, the Chinese People's Republic embarked on a programme for the reclamation of new or virgin lands especially in the north and west, to which millions of people have migrated during the last two decades. This has produced only minor modifications in the population map, but they will probably augment.

Migration to the north-east, to Manchuria, is no new phenomenon. It has gone on for centuries, its empty spaces and black or brown soils being attractive to farmers and its forests offering enormous timber supplies. Chinese immigration gained momentum in the latter part of the nineteenth century and particularly during the first three decades of this century when many millions of colonists arrived, and Manchuria was not unlike the nineteenth-century American West. The population grew rapidly and in the 1930s manufacturing and mining workers were more numerous than rural immigrants, and coal, iron and oil shale became the bases of a large complex of heavy industries. By 1953 the population of the various provinces which make up Manchuria had reached 42 million, and since then migration has continued, notably to the northern regions of Heilungkiang province (Heilungkiang means "new lands") adjacent to the Soviet Union, where recent border clashes have inflamed Sino-Soviet relations, and have kept alive the notion that China has envious eyes for the vast open spaces of Siberia. Today the old Manchuria probably has about as many people as the United Kingdom.

Sinkiang and Tibet in the far west have also received many Chinese migrants, and the Production and Construction Corps has made strenuous efforts to develop the agricultural production of areas like the vast Tarim Basin of Sinkiang and the Tsaidam Basin of Chinghai province.

Internal migration has also occurred as a result of the communist government's policy of industrialization. Efforts have been made (a) to take the industries to the sources of raw material and fuel in order to reduce transport costs, (b) to disperse small-scale industries into rural areas in order to transform rural China, and (c) to establish many new industries, especially heavy industries, in the interior west and north-west in order to effect a better balance in the distribution of industry, which was far too localized in the coastal provinces. New industrial centres in the interior, like Paotow in Inner Mongolia and Lanchow in Kansu, have needed manpower, but the volume of migration associated with industrial dispersal has generally been smaller than the development of the virgin lands.

Although neither policy has provoked a major redistribution of the Chinese population, both are significant in the context of the population geography of developing countries, as they demonstrate a deliberate attempt to reduce the preeminence of the coastal provinces and their large cities, which were in the past partially dominated by foreign capital. The planners were unable to arrest the growth of these large cities, but they are effecting a more even utilization of resources and consequently there is every reason to expect some reduction in the over-concentration of population.

On the other hand, not all migration to cities has resulted from the "pull" of industrialization; perhaps more resulted from the "push" of enforced collectivization. Millions of peasants also entered the cities during the "great leap forward" of the late 1950s, but the problems of housing and employing these rural–urban migrants proved very severe and consequently many were forced to return to the land, especially when another food crisis reared its ugly head.

Urban Population

In 1953, only 13.2 per cent of the population of Mainland China were classified as urban, a relatively low percentage even for a developing country. This meant, however, that 77.3 million people were living in urban places, a figure which rose to about 120 million by 1960, and, according to the estimate of Kingsley Davis, to about 177 million by 1970, far more than the total populations of all but a few countries.

Typical Chinese towns are small market and administrative centres, which are containing an ever-growing proportion of the total population (Table 6.4). But China is also a land of large cities; by 1960 there were more than 120 with over 100,000 inhabitants including 17–18 millionaire cities (Table 6.5), and in all these large cities contained

TABLE 6.4. GROWTH OF URBAN POPULATION OF CHINA, 1950–70
(AFTER K. DAVIS)

Size of locality (Population in thousands)		1950	1960	1970
Under 100,000	Population	21,135	39,571	68,610
	% of total population	3.8	5.9	9.1
100,000–499,999	Population	14,190	17,040	22,790
	No. of localities	76	87	96
	% of total population	2.5	2.5	3.0
500,000–1,000,000	Population	9,915	14,101	8,800
	No. of localities	15	19	12
	% of total population	1.8	2.1	1.2
Over 1 million	Population	16,450	40,150	76,525
	No. of localities	8	18	31
	% of total population	2.9	6.0	10.2
Total urban population		61,690	110,862	176,725

SOURCE: K. Davis, *World Urbanization 1950–1970*, vol. 1: *Basis Data for Cities, Countries and Regions*, Berkeley, 1969.

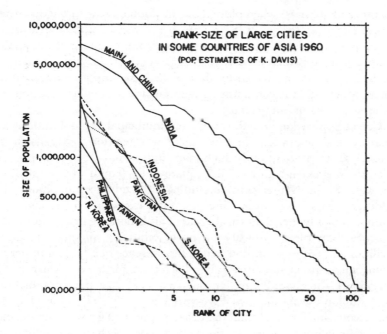

Fɪɢ. 6.4. Rank-size of large cities in some countries of Asia, 1960. The large countries of China and India have fairly smooth curves with no marked primacy, whereas primacy is very clear in the Philippines, Taiwan and North Korea.

more than one-tenth of the total population and two-thirds of the urban population. As numerous as those of the United States and more than twice as many as in India, China's millionaire cities are now a distinctive feature of the population map (Fig. 6.3). Sen-Dou Chang notes that their number has increased more rapidly than that of smaller cities—between 1953 and 1958 they increased from 9 to 15 whereas cities of 100,000–1 million inhabitants only increased from 91 to 99—but their populations have grown more slowly, an opposite trend to other parts of the developing world. Yet most Chinese millionaire cities are provincial and cultural capitals, important industrial centres and bases for national construction.

An interesting feature of city size in China is its linearity (except for minor irregularities) when plotted on the double logarithmic diagram, in a similar way to that of India (Fig. 6.4). Partly because of the little difference in size of Shanghai and Peking, the two largest cities, the index of urban primacy is low and declining, whether the population of the largest city is divided by that of the next largest or by the next three. Moreover, the communist government is particularly anxious to avoid excessive urban primacy.

Urban population growth arises from municipal expansion, natural increase and migration. In 1958 there was territorial expansion of municipal territories, and Buchanan states that the authority of Tientsin was extended over 7680 square miles (equal to two-thirds of the area of the Netherlands) including 11.4 million inhabitants. In addition, cities have natural increase rates exceeding 3 per cent per annum, much higher than rural areas. This is because urban mortality is lower than rural mortality owing to relatively adequate medical facilities and better sanitation, while the presence of a large number of young migrants in the cities raises the urban birth rate. During the period 1949–56 about 20 million people moved into the cities, including 8 million during the First Five-year Plan (1953–57), a huge migration accounting for nearly half the urban population growth; but during the 1960s many returned to the countryside, perhaps an indication that urbanization has recently slowed down. Legislation to arrest "blind infiltration" of "non-productive" peasants into cities may be effective in this respect.

Many widely scattered cities have experienced rapid growth in recent decades: Peking, Lu-ta, Sian, Taiyuan, Lanchow and Tzepo are examples (see Table 6.5). In particular, the government has encouraged urbanization in the less urbanized interior (e.g. in Kweichow, Kwangsi and Kansu provinces) rather than in the industrialized and more urbanized north-east. But rapid population growth of cities has not been accompanied by a commensurate increase in housing. The population of Sian, for instance, multiplied three times between 1950 and 1965, but the total floor space of dwelling units only doubled. Old walled sections of cities have undergone repairs instead of renewal, and new extensions have cost heavily in the loss of fertile land. No city of Mainland China, however, faces quite as many difficulties of growth as are apparent in Hong Kong. Moreover, Chinese cities exhibit less

TABLE 6.5. POPULATIONS OF MAJOR CITIES OF CHINA, 1950-70 (AFTER K. DAVIS)

	Population (in thousands)			Percentage Annual growth	
	1950	1960	1970	1950-60	1960-70
Shanghai	5300	7200	8500	3.1	1.7
Peking	2150	5500	8000	9.8	3.8
Tientsin	2200	3500	4500	4.8	2.5
Shenyang (Mukden)	1700	2500	3750	3.9	4.1
Wuhan	1200	2500	4250	7.6	5.4
Chungking	1400	2300	3500	5.1	4.3
Lu-ta	700	2000	4000	11.1	7.2
Canton	1500	1900	2300	2.4	1.9
Harbin	1000	1800	2750	6.1	4.3
Nanking	950	1500	2000	4.7	2.9
Sian	600	1500	1900	9.6	2.4
Taiyuan	600	1400	2725	8.8	6.9
Chengtu	750	1200	2000	4.8	5.2
Tsingtao	850	1200	1900	3.5	4.7
Tzepo	250	1100	1750	16.0	4.8
Changchun	750	1050	1500	3.4	3.6
Fushun	650	1000	1700	4.4	5.4
Kunming	625	1000	1700	4.8	5.4
Lanchow	300	950	1500	12.2	4.7
Tsitsihan	300	950	1500	12.2	4.7
Tsinan	650	920	1500	3.5	5.0
Anshan	475	900	1500	6.6	5.2
Suchow	375	900	1500	9.1	5.2
Chengchow	500	850	1500	5.4	5.8
Tangshan	500	850	1200	5.4	3.5
Hangchow	640	837	1100	2.7	2.8
Shihkiachwang	275	750	1500	10.6	7.2
Soochow	400	740	1300	6.3	5.8
Kweiyang	260	700	1500	10.4	7.9
Kirin	350	650	1200	6.4	6.3
Changchiakou	250	500	1000	7.2	7.2

SOURCE: K. Davis, *World Urbanization 1950-1970*, vol. 1: *Basic Data for Cities, Countries and Regions*, 1969, pp. 183-5.

marked social contrasts than Indian, African and Latin American cities; the gap between millionaires and misery is absent, and the juxtaposition of old and new in Chinese cities is less indicative of poverty and wealth than in many other developing countries. Nevertheless, the great surge of urban growth in China is a reflection of the high and rising level of population pressure in the country.

Population Growth

Analysis of population pressure is, of course, partly dependent upon considerations of population growth, but, as already intimated, these are largely in the realm of speculation, because little is known precisely about vital rates. There is little doubt that vital registration takes place, as demanded by a Vital Registration Law passed in January 1952, but the only general birth and death rates published are for 1952–57 (Table 6.6). Before publication of these rates it was generally assumed

TABLE 6.6. VITAL RATES IN COMMUNIST CHINA, 1952–70

	Birth rate	Death rate	Natural increase rate
1952	37	18	19
1953	37	17	20
1954	38	15	23
1955	35	12.4	22.6
1956	32	11.4	20.6
1957	34	11	23
1965–70	33.1	15.3	17.8

SOURCE: S. Chandrasekhar, *China's and Population: Census Vital Statistics,* 1961, p. 3, and U.N., *Demographic Yearbook,* 1970.

that the crude birth rate of China was above 40 per thousand, and therefore some were doubtful of their veracity. However, experts now judge that a general birth rate of the order of 30–35 per thousand seems to be a reasonable assumption, given that China is enjoying relatively peaceful internal conditions, that there has been substantial improvement in sanitation and health services, that the food situation has oscillated from poor to moderate and that family planning has not yet become a major factor. Pan also points out that birth rates vary between the regions of China, and that a negative relationship holds between crop-yield density and the birth rate; the highest birth rates are in Manchuria, Szechwan and Honan and the lowest in Shantung, Shensi and Shansi.

It may also be mentioned that Chinese communities overseas are experiencing declining fertility: Taiwan, Hong Kong and Singapore are notable examples, where family planning is playing an important role. In addition, however, there is the significant influence of youthful age structures upon fertility declines.

There is perhaps more unanimity over the published death rates of China. Whilst it is generally felt that medical and sanitation improvements, control of food allocation and civil order have resulted in a fairly dramatic decline in mortality, published crude death rates of 18 per thousand in 1952 and 11 per thousand in 1957 seem unreasonably low and probably reflect under-reporting of deaths; estimated death rates in pre-communist China were 25–35 per thousand. Nevertheless, there can be little doubt that mortality has dropped substantially, especially in large cities like Shanghai (where it was said to have fallen from 19.4 per thousand in 1953 to 6.7 per thousand in 1959), and it may well be that 11 per thousand is a reasonable assumption for China's death rate now, if not in 1957. Obviously the youthfulness of the population

TABLE 6.7. AGE AND SEX STRUCTURES OF SELECTED ASIAN COUNTRIES

	Year	Percentage age composition			Males per 1000 females
		under 15	15–59	60+	
Burma	1960	41.3	53.5	5.2	1040
Cambodia	1962	43.8	51.3	4.8	999
Sri Lanka	1963	41.5	52.0	5.9	1082
China (Mainland)	1953	35.9	59.7	4.4	1076
China (Taiwan)	1966	43.3	52.3	4.4	1113
India	1961	41.1	54.1	4.8	1063
Indonesia	1961	42.1	53.8	4.1	973
Iran	1966	46.0	47.5	6.5	1036
Japan	1965	25.7	64.6	9.7	964
Korea (Republic)	1966	43.5	51.3	5.2	1014
Malaya	1957	43.8	51.6	4.6	1065
Sabah	1960	43.5	52.6	3.9	1086
Sarawak	1960	44.5	50.3	5.2	1019
Pakistan	1961	44.5	49.5	6.0	1111
Philippines	1960	45.7	50.0	4.3	1018
Thailand	1960	43.2	52.2	4.6	1004

SOURCE: U.N., *Demographic Yearbook*, 1970.

has assisted this decline, although it would appear that China has a lower proportion of young people than most developing countries of Asia (Table 6.7); in 1953 the population under 15 amounted to 35.9 per cent of the total, but the percentage will be higher now.

One aspect of improved mortality conditions in China is revealed in the age pattern of sex-ratios. In 1953 there were 1076 males per thousand females—in Table 6.7 it will be seen that preponderance of males is a common feature of Asian countries (except Japan, Indonesia and Cambodia)—and this was probably a reflection of a variety of factors including under-counting of females, the desire for male children, occasional female infanticide, inadequate care of female children, high mortality of females and in particular high maternal mortality. All these reasons are closely connected with the problem of the traditionally low status of women, common in most of Asia. However, the changed status of women in communist China (associated with the abolition of concubinage and arranged marriages, the raising of the age of consent to 18 for females, and the facilitation of divorce and remarriage of widows) has had the effect of reducing the disadvantage of female babies and therefore reducing the preponderance of males in the early age groups (Table 6.8). Unfortunately the complete data on age and sex structure for the 1953 census have never been published, so it is difficult to be sure.

TABLE 6.8. CHINA: SEX-RATIOS BY AGE GROUPS, 1953

Age Group	Males per 100 females
Under 1	104.9
1–2	106.2
3–6	110.0
7–13	115.8
14–17	113.7
18–35	111.5
36–55	106.8
56 and over	86.7

SOURCE: S. Chandrasekhar, *China's Population: Census and Vital Statistics*, 1961, p. 43.

If a birth rate of 33–35 per thousand and a death rate of 11–12 per thousand are assumed, then the natural increase is about 2.2–2.4 per cent. This means about 15–17 million extra people each year, possibly a quarter of the annual increase of mankind and much more than the combined populations of Australia and New Zealand. Such an increase may mean that China will have more than 900 million by 1975 and more than 1000 million by 1980, but nobody can be certain. J. S. Aird has concluded that "if all the possibilities . . . are incorporated into alternate estimates and projections, the totals at the upper and lower limits describe an extremely wide range. Estimates for recent years may differ by as much as 100 to 150 million. Estimates which go back to 1750 may have a range of over 250 million with smaller magnitudes. Projections for 1985 have a spread of more than half a billion with no guarantee that all the possibilities have been covered."

Population Policy

Whatever the estimates, China faces enormous problems resulting from population growth, as, for example, in the development of education, without which one cannot easily foresee any great transformation from the "self-perpetuating mechanisms of traditional societies" (Taeuber): large families encouraging the preservation of illiteracy and traditional customs. Before the communists came to power four-fifths of the Chinese population were illiterate, and this was seen, along with the lack of education and technical skills, as the prime cause of over-population in the old China, preventing diversification of the economy and condemning its peasants to poverty. Consequently, the communist regime undertook a crash programme to eliminate illiteracy, to expand the school system and to train skilled and semi-skilled workers. Some idea of the problem may be envisaged from the fact that in 1953 there were about 118 million children aged 5–14, and that this number has grown quickly. China faced this daunting challenge and in less than a decade enrolment in primary schools increased by 60 million. But the increasing proportion of young people, resulting from lowering mortality, means that China has something like 100 million more children than it would have if it had an age structure akin to those of developed countries, although it has a smaller proportion in the working age groups, and the return from the cost of education has been less owing to shorter working lives.

Problems of this nature have undoubtedly influenced Chinese thinking about population policy, although this has vacillated over the years, partly as a result of the contrast between the theoretical position of communists ("population is the most precious of all the categories of capital") and the reality of massive population growth. In 1954, soon after the publication of the 1953 census figures and the initial reaction of jubilation, a birth-control policy came into effect, the communist leaders recommending later marriage than the lower legal age (21 for males and 18 for females) and also the use of contraception in order to prevent large families and to enable the spacing of births at longer intervals. In this birth-control campaign the Chinese leaders insisted that the population was not too large, but was growing too quickly to permit marked improvement in levels of living. In addition, it was suggested that the campaign was designed to improve the health of mothers and children, to allow greater use of female labour and to provide better educational facilities for youths and children. In support of this policy Marx was evoked and Malthus roundly denounced.

In 1958, about the time of the "Great Leap Forward", the birth-control policy was abandoned. Observers have given a variety of reasons for this: the difficulty of justifying birth-control with Marxism, the failure of the campaign and the excellence of the 1957 harvests. It was stated that there was a manpower shortage and women were accordingly "liberated" from their domestic tasks to work in factories and in fields. At this time the Chinese communists saw no problem at all in increasing food production. With reforming zeal, military-like communes were established, partly designed to break up the traditional family system; the segregation of male and female production brigades might also have been seen as a means of delaying marriages.

Unfortunately, there followed a series of disastrous agricultural years, so in 1962 a second birth-control campaign was launched, proclaiming the need to cut down the size of the Chinese family, and emphasizing the desirability of later marriages. People with large families have been called unpatriotic, the two-child family being considered the optimum, with a gap of 3–5 years between the children. It is suggested that voluntary sterilization should be practised by males after 2 or 3 children are born, and there is also greater interest in induced abortion and IUDs, which are apparently acceptable to the Chinese. But the main cry is for later marriages, a form of family planning which is probably unique to China, but which is highly effective as it reduces the size of families and lengthens the time between generations. Letters have been published in newspapers under such headings as "I resolutely persist in late marriage", and a Peking daily has warned that "some young people have not understood fully the harm of falling in love and getting married early". Furthermore, the authorities have reduced the incentive to raise large families by refusing additional rations or maternity benefits for the fourth child and subsequent children.

The early policies of the new China had little impact upon birth rates, because the means of implementation were minimal. These means are now more readily available, but the real difficulty is in extending the aims of the authorities to the rural masses, whose agricultural practices, such as rice cultivation, have involved considerable manual labour and necessitated large families. Acceptance of birth control must therefore be linked with programmes of mechanization, which are not easy to implement quickly. China is better organized than India to do this, and she will probably, like the USSR, find ways of reconciling birth control with Marxism. The youth of the villages have values very different from those of their elders, and whilst one must expect some continuity of the values and customs of the old China in the first new generation, there is ample evidence of the receptivity to change. Moreover, there is also evidence that fertility is declining fairly decisively in other countries of East and South-east Asia where Chinese populations predominate, partly as a consequence of organized family planning programmes; between 1955 and 1970 Taiwan's birth rate fell from 45.3 per thousand to 28.1, Hong Kong's from 36.3 to 18.9 and Singapore's from 44.3 to 23.3. However, apart from being small, these are countries where mortality is relatively low and age structures are very youthful, where there is considerable economic development and social change as well as effective organization to provide family planning information and services, and a general desire for small families.

Many experienced demographic observers believe that the time is ripe for China to effect a dramatic reduction in its population fertility. Political control, social change and economic motivation are all strong, and it is possible that China will show the way to many other developing countries. Much will depend upon the lead given by its politicians.

External Migration

It is extremely unlikely that emigration could relieve China's population pressure, either nationally or provincially, even if her frontiers were opened to the free emigration of her people. In fact, since the communists took over power in 1949 and the first flood of millions of refugees found their way to Hong Kong, Taiwan and countries of South-east Asia, Mainland China has become an almost entirely closed population.

Emigration from China dates back at least to the twelfth century, but it was intermittent partly because in some dynastic periods it was prohibited. During the nineteenth century the emigration of Chinese traders and labourers gained momentum, especially after 1860 when the Manchu government withdrew the ban on emigration. They went mainly to South-east Asia, Australia and the Americas, although during the early part of this century they spread to most countries of the world. Ta Chen estimated that there were about 8,179,000 Chinese living abroad in 1922, but the imposition of immigration laws and quotas, especially in North America, Australasia and Europe, greatly restricted the movement of Chinese, and large numbers returned home prior to the Second World War. These laws and quotas are evidence of the cultural and racial prejudice and national fears of minority problems which largely confine Asians to their own continent. Asians have been denied many outlets for emigration, and, unlike so many European refugees after the Second World War, few have found succour outside of Asia. Chinese emigration increased rapidly after the war, but it was mostly to Hong Kong, Taiwan and Singapore, which were sometimes used as stepping-stones to Britain or the United States.

In the mid-1960s there were probably nearly 30 million Chinese living outside of Mainland China (Table 6.9), but the numbers cannot be stated precisely. The largest number by far are living in Taiwan where they constitute about 98 per cent of the island's 13.8 million

TABLE 6.9. DISTRIBUTION OF CHINESE OUTSIDE OF MAINLAND CHINA, 1963
(INCLUDING ONLY COUNTRIES WITH MORE THAN 100,000 CHINESE)

ASIA	27,606,000		
Taiwan	11,746,000	Vietnam	1,035,000
Thailand	3,799,000	Burma	420,000
Hong Kong	3,197,000	Cambodia	260,000
Indonesia	2,545,000	Sarawak	229,000
Malaya	2,461,000	Macau	161,000
Singapore	1,303,000	Philippines	152,000
		Borneo	105,000
ANGLO-AMERICA	295,000		
USA	237,000		
LATIN AMERICA	149,000		
OCEANIA	53,000		
AFRICA	44,000		
EUROPE	21,000		

SOURCE: Chang, S-D., The distribution and occupations of overseas Chinese, *Geog. Rev.* **58,** 99 (1968).

inhabitants (1969). The remarkable population growth of the island, which increased more than four times between 1904 (the first census) and 1964, results partly from successful economic development and partly from Chinese immigration; about 2 million arrived from the Chinese mainland following the defeat of the Kuomintang, and many of their older members still dream of returning.

The other country where Chinese form an almost homogeneous ethnic element is the British Crown Colony of Hong Kong, in which millions of Chinese took refuge before and after the Second World War. It is astonishing that Hong Kong now has about 4 million inhabitants, whereas in 1842 Hong Kong Island contained only 12,000 people and in 1945 there were only 400–600,000 people in the colony after a disastrous war during which many fled from Japanese occupation to China. The postwar injection of capital and entrepreneurial skill by Chinese immigrants, particularly from the great trading city of Shanghai, has contributed substantially to Hong Kong's economic miracle.

Although overseas Chinese now have a widespread distribution, according to Sen-Dou Chang about 96 per cent (excluding those in Taiwan) live in South-east Asia (including Hong Kong and Macau)

and 97 per cent within the tropics; the United States is the only mid-
latitude country with more than 100,000 Chinese. The great majority
of overseas Chinese are more numerous on islands or along coasts than
in the interior, and in towns (particularly ports) rather than rural
areas, despite their rural origins particularly in the Si Kiang delta,
eastern Kwantung, Fukien and the hinterland of Amoy. Their main
occupations are as retail traders and restaurant owners and workers,
though in some countries they work in agriculture, manufacturing or
mining.

Problem of Population Pressure

With her frontiers sealed, there is little question of large-scale
emigration acting as a relief to China's population pressure. The cost
and problems of organization of any substantial overseas migration
would be colossal. There is also the political difficulty. W. S. Thompson,
who sees population pressure as a major cause of a feeling of privation
and of a need for political expansion, has stressed the danger of population politics: "no country in South and East Asia can start large-scale
emigration without acquiring actual political control of the area to be
colonized, and such control can be achieved only by conquest." He and
other American demographers are in no doubt that numerical strength
will influence Chinese attitudes to other Asian powers, including the
USSR, especially as her industrialization proceeds, her manpower is
increasingly trained, and her zeal for communism is still strong.
Thompson is not alone in being afraid that if China is frustrated in her
desire to achieve higher standards of living she may eventually resort
to force to gain access to additional resources. Soviet Asia, with only
59 million people on 6.5 million square miles, is an obvious attraction.
Migration to this vast area from European Russia was only on a modest
scale until recent years, when it has gained priority, and consequently
there is a sharp-edge density between the expanding masses of China
and the scattered populations of Soviet Asia. Irene Taeuber believes
that "the greatest of the many danger spots in the world population of
the coming century is the long, fortified and already vacated frontier
zone that separates the Asian peoples of the southern portion of the
continent of Asia from the European peoples of the northern portion of

that continent. The wall against migrants from a developing Asia is already erected by the Soviet Union; the critical confrontation is already fact." She also wonders whether the expansion, militarism and migrations which characterized Europe midway in her modernization may become true for Asia. Fears certainly exist, and are constantly kept alive by the political isolation of China and frontier incidents with India and the Soviet Union.

In contrast with these pessimistic views, there are many, like Buchanan, who are confident of China's ability to accommodate her growing masses, and point to the reappraisal of her resources which has revealed the immense supplies of raw materials and has opened the door to economic diversification. They feel that the policy of agricultural intensification through increased use of fertilizers, machinery, irrigation and labour will permit a much larger population, and some stress the fact that China, with about 82 persons per square km., is less densely peopled than many European countries, and that China's population per square unit of cultivated land is less than half of that of Britain. On the other hand, Britain is, of course, much more urbanized and industrialized, and China's capacity to carry one thousand million people will greatly depend upon the rapidity of economic change within this vast country.

Select Bibliography

AIRD, J. S., *The Size, Composition and Growth of the Population of Mainland China*, U.S. Bureau of the Census, International Population Statistics Reports, Series P-90, No. 15, Washington 1961.

AIRD, J. S., Estimating China's population, *Ann. Am. Acad. Polit. Soc. Sci.* **369**, 61 (1967).

BARCLAY, G. W., *Colonial Development and Population in Taiwan*, Princeton, 1954.

BERELSON, B. *et al.* (Eds.), *Family Planning and Population Programs*, Chicago, 1966.

BUCHANAN, K., *The Chinese People and the Chinese Earth*, London, 1966.

CHANDRASEKHAR, S., *China's Population: Census and Vital Statistics*, London, 1961.

CHANDRASEKHAR, S. (Ed.), *Asia's Population Problems*, London, 1967.

CHANG, S-D., The distribution and occupations of Overseas Chinese, *Geog. Rev.* **58**, 89 (1968).

CHANG, S-D., The million city of mainland China, *Pacific Viewpoint* **9**, 128 (1968).

CHEN, C., *Taiwan: An Economic and Social Geography*, Taipei, 1963.

CHEN, T., *Population in Modern China*, Chicago, 1946.

CLARK, C., L'accroissement de la population de la Chine, *Population* **19**, 559 (1964).

CLARK, C., La population de la Chine depuis 1915, *Population* **21**, 1191, 1289 and 1292 (1966).

CRESSEY, G. B., *Land of the 600 Millions—A Geography of China*, New York, 1956.
DURAND, J. D., The population statistics of China, A.D. 2–1953, *Pop. Studies* **13**, 209 (1960).
DWYER, D. J., Problems of urbanization: the example of Hong Kong, *IBG Special Publication* No. 1, Sir Dudley Stamp Memorial Volume, 169 (1969).
FREEDMAN, R. and ADLAKHA, A. L., Recent fertility declines in Hong Kong: the role of the changing age structure, *Pop. Studies* **22**, 181 (1968).
FREEDMAN, R. and PENG, J. W., Fertility trends in Taiwan: tradition and change, *Pop. Studies* **16**, 219 (1963).
FREEDMAN, R., TAKESHITA, J. Y. and SUN, T. H., Fertility and family planning in Taiwan: A case study of the demographic transition, *Am. J. Sociol.* **70**, 16 (1964).
HAUSER, P. M. (Ed.), *Urbanization in Asia and the Far East*, UNESCO, 1957.
Ho, P., *Studies on the Population of China, 1368–1953*, Cambridge, Mass., 1959.
HSIEH, C., *Taiwan—ilha Formosa: A Geography in Perspective*, London, 1964.
Lo, C. P., Changing population distribution in the Hong Kong New Territories, *Ann. Assoc. Am. Geog.* **58**, 273 (1968).
MALLORY, W. H., *China: Land of Famine*, New York, 1926.
MILBANK MEMORIAL FUND, *Population Trends in Eastern Europe, the USSR and Mainland China*, New York, 1960.
ORLEANS, L. A., The recent growth of China's urban population, *Geog. Rev.* **49**, 43 (1959).
ORLEANS, L. A., *Every Fifth Child: The Population of China*, London, 1972.
PAN, C-L., An estimate of the long-term crude birth rate of the agricultural population of China, *Demography* **3**, 204 (1966).
PRESSAT, R., La population de la Chine et son économie, *Population* **13**, 569 (1958).
SHABAD, T., *China's Changing Map*, London, 1956.
SHABAD, T., The population of China's cities, *Geog. Rev.* **49**, 32 (1959).
THOMPSON, W. S., *Population and Progress in the Far East*, Chicago, 1959.
TREGEAR, T. R., *A Geography of China*, London, 1965.
TREWARTHA, G. T., Chinese cities: number and distribution, *Ann. Assoc. Am. Geog.* **41**, 331 (1951).
TREWARTHA, G. T., Chinese cities: origins and functions, *Ann. Assoc. Am. Geog.* **42**, 69 (1952).
TREWARTHA, G. T., New maps of China's population, *Geog. Rev.* **47**, 234 (1957).
TREWARTHA, G. T. and ZELINSKY, W., Population distribution and change in Korea, 1925–1949, *Geog. Rev.* **45**, 1 (1955).
ULLMAN, M. B., *Cities of Mainland China: 1953 and 1958*, US Bureau of Census, International Population Statistics Reports, Series P-95, No. 59, Washington 1960.
UNITED NATIONS, BUREAU OF ECONOMIC AND SOCIAL AFFAIRS, *Future Population Estimates by Sex and Age, Report IV, The Population of Asia and the Far East, 1950–1980*, New York, 1959.
UNITED NATIONS, ECONOMIC COMMISSION FOR ASIA AND THE FAR EAST, *The Demographic Situation and Prospective Population Trends in Asia and the Far East*, Asian Population Conference, New Delhi, 1963.
VAUGHAN, T. D. and DWYER, D. J., Some aspects of postwar population growth in Hong Kong, *Econ. Geog.* **42**, 37 (1966).
WYNNE, W., *The Population of Manchuria*, US Bureau of Census, International Population Statistics Reports, Series P-90, No. 7, Washington 1958.

7

SOUTH-EAST ASIA

Unity and Diversity

It is appropriate that this last major region of study should illustrate clearly the underlying theme of this volume: the marked areal disparities which have evolved in the patterns of population in developing countries.

Lying almost entirely within the humid tropics, South-east Asia exhibits much climatic uniformity, but its 1.5 million square miles of land area—half in mainland South-east Asia and half in insular South-east Asia, but in all less than half the area of Brazil—is very much less compact than any of the major regions so far considered. With a complex pattern of peninsulas and islands separated but connected by seas and straits, South-east Asia extends over a surface area many times that of its land area, and this physical fragmentation is intensified by the multiplicity of mountain ranges isolating river basins and coastal plains, the main areas of settlement. This has helped to produce an extremely patchy population distribution, peoples and cultures evolving in scattered pockets which have sometimes been distinct political units.

As C. A. Fisher puts it, "South-east Asia is a region which the land divides but the sea unites", and this interpenetration of land and sea has increased the accessibility of the region to outsiders, as in the Caribbean. As a result, the impact of external forces upon the economies and societies has been most profound. Located between the two great culture realms of India and China, South-east Asia's own cultures have been deeply but diversely influenced by both, and have sometimes been replaced by them. Moreover, Western colonial conquest, rule and trade were all facilitated by the accessibility of the region. The colonial divisions made by the Spaniards, Dutch, British, French and Americans bore little relation to the ethnic pattern, and although Europeans never settled in large numbers, their political and economic structures caused sharp contrasts between local modernized areas and much larger areas with more traditional modes of life. Today, many South-east Asians allocate Europe or the West much of the blame for the present backwardness; it is felt that the present condition of the region largely results from the development of the advanced countries of the West at the expense of the countries of South-east Asia. Chesneaux suggests that "pre-developed" is a more suitable adjective for much of South-east Asia than "underdeveloped", as a large part of the region knew a high degree of development prior to European contact; many authors have emphasized the contemporaneity of Angkor and the Khmer civilization with the European Dark Ages.

TABLE 7.1. THE POPULATIONS OF SOUTH-EAST ASIA

	Area (thousand km²)	Population (Millions)		Density (per km²)
		last census	estimated 1970	
Brunei	6	0.1 ('71)	0.1	21
Burma	678	16.8 ('41)	27.6	41
Cambodia	181	5.7 ('62)	—	—
Indonesia	1,492	118.3 ('71)	121.2	81
Laos	237	—	3.0	13
Federation of				
Malaysia	332	10.4 ('70)	10.8	39
Malaya	131	8.8 ('70)	9.1	70
Sabah	76	0.7 ('70)	0.7	9
Sarawak	125	1.0 ('70)	1.0	8
Philippines	300	36.7 ('70)	38.5	128
Singapore	0.6	2.0 ('70)	2.0	3528
Thailand	514	34.1 ('70)	35.8	66
Timor (Port.)	15	0.5 ('60)	0.6	38
North Vietnam	159	15.9 ('60)	21.1	133
South Vietnam	174	—	18.3	105

SOURCE: *UN Demographic Yearbook*, 1970.

The recent achievement of independence in South-east Asia has added to the complexity by the creation of new national entities, so that the 287 million people (1970) living in the region—about as many as in Latin America on a much smaller area, but only half the population of India—are divided among ten independent countries and two colonial enclaves (Brunei and Portuguese Timor). Inevitably, the scatter of population sizes is great (Table 7.1), from 100,000 in Brunei to over 121 million in Indonesia, and in addition the various states differ substantially in political systems and alignments, economic development and social advance.

Evolution of Population

Like many other regions of the developing world, South-east Asia suffers from a lack of accurate data. Although censuses were held in Java in 1815 (under the direction of Stamford Raffles), in the Philippines in 1881, in Burma in 1901, in the Dutch East Indies in 1905 and in Thailand and Malaya in 1911, no censuses have yet been held in Laos or South Vietnam, and none since 1941 in Burma. Moreover, most census data have not a high level of reliability, and the only areas with reasonably complete vital statistics are Malaya and Singapore.

With only fragmentary data, it is not easy to decipher the evolution of population in recent times. No clear picture is available of population numbers in South-east Asia prior to the nineteenth century, but it seems that historic vicissitudes probably caused substantial fluctuations in numbers, the climax of kingdoms being associated with population peaks followed by marked declines. In some cases these peaks have been recovered only recently. Even if such fluctuations are taken into account, there is little doubt that South-east Asia has always been relatively sparsely peopled. Certainly, the fragmentation of physical environments must be held partially responsible, but so also must the delay in the transition from shifting to sedentary cultivation. In other words, a blend of physical and human factors account for the low population total in South-east Asia at the beginning of the nineteenth century (Table 7.2).

Myrdal's figures of population growth in South-east Asia since 1800 are admittedly in some cases only free guesses or vague estimates, but

TABLE 7.2. POPULATION GROWTH IN SOUTH-EAST ASIA, 1800–1960

	Estimated population (in millions)					Annual growth (%)			
	1800	1850	1900	1950	1960	1800–50	1850–1900	1900–50	1950–60
Burma	(4.5)	(6.0)	(10.5)	18.8	21.5	0.6	1.1	1.2	1.4
Thailand	(6.0)	6.0	8.0	18.5	26.3	0.0	0.6	1.8	3.1
Former French Indo-China	(7.0)	8.0	16.0	29.8	36.0	0.3	1.4	1.3	1.9
Malaya and Singapore	(0.3)	(0.5)	2.1	6.2	8.5	1.0	2.9	2.2	3.2
Java and Madura	4.0	10.0	28.9	50.4	93.5	1.8	2.1	1.1	2.0
Rest of Indonesia	4.5	6.0	10.0	26.1		0.6	1.0	1.9	
Philippines	(1.7)	3.5	7.2	19.9	27.8	1.4	1.4	2.1	3.1
South-east Asia	28.0	40.0	82.7	169.7	213.6	0.7	1.5	1.4	2.1

SOURCE: G. Myrdal, *Asian Drama*, 1968, pp. 435 and 1396.

they may not be far removed from reality; they also give some credibility to John Crawford's estimate in or about 1830 of a total of 25,824,000 people. If this order of population size is accepted for the early nineteenth century, it appears to have multiplied about ten times since then. In places where European domination was established early, like Java and the Philippines, population growth has been even more rapid. By 1975 Java's population will probably be twenty times that of 1800. The main reason for early population growth in these countries was the decline in mortality caused by a reduction in internecine wars and the introduction of basic sanitation and hygiene, along with the stimulus of new economies and new agricultural techniques. These developments later affected Malaya, Singapore and Indo-China but extended only gradually to other parts of South-east Asia.

Consequently, it is likely that there were no more than 40 million people in the whole region in 1850 and about 80 million in 1900—tiny totals in comparison with those in Mainland China (about 430 and 436 million in 1850 and 1900) and India–Pakistan (about 233 and 285 million respectively), where overall population densities were also much higher. So South-east Asia entered this century with only a modest population total, but through rapid population growth it is making up some of the discrepancy with the adjacent regions. Population growth has indeed been more rapid than other parts of Asia, and South-east

TABLE 7.3. GROWTH OF ASIA'S POPULATION, 1930–70
(IN MILLIONS)

	1930	1940	1950	1960	1970
South-east Asia	127	150	173	219	287
Middle South Asia	371	422	479	587	762
South-west Asia	31	38	45	59	77
China, Mongolia, Hong Kong	501	533	503	654	791
Japan	64	71	83	93	103
Other East Asia	26	30	38	47	61
ASIA (excluding the USSR)	1120	1244	1381	1659	2081

SOURCE: *UN Demographic Yearbook*, 1970.

Asia's proportion of the continental population rose from 11.3 per cent in 1930 to 13.8 per cent in 1970 (Table 7.3). Already its population has multiplied more than three times this century, largely as a result of further declines in mortality and immigration from China and India, and the populations of Thailand, the Philippines, Malaya and Singapore have quadrupled.

Despite rapid population growth, South-east Asia is still much less populous than East or South Asia; its average population density—admittedly not a very meaningful measure in a region with such uneven population distribution—is only half that of South Asia. In the past immigrants have been attracted from these adjacent regions, but now politicians have closed the gates. In any case the region could never receive sufficient immigrants to relieve population pressure in these neighbouring regions, even if this were politically possible or desirable. Furthermore, all the countries of South-east Asia are now experiencing fast population growth and some are suffering from population pressure of their own.

Apart from overall population growth, the nineteenth and twentieth centuries have also witnessed a movement of peoples into lowlands, deltas and coastal fringes, provoking great unevenness in population distribution, which has been further augmented in recent decades by the process of urbanization. Both phenomena will be examined later.

Diversity of Indigenous Peoples

Although South-east Asia has never been densely peopled, like tropical Africa it contains great diversity of peoples. No simple explanation is possible, although any explanations must be sought in the past. In particular, much of the racial complexity arises from the pressure of Han peoples from the north attracted by the relative emptiness of the region and causing southward tribal movements of pre-Chinese peoples. In a series of migrations from the second milennium BC Alpine-Mongoloids pressed down the river valleys of the mainland from the Tibet–Yunnan area, undergoing modifications as they moved so that today purer Mongoloids are found in the northern and coastal areas. These more Mongoloid peoples, termed Pareœans (or southern Mongoloids), may be distinguished from the olive or dark-skinned

Nesiots (or Indonesians) who comprise some Caucasoid-Mediterranean elements, but together they constitute the basal population of much of South-east Asia. Many of the later Mongoloid arrivals from the north could find no alternative than to occupy the inferior hill lands of the mainland, their descendants being peoples like the Karen, Naga and Kachin of Burma and the Man and Miao of Laos, some of which are regarded as problem minorities.

Early Negrito and Veddid elements are now tiny and much diluted minorities, although the small, dark, woolly-haired Negritos have contributed to the make-up of many peoples within the region. Their mixing with dark, wavy-haired Australoid peoples probably resulted in the Melanesoid peoples found in the eastern islands of Indonesia and in New Guinea. Negrito characteristics are best seen today among the primitive food-gathering Semang of Malaya, the Aeta of the Philippines and the Orang Akit of Sumatra, while Veddid characteristics are visible among the Senoi food gatherers of Malaya.

The distribution of the major ethnic groups in South-east Asia in no way accounts for the patterns of culture groups; although many of the peoples are predominantly Pareœan in physique there are great differences between the cultures, for example, of the Malays and the Khmers of Cambodia. In particular, South-east Asia contains very striking linguistic and religious diversity, more comparable with India than with China.

The complicated pattern of languages (Fig. 7.1) reflects their long evolution. Two thousand years ago peoples of the mainland spoke Mon-Khmer languages of the Austro-Asiatic group, while in the Malay peninsula and the islands Malayo-Polynesian languages of the Austronesian group were spoken. This relatively simple pattern was subsequently destroyed by the arrival of the immigrant northerners bringing Sino-Tibetan languages, especially Tibeto-Burmese, Thai and Vietnamese languages. These now prevail in all the major lowlands of the mainland, except Cambodia where Khmer persists. Austro-Asiatic languages survive elsewhere among peoples of the forested uplands, such as the Annamite chain. In contrast, the Malayo-Polynesian languages have maintained themselves in the Malaysian world, but not without much differentiation, especially between the Indonesian and Oceanic or Melanesian languages, so that despite ease of linguistic diffusion

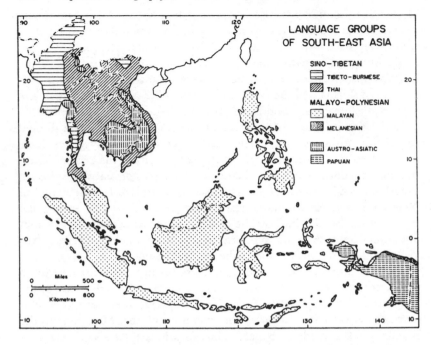

Fig. 7.1. Language groups of South-east Asia. The simplicity of the distributional pattern of language groups masks great complexity of distribution of languages.

among the islands Indonesian Malay includes some 25 languages and about 250 dialects.

Indian influence has been exerted linguistically through the introduction of many words as well as many forms of writing. Indian scripts have remained in use in the Cambodian, Burmese, Thai, Shan and Laotian languages and in some regional Indonesian languages, although in others the Arabic script is now employed. European influence is seen in the fact that the national languages of Indonesia, Malaya, Vietnam and the Philippines now use the Roman alphabet.

Evidence of Indianization in South-east Asia is also seen in the introduction, probably mainly by merchants, of three major religions, namely Hinduism, Buddhism and later Islam (Fig. 7.2), although it

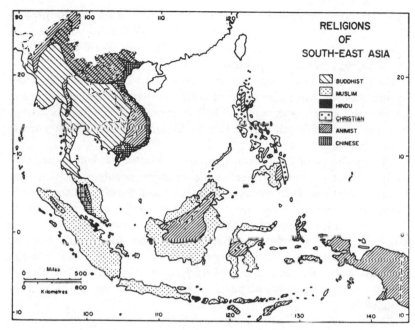

Fɪɢ. 7.2. Religions of South-east Asia. The region is a meeting-place of the great religions.

must be stressed that all these religions have undergone substantial modification in this part of the world. Great temples bear witness to the former spread of Hinduism in South-east Asia, but despite its widespread influence it survives today as a living religion only on the Indonesian island of Bali. Buddhism was also more extensive than now, but it lost its grip on the Malay world (although syncretic Hindu–Buddhist traditions survive, as, for example, in Java) and is restricted to mainland South-east Asia, but there it is generally predominant and exercises considerable political force especially in Cambodia, Burma and Vietnam. Gujarati traders contributed to the spread of Islam over Malaya and most of the islands, which were converted by the end of the sixteenth century, and only the success of Christian missionaries in the northern two-thirds of the Philippines, northern Sumatra and northern Celebes along with the persistence of animistic beliefs in the forested interiors has prevented the complete conversion of insular South-east Asia to Islam. Nevertheless, more than half of all South-east Asians are Muslims, and in this extreme corner of the Islamic world live one-fifth of the world's Muslim population.

Chinese religious influences in South-east Asia are much more localized in the Annamite lands of North Vietnam where a mixture of Confucian, Taoist and animist beliefs prevails. It is in this deeply Sinicized part of South-east Asia that communism has recently made most advance.

The profusion of indigenous peoples in South-east Asia means that each of the new states is faced with minority problems, which may result in rebellion, as in the case of the Karen of Burma and the peoples of the Outer Islands of Indonesia. Moreover, partly as a reaction to the West, the cultural revolutions and nationalist movements have given emphasis to the significance of local languages, historical roots and religious activity, thus intensifying existing diversity. In some countries only the persuasiveness of a powerful ruler or the concentration of power in a single political party has averted further political fragmentation.

Plural Societies

Supplementing the ethnic diversity of South-east Asia has been the large-scale immigration of Chinese and Indians. Although they were present in the region long before Europeans, it was not until the nineteenth century that Chinese and Indians came in very large numbers, to work in the plantations and mines which formed the basis of the European export-orientated economies. Many came as indentured labourers, for example in the rubber plantations and tin mines of Malaya, but many others came as merchants and shop-keepers, as in Singapore and Java, while a few came as colonists in sparsely peopled areas such as western Borneo.

Since independence some of the colonial-type economies have been considerably transformed and immigration has been severely curtailed through legislation, and consequently the immigrant communities of Chinese and Indians are changing in demographic composition. They are no longer so dominated by adult males and are now multiplying

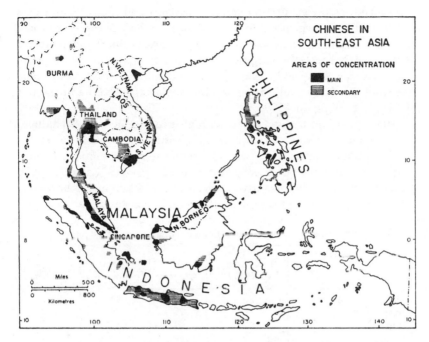

Fig. 7.3. Chinese in South-east Asia. They number well over 12 million, and are particularly numerous in Thailand, Indonesia, Malaya, Singapore and Vietnam.

through natural increase alone. Sometimes this means a decline in their relative size; Caldwell noted that "between the 1921 and 1957 censuses of Malaya the foreign-born population fell from 47 per cent to 17 per cent, the sex ratios from 159 to 107 males per 100 females and the proportion of the community made up by males in the 15–54 years of age range from 42 per cent to 26 per cent". Nevertheless, South-east Asia still has the numerous problems of "plural societies" or "semi-societies" where peoples "mix but do not combine".

There are now well over 12 million Chinese in South-east Asia (Fig. 7.3 and Table 6.9) and several million Indians, and through their commercial success as traders and moneylenders (although it must not be imagined that all are successful—some are labourers), they became a powerful middle group between the peasants and the colonial rulers, concentrating in large primate cities (Bangkok is half Chinese) especially in countries where their numbers are not great. Since independence they have become the targets of xenophobic nationalism in many countries, as evidenced by the expulsion of Indians from lower Burma, the wholesale killings of Chinese in Indonesia in 1965–66 and the riots in Kuala Lumpur in 1969.

Although the numbers of aliens are higher in Indonesia and Thailand, it is Malaya which best exemplifies the features of a plural society: in 1960 Malays comprised 43 per cent of the total population, Chinese 44 per cent, Indians 11 per cent and others 2 per cent (Table 7.4). The proportions differ significantly between Old Malaya in the north, the "Malay home zone" where immigrants are few and economic develop-

TABLE 7.4. PERCENTAGE OF ETHNIC GROUPS IN MALAYSIA, 1960

	"Indigenous" Malaysians	Chinese	Indians	Others
Federation of Malaya	50	37	11	2
Singapore	14	75	9	2
Sarawak	68	31	—ᵃ	1
Sabah	76	23	—ᵃ	1
Malaya	43	44	11	2
Borneo territories	71	28	—	1
Malaysia	46	43	9ᵃ	2

ᵃ The small number of Indians in Sarawak and Sabah are included in "others". The percentage of Indians calculated for the whole of Malaysia is based on those enumerated in Malaya.

SOURCE: J. C. Caldwell, Malaysia's population problem, chapter 7 in S. Chandrasekhar (Ed.), *Asia's Population Problems*, 1967, p. 167.

ment limited, and the more developed New Malaya in the south and west which has three-quarters of the total population and four-fifths of the urban population and where Malays have been reduced to one-third of the population. In Singapore, which now has a total of more than 2 million people, the Malays form only 14 per cent, in contrast to the 75 per cent Chinese, so that Singapore is (and always was) unquestionably a Chinese city. This fact undoubtedly influenced the breakaway of Singapore from the Federation of Malaysia in 1965, a federation formed to some extent as a reaction to the problems of the immigrant communities in the former British sector of South-east Asia.

Elsewhere in South-east Asia the proportions of immigrants are smaller, but their economic significance in countries like the Philippines, Indonesia and Thailand is out of all proportion to their numbers. This is also the case with the small European residential population, who probably numbered no more than 300,000 even in the colonial days prior to the Second World War, and must be much fewer now. Yet their political, economic, cultural and demographic impact was enormous. In the context of human diversity, it is appropriate to mention here their contribution to the Eurasian, "Indo-European" or *mestizo* communities, who are much more numerous in the Philippines and Indonesia than any other part of South-east Asia.

Population Distribution

No other major region of the world exhibits quite the same patchiness of population distribution as South-east Asia (Fig. 7.4). The general pattern is of large areas of low population density and small pockets of high density, the small areas containing the majority of the population. Indonesia is an excellent example of these dramatic differences in population density. At one end of the scale is the island of Java, containing 63 million people in 1961, or nearly one-third of the total population of South-east Asia on less than one-thirtieth of the land area of this region. With an average density greatly exceeding one thousand per square mile, with farm holdings averaging only one acre, and with at least six persons per acre of rice land, Java is one of the most closely peopled areas of the world; it contrasts particularly with Australia, which has about one-sixth as many people on an area 65 times larger. Java, with 65 per cent of the population of Indonesia on 7 per cent of its land area, also contrasts with other parts of that country; West Irian (the western part of the island of New Guinea) has less than 1 per cent of Indonesia's population on 22 per cent of its land area, and Kalimantan (Borneo) has only 4 per cent of the country's population on 28 per cent of its land area.

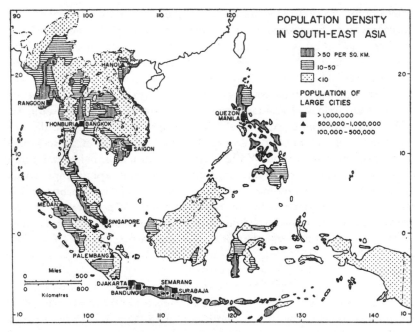

Fig. 7.4. Population density in South-east Asia. The region is characterized by extreme patchiness of population distribution.

While the sharpness of density contrasts are unusually dramatic in Indonesia, clear contrasts exist elsewhere in South-east Asia. In the Philippines, for example, the large southerly island of Mindanao has long been much less peopled than most other islands in the group. In mainland South-east Asia the main discrepancies have been between many of the long-occupied and densely peopled lowland areas, like the deltaic areas of the Red River in North Vietnam and the Menam in Thailand, where densities rise over 500 per square mile, and the extensive sparsely peopled upland areas with average densities rarely in excess of 25 per square mile. Not all deltaic areas and coastal lowlands are equally densely peopled; while the Red River lowland and the small deltas along the Vietnamese coast are comparable in density with the deltaic lowlands of China, the lower Irrawaddy in Burma and the lower Mekong in Cochin China (South Vietnam) were relatively thinly peopled until clearances in the nineteenth century, a fact today reflected in their lower population densities.

All these highly localized, extremely scattered and sometimes very narrow (e.g. Celebes) lowland areas form "favourable ecological niches" (to use an expression of Buchanan) permitting intensive agriculture and dense populations. Consequently, crude population densities and densities per unit area of cultivated land of individual countries are very different, especially in sparsely inhabited countries like East Malaysia, Brunei and Laos, where the density per square kilometre of cultivated land may be more than twenty times the crude density.

In this essentially humid tropical region, where agriculture employs two-thirds of the working population, the range of agricultural economies has exerted a major influence upon population distribution. Wet rice monoculture, in particular, has been a prominent localizing factor. Although the neat patterns of *sawahs* (irrigated rice fields) have been known for centuries in some areas, and have been closely associated with ancient civilizations, rice cultivation spread slowly and unevenly from the older core areas, often replacing an earlier yam–taro–sago complex of crops, and was sometimes introduced only by Europeans. Nevertheless, paddy now covers one-half to three-quarters of all the cultivated land in mainland South-east Asia, as much as nine-tenths of the cropland in Cambodia, and is only seriously challenged as a food crop in eastern Indonesia, where maize and sago are important. Rice is grown in a wide variety of ways, and the extent to which irrigation works supplement monsoonal rainfall varies with the density of population; whereas complex systems of irrigation have been developed in the Red River lowlands and in Java, in the past less interest in irrigation works has been shown by the Thais and the Burmese. Rice encouraged an earth-bound peasantry dependent on their considerable skills and on stable government, but too often its cultivation is associated with small, highly fragmented farms, high rates of tenancy and absentee landlordism. All these features can be seen, for example, in the central plain of Luzon, the "rice bowl" of the Philippines. Holdings are often less than one acre, when about 2.5–5 acres are normally required to sustain a peasant household, and productivity is not nearly as high as is generally imagined. Certainly, more intensive use of fertilizers would raise productivity and reduce the hunger suffered by many. Another problem of rice cultivation is that although it involves very large amounts of labour, especially in transplanting of rice and interplanting of crops, it also involves seasonal underemployment. Sometimes this problem is diminished by associated garden cultivation, which helps to diversify diets, but owing to imports of cheap manufactured goods artisanal industries have unfortunately lost much of their former significance as supplementary employment, and the development of rural industries is frequently impeded by the limited and local availability of power supplies.

Sedentary dry farming is not nearly as common as paddy cultivation in South-east Asia, and is found mainly in less humid areas with 40–80 inches of rainfall with a distinct dry period, like north-east Thailand and central Burma, where leaching of soils is not excessive. However, European stimulus to the sedentarization of shifting cultivators and the establishment of permanent cultivation, as in parts of Indonesia, has sometimes resulted in excessive deforestation, soil erosion and extension of savannas.

The process of savannization is particularly advanced in the Philippines and Indonesia, but it cannot be blamed entirely on sedentarization, for it is sometimes caused by the intensification of shifting cultivation under increasing pressure of population. Shifting cultivation or bush fallowing is still the principal form of subsistence farming in many of the islands of Indonesia as well as in the upland districts of mainland South-east Asia, where there have been relatively few attempts to extend sedentary agriculture into mountains, for many reasons including the dominant character of lowland rice cultivation and its intimate links with civilizations, the limited role of cattle in South-east Asia, the localization of less advanced peoples in mountains, and also the unusual prevalence of malaria in these areas. As mentioned before in the case of tropical Africa, the rotational nature of shifting cultivation inhibits high population carrying capacity. Indeed, it has been estimated that cultivation by a family of 2.5 acres per annum followed by 9 years of fallow would give a maximum density of about 130 per square mile, but this can only be a very rough guide. Some forms of shifting cultivation practised by older peoples are very primitive, and in many remote forest areas in New Guinea, the Moluccas, the Lesser Sundas and elsewhere are backward peoples practising hunting and collecting at very low densities of population.

The effects of traditional agricultural systems upon patterns of population distribution were intensified by the impact of Europeans introducing money economies, external orientation towards overseas markets, plantations, mining and forestry. An excellent illustration of this impact may be seen in Malaya where nine tenths of the population are now concentrated on only two-fifths of the area.

Producing crops like rubber, tea, coffee, sugar and coconuts, plantations evolved especially in western Malaya, north-east Sumatra, Java and Luzon in the Philippines. As Myrdal has suggested, they were "large-scale, capital intensive, highly specialized commercial enterprises employing wage labour" and were therefore a process of industrialization. Their great expansion in South-east Asia during the second half of the nineteenth century was facilitated by the relative ease of obtaining numerous Indian and Chinese labourers, except in Java where there was an adequate supply of local labour. Consequently, plantations were partly responsible for the problems of plural societies, but at the same time they became new nuclei of population growth, stimulating economic growth including the expansion of commercial rice cultivation in the deltas, especially of Burma and Thailand. Plantations help to explain the relative advance of Malaya and Singapore over most other countries in South-east Asia as well as many of the contrasts in population geography.

Chinese and later Western enterprise in mining and forestry had comparable effects upon population distribution, creating poles of development. Tin mining in western Malaya and to a lesser extent in Thailand, Tonkin and Indonesia, the oil industry in Burma, Brunei, Sarawak, Sumatra and Java, and the teak industry of Burma and Thailand are obvious examples. Unfortunately, plantation agriculture, mining and forestry have not helped sufficiently to develop manufacturing in South-east Asia, because they were so linked with Europe that they gave greater help to industrialization there. In Java and elsewhere industrialization was positively impeded by imports of manufactured goods. The consequence is that modern manufacturing, mostly of consumer goods, has evolved mainly in large cities, but even there the tertiary sector usually excessively outweighs the secondary sector.

Urban Populations

The peoples of South-east Asia remain preponderantly rural, and today it is still one of the least urbanized parts of the developing world. In 1960 about one in six lived in urban areas and about one in ten lived in large cities with 100,000 inhabitants or more—levels similar to those in South Asia, and exceeding only those in tropical Africa and possibly China.

One major reason for this situation is that although, as McGee rightly points out, "South-east Asia has had a very long and rich history of urban life" since the first century AD, the pre-industrial sacred cities like Angkor Thom and market cities like Malacca, which evolved partly in response to Chinese and Indian influences, were highly scattered and many societies knew no urban life before the arrival of the Europeans. Moreover, these pre-industrial cities did not increase in number or size until the great expansion of Western territorial power over South-east Asia (except Thailand) during the nineteenth century, when many cities were created, especially ports linking the colonies with the West. Administrative, commercial and, latterly, industrial functions have contributed to the growth of some of these ports, so that they have become dominant in the urban hierarchy eclipsing many of the smaller towns. But Europeans were not only responsible for port growth, they created many other towns, including hill stations, which are particularly widespread in South-east Asia, and mining towns.

As elsewhere in the developing world, study of urbanization is plagued by differences in definition of urban populations or lack of definition. Those definitions based upon size have been shown to be inadequate, because large localities of 10,000 inhabitants may be less urban than localities of 1000, and those based upon density are also seen to be insufficient when rural densities in deltaic areas exceed urban densities. Moreover, calculation of urban populations on the basis of functions is impeded by limited data.

Despite difficulties of data, it is apparent that levels of urban population vary substantially from country to country, from one-twelfth to one-eighth of the total population in Cambodia, Thailand and Laos to over two-fifths in Malaya and Brunei and nearly all of the city-state of Singapore (Table 7.5). Although the level of urban

TABLE 7.5. ESTIMATED URBAN POPULATIONS OF SOUTH-EAST ASIA *ca.* 1960

	Urban population (%)	Population in localities with 100,000 or more (%)	Urban primacy P_1/P_2
Brunei	43.5	—	—
Burma	14.3	5.4	4.4
Cambodia	10.1	6.2	—
Indonesia	14.9	9.7	2.6
Laos	8.6	4.9	—
Federation of Malaya	42.8	—	1.5
Philippines	21.5	14.3	10.8
Sabah	14.9	—	—
Sarawak	14.9	—	—
Singapore	100.0	100.0	—
Thailand	11.4	6.5	3.5
Portuguese Timor	10.1	—	—
North Vietnam	14.2	6.3	1.7
South Vietnam	20.9	10.5	12.0

SOURCE: K. Davis, *World Urbanization 1950–1970*, vol. 1: *Basic Data for Cities, Countries and Regions*, 1969, various tables.

population is generally rising, Ginsburg has noted that the rate of urban growth as a percentage of the total population has not been spectacular owing to the high rate of total population growth. In general, the level of urban population is closely associated with the level and type of economic development: rice producing states like Burma, Cambodia and Thailand, which are among the less developed states in South-east Asia, have low levels of urban population, while countries with more diversified, developed economies, such as Malaya, Indonesia and the Philippines, have higher levels. The level of urbanization in Malaya is somewhat anomalous for it is much higher than anywhere else in South-east Asia, or for that matter in the humid tropics except Venezuela.

In view of its generally low level of urban population, South-east Asia contains a surprising number of large cities, a number which is increasing rapidly. Although there were no millionaire cities before the Second World War, by the mid-1960s there were nine—Rangoon,

Djakarta, Surabaja, Bandung, Manila, Singapore, Bangkok, Hanoi and Saigon—three of which are located on the island of Java (see Fig. 7.4). Except in the case of Singapore, these millionaire cities do not yet contain so high a proportion of the total populations of their respective countries as many of the millionaire cities of Latin America, but they are growing rapidly: Djakarta grew from 533,000 in 1930 to 4,750,000 in 1970, Manila from 1,367,000 in 1948 to 2,136,000 in 1960, Bangkok from 782,000 in 1947 to 1,800,000 in 1965 and Singapore from 680,000 in 1947 to 1,913,000 in 1966.

The number of cities with 100,000–1 million inhabitants is also increasing and, by the late 1960s there were more than sixty in South-east Asia, of which about twenty-five were in Indonesia. Many are growing so rapidly that they will soon join the ranks of millionaire cities: Semarang, Medan and Palembang in Indonesia, Kuala Lumpur in Malaysia and Haiphong in North Vietnam. Medan grew more than six times between 1930 and 1961, from 76,600 to 479,000.

Urban primacy is evident in all countries of South-east Asia, with the exception of Malaysia and Indonesia, and the dominance of primate cities is growing. Bangkok, together with its twin city Thonburi, are at least twenty times larger than the next city in Thailand, and Manila is between ten and twelve times the size of Cebu, the second city in the Philippines (see Fig. 6.4). Saigon, Rangoon, Phnom Penh and Vientiane are also clearly primate cities in South Vietnam, Burma, Cambodia and Laos respectively. They are the main foci of urban growth, which has accelerated particularly in response to decolonization and nationalism. Cosmopolitan cities, these "metropoles" epitomize the characteristics of plural societies, with Indians, Chinese, Europeans, Americans and a great variety of South-east Asian peoples living within them in more or less segregated societies, a feature which became common under colonial rule and which has inhibited social change. The great cities show many signs of modernization, but they are alien to the countries in which they exist, and may be accused of parasitism. In 1960 the Bangkok metropolitan area contained two-thirds of the doctors in Thailand and four-fifths of the university graduates but only 8 per cent of the country's population. So far there has been no abandonment of Western-oriented capitals in favour of more indigenous cities—partly because of the cost of translocation—but there is an awareness of the danger of dichotomy between the capital and the nation.

In contrast to the large cities with their international culture, small towns in South-east Asia are mostly provincial centres more closely connected with their hinterlands. They have less aliens, except in the case of mining townships, and they are places where urban and rural mix. Frequently they act as steps in the migration to large cities.

Urban population growth arises from high and sometimes rising natural increase, extension of urban areas and in-migration, the relative significance of which varies from country to country. Natural increase is an important component of urban population growth in South-east Asia, and according to Simkins accounted for the bulk of city growth in the Philippines during the period 1948–60. Data on fertility and mortality trends in urban centres are fragmentary, but it appears that early urbanization was not associated with high natural increase, because urban places contained high proportions of males and therefore not unusually high fertility and also because it was some time before mortality began to drop substantially. As urban sex-ratios became more balanced fertility rose, but much less markedly than the decline in mortality, which was in response to the localization of medical facilities and of Chinese populations. In Singapore the death rate fell from 24.2 per thousand in 1931 to about 5.5 per thousand today, and similar evidence is also available in Malaya and the Philippines, making mortality the main determinant of rising urban natural increase. As city life has evolved in South-east Asia urban fertility has also diminished. In Indonesia, for instance, the urban birth rate in 1961 was 38.5 per thousand in comparison with the rural birth rate of 43.8 per thousand. However, fertility in towns has declined much less clearly than mortality, and more among alien elements than indigenous peoples. Caldwell and Swee-Hock both note in Malaysia, for example, that the urban–rural fertility differential is greater among Chinese and Indians than Malays. Undoubtedly, the acute congestion and problems of employment in many South-east Asian cities have encouraged a reduction in family size, despite the persistence of traditional social attitudes favouring large families.

A second component in urban population growth is the extension of urban areas, following centrifugal expansion and the inability of some cities to absorb the influx of migrants. Many great cities in South-east Asia have enlarged their boundaries in recent decades—McGee cites the example of Bangkok which grew in size from 49.5 square kilometres in 1947 to 124.7 square kilometres in 1960—incorporating more settlements within their municipal control. Nevertheless, many cities are fringed by squatter camps and other settlements which are not officially under their control.

In-migration has played a vital role in urban growth in South-east Asia. Emphasis has already been laid on the alien creation of many South-east Asian cities and the concentration of aliens within them, but since the cessation of large-scale immigration of Chinese and Indians and the increase in rural–urban migration the proportion of aliens has diminished. However, the pluralistic composition of large city populations remains, for the rural–urban migrants comprise diverse ethnic elements.

Most South-east Asian countries are experiencing rapid rural–urban migration. It is common for half of a city population to have been born elsewhere; at the time of the 1961 census of Indonesia 51 per cent of the 2.9 million inhabitants of Djakarta were born there, but half of these were under 5 years old. Motives for migration vary greatly, but researchers usually place great stress on push factors including the frequency of high agricultural densities in the "ecological niches", fragmentation of farms, high rates of tenancy, low productivity of land and labour, as well as the prevalence of political insecurity leading to the flight of refugees to cities, as in Burma, Indonesia and Malaysia. In North Vietnam, however, American bombing has had the opposite effect, causing people to desert the big cities.

Obviously many migrants are attracted by the "pull" of the cities, but some are quickly disillusioned, for while industrialization has increased in many cities of the region it has not been sufficient to overcome the common problems of unemployment and underemployment. As in South Asia, the phenomenon of hidden unemployment, or the super-abundance of workers doing menial jobs such as pedi-cab driving and domestic service, is also general in the cities.

As in most other regions of Asia and in Africa, rural–urban migration involves a preponderance of young adult males, largely because tradition places restrictions on the employment of women outside the home.

TABLE 7.6. SEX-RATIOS IN COUNTRIES OF SOUTH-EAST ASIA

	Year	Males per 1000 females
Burma	1953	1040
Cambodia	1962	999
Indonesia	1971	982
Malaysia: West		
Malaysia	1970	1014
Sabah	1970	1075
Sarawak	1970	1014
Philippines	1970	990
Singapore	1970	1049
Thailand	1960	1004

SOURCE: *UN Demographic Yearbooks.*

Immigrant communities in cities have also had a surplus of males, and consequently most cities in South-east Asia have imbalanced sex-ratios especially in the 15–44 age group and especially in their central areas. Of course, cities offer fewer employment opportunities for the young and old than rural areas, and in addition urban sex-ratios are influenced by general sex-ratios (Table 7.6) which usually reveal an excess of males (except in Cambodia, Philippines and Indonesia), for reasons mentioned in the chapter on South Asia. On the other hand, male preponderance in cities is not so striking as in many cities of South Asia. In most it does not exceed 1100 per thousand females, and where it does it is dwindling, as in Singapore where the sex-ratio is more normal now than ever before. In the Philippines, where Christianity prevails, female emancipation is more advanced and rural-urban migration is less significant, cities often have a preponderance of females; in 1960 Manila City contained only 93 males per 100 females. Future sex-ratios in South-east Asian cities will greatly depend upon the role and status of women in society.

The influx of migrants into cities has caused grave housing difficulties, and in particular the evolution of squatter camps and tenement slums. Squatter camps contain many of the poorest and most recent of the city's inhabitants, and are symptoms of both rapid urban growth and the ineffectiveness of policies of economic development. At the beginning of the 1960s they accounted for a quarter of the populations of the cities of Singapore, Djakarta, Kuala Lumpur and Manila. They have no general location: found on the fringes of Rangoon, Manila and Djakarta, elsewhere they have more central locations. Whatever their location, they lack all public amenities and have appalling sanitation.

The tenement slums of inner city areas are not much better. In old dilapidated housing large proportions of city populations live at densities often exceeding 100,000 per square mile. Chinatown in Singapore and Bangkok and the Indian quarter of Rangoon admirably illustrate these conditions, for alien elements are the main occupants of tenement slums. In Singapore and a few other cities low-cost housing programmes and squatter resettlement are ameliorating the situation, but elsewhere little progress has been made, and the striking contrasts persist between the squalor of the many and the opulence of the few.

Internal Migration

Apart from rural–urban migration, South-east Asia experiences other types of migration, but in view of the unevenness of population pressure none is more important than migration from densely peopled to sparsely peopled areas within the same country. Although spontaneous long-range migrations of this sort are not common they have sometimes occurred, as in the resettlement of the Irrawaddy delta in Burma, of the lower Menam in Thailand and of the island of Mindanao in the Philippines. Comprising 32 per cent of the land area of the Philippines, Mindanao was sparsely inhabited until this century but the situation has changed dramatically owing mainly to spontaneous migration and subsidiarily to government-sponsored settlement schemes. Its population rose from 933,000 (9.0 per cent of the country's population) in 1918 to 2.7 million (14.1 per cent) in 1948 to 5.1 million (18.6 per cent) in 1960, when its population density had reached the country's average. Between 1948 and 1960 Mindanao accounted for 30 per cent of the total population growth of the Philippines, and acted as a safety valve for population pressure in other islands, especially Luzon. By 1960 only 4.2 million of the 11 million acres of arable land on Mindanao were in cultivation, and perhaps another 4 million individuals could be settled there in rural areas, so the safety valve will not be open long.

The enormous disparity between the great density of population on the island of Java and the low densities of many of the other islands of Indonesia has inspired schemes for population transfer, known locally as "transmigration", since the early years of this century, but unfortunately they have not met with any real success. The movement of 20,000–50,000 persons a year to the other islands, notably Sumatra, has not been enough to relieve Java's population pressure or to substantially reduce its population growth, which is well over one million persons a year. By 1980 Java will probably have between 90 and 100 million people and even with an annual out-migration of 200,000 persons from 1960 onward the projected 1980 total would be reduced by only 5 million. So far difficulties of organization, transportation and costs have impeded migration on this scale, even if there were enough Javanese willing to migrate. Moreover, despite Indonesian efforts to encourage transmigration, partly as a pretext to stave off a birth-control programme, it has had little effect upon the economic development of other islands, and owing to the non-assimilation of Javanese colonists it has not really assisted in the policy of national consolidation.

Although government resettlement schemes have locally influenced population distribution schemes in Malaya, they were the result of political troubles, and have not diminished the growing concentration of population, particularly in New Malaya.

On the whole, migration offers no solution to the problems of growing population pressure, although it has long been regarded as such in Indonesia, the Philippines and elsewhere. However, in the face of rising population growth there is now a growing realization that migration is no substitute for family limitation.

Mortality

It has already been mentioned that mortality decline is the key influence upon rising natural increase rates in South-east Asia, but the decline has not been everywhere equal. While relatively prosperous countries like Singapore and Malaysia, quite well provided with hospitals and doctors, have achieved crude death rates below 10 per thousand (Table 7.7), and substantial progress has been achieved in the Philippines and Thailand (death rates 10–15 per thousand), in most

TABLE 7.7. VITAL RATES IN SOUTH-EAST ASIA, EARLY 1970's

	Birth rate	Death rate	Infant mortality rate	Current annual rate of popula- tion growth
Burma	40	17	—	2.3
Cambodia	41	20	127	2.2
Indonesia	47	19	125	2.9
Laos	42	17	—	2.5
Malaysia	37	8	49	2.8
Philippines	45	12	67	3.3
Singapore	23	5	26	2.2
Thailand	43	10	31	3.3
North Vietnam	—	—	—	3.1
South Vietnam	—	—	—	2.6

SOURCE: Population Reference Bureau, 1972 World Population Data Sheet.

other countries much less medical advance has been experienced and death rates exceed 16 per thousand. It should not be construed from this that economic advance is a prerequisite for mortality decline, for other important factors are the better health facilities inherited from colonial times (except in Thailand) and the progress made in malaria control after the Second World War. Moreover, it should be remembered that low crude death rates are partly attributable to extremely youthful age compositions, in which 40–47 per cent are aged under 15 and rarely more than 5 per cent aged 60 and over (see Table 6.7). In consequence, age-specific mortality rates.are not low, and in fact are very high in countries like Burma, Laos and Indonesia where the provision of medical personnel and facilities is quite inadequate and also in Vietnam ravaged by war. In such countries infant mortality rates are well above 100 per thousand, and as in all countries with high birth rates the mortality of children aged 1–4 is also high. This is even the case in countries and cities with relatively low mortality like Malaya, Thailand and Saigon (Table 7.8), and is even more striking in rural areas.

Within South-east Asian countries there is considerable differential mortality, but the poor quality of mortality statistics, especially under-registration, impedes analysis. As in South Asia, female mortality is

TABLE 7.8. ANNUAL MALE DEATH RATES IN PARTS OF SOUTH-EAST ASIA

Age	Federation of Malaya, 1955–57	Saigon 1958–59	Thailand 1958
Less than 1	84.9	66.9	65.7
1–4	10.5	12.2	16.2
5–9	2.8	2.9	4.2
10 11	1.7	1.7	1.9
15–19	2.1	2.1	2.1
20–24	2.8	3.6	3.9
25–29	3.5	4.4	4.9
30–34	4.5	5.3	5.1
35–39	5.6	6.7	5.9
40–44	8.4	9.7	8.0
45–49	12.6	13.3	10.7
50–54	16.7	20.0	14.2
55–59	27.2	30.6	22.6
60–64	35.3	43.5	40.9
65–69	59.7	60.6	45.7

SOURCE: H. Wiesler, Mortality in South-East Asia, in United Nations, *World Population Conference*, 1965, vol. II, 1967, p. 385.

usually higher than male mortality, although not among Chinese populations whose male–female mortality differential is like that of developed countries; in Malaya in 1957 the average expectation of life of Chinese females and males was 67.8 and 60 years respectively, in contrast to 56.2 and 60.1 years for Indian females and males and 53.9 and 53.2 for Malay females and males. It may be that the Malaysian government's policy of expansion of health services to rural areas, where the Malays mainly live, will reduce the obvious ethnic disparity in mortality, but in mid-1965 only 9 out of 1200 doctors in theFederation of Malaysia worked in rural areas. Yet in Malaysia, and the Philippines, there is a better spread of medical facilities than in most other South-east Asian countries; in Thailand in the 1950s the number of hospital beds per 100,000 peopled varied from 190 in Bangkok to 0.1 in other areas. Too often the poorer country folk are deprived of any medical attention.

Strong areal variations in mortality are likely to remain in the near future owing to the difficulties and costs of the implementation of

medical and health schemes in rural areas, and the problems of over-
coming widespread malnutrition, insanitary housing, lack of sewerage
disposal and impure water supplies. Despite great advances in the
control of malaria (which has influenced settlement patterns, as in
Borneo), smallpox and the plague, diseases due to deficiencies of diet,
sanitation and housing remain very common. There is still much progress to be made.

Fertility

High fertility has long been the norm in South-east Asia, with birth
rates well in excess of 40 per thousand, and it is only in the 1960s that
substantial fertility decline has occurred in Malaya and Singapore. In
Singapore the birth rate declined from 42 per thousand in 1958 to
22 per thousand in 1971, but this was quite exceptional.

High fertility has been influenced by a host of factors, but particularly significant are universal marriage, which is partly influenced by
the surplus of adult males, and early marriage. The latter is not general
in the Philippines, Thailand, Singapore or among the Chinese in
Malaya, but it is in Indonesia and among the Malay population; about
half of all Malay girls aged 15–19 are married (a lower proportion than
in either India or Pakistan), but the effect of early marriage is offset to
some extent by the unusual prevalence of divorce among Malays
which, although associated with multiple marriages, leads to lower
cumulative fertility.

The later marriage of the predominantly urban Chinese populations
in South-east Asia, notably in Malaya and Singapore, has been an
important factor lowering their fertility, but in addition since the late
1950s they have made a great increase in their use of family planning.
Evidence from Malaya also suggests that the Indian population has
experienced fertility decline especially in urban areas (Table 7.9),
but in a plural society like Malaya it is no easy matter to distinguish
the relative differentials. Nevertheless, surveys indicate that there is a
clear desire for family planning in all groups of the population of
Malaya, and so we may expect further fertility declines in the near
future.

Although there are a number of natural checks upon fertility,

TABLE 7.9. TOTAL FERTILITY RATES IN WEST
MALAYSIA, 1957–61 AND 1962–66

	1957–61	1962–66
Metropolitan areas	5170	4615
Malays	5430	5550
Chinese	5015	4250
Indians	6165	5175
Non-metropolitan urban areas	5830	4805
Rural areas	6280	5775

SOURCE: L-J Cho, J. A. Palmore and L. Saunders, Recent
fertility trends in West Malaysia, *Demography* **5,** 742–3 (1968).

including late weaning and poor health conditions, which cause high
mortality in the reproductive age groups, and a high proportion of
widows (e.g. between one-fifth and one-quarter of all women aged
45–49 in Malaya and Thailand), family planning has not had much
success in South-east Asia outside of Singapore and Malaysia and the
major cities. In the Catholic Philippines, despite the existence of family
planning clinics and widespread awareness of contraceptive techniques,
there would seem little likelihood of an early important reduction in
fertility, a conclusion which must for the present be even more obvious
in other countries like Indonesia, Laos and Burma where family
planning is rare.

The Future

With little chance of an immediate general fall in fertility, except in
Malaysia and Singapore, and the certainty that death rates can be
reduced further without any major economic development, it seems
that rapid population growth is assured in South-east Asia at least for a
decade or so. At present, the 1970 totals for individual countries are
mainly somewhere between the "conservative" and "modified" projections made by the United Nations in the late 1950s, and this may well
remain the case for the 1980 totals (Table 7.10). On the other hand, the
population growth of Thailand has probably been under-estimated and
that of Malaya exaggerated. However, it should be recalled that all

TABLE 7.10. PROJECTED POPULATIONS OF SOUTH-EAST ASIAN COUNTRIES, 1960–80 (IN MILLIONS)

	1960		1970		1980	
	(a)	(b)	(a)	(b)	(a)	(b)
Burma	21.5	24.6	25.9	32.8	32.3	45.3
Indonesia	90.7	93.3	111.0	119.9	137.4	159.7
Malaya	7.0	7.0	9.7	9.9	14.0	14.4
Philippines	26.6	27.3	36.3	39.0	50.8	57.0
Thailand	23.7	24.4	31.1	33.5	41.6	47.5
South Vietnam	13.9	14.0	17.3	18.1	21.2	23.3

SOURCE: United Nations Department of Economic and Social Affairs, *Future Population Estimates by Sex and Age*, Report III, The Population of South-east Asia (including Ceylon and China: Taiwan) 1950–1980, 1958, pp. 26–7.

projections are tentative; a forecast made in 1937 for the population of Java in the year 2000 was actually achieved by 1955. In the mid-1960s at least five sets of medium-range projections were available for Thailand, and the range of projected totals for 1977 was from 33.9 to 48.9 million, strikingly wide by any standards.

Despite uncertainty about the future trends of fertility and mortality in South-east Asia, there can be little doubt that if the present nationalism persists international migration will play only a small role in population change, so that effectively the various countries may be regarded as closed populations. They will have to solve their own population problems, not merely general problems of matching population growth with economic growth, or of coping with a broadening base to the population pyramid, but also geographical problems resulting from the marked localization of population concentrations. As in Latin America and Africa, South-east Asia possesses extensive areas which are underutilized and underpopulated. Its present population distribution strongly reflects past patterns of human occupation and the evolution of certain types of economy. It is a dominant influence upon future population distribution, but it is not immutable and the future distribution will owe much to economic and social change. Reorientations of economies and increased emphasis on social welfare, particularly through education, should soon have pronounced effects. In addition, however, like South-west Asia, South-east Asia is in a state of political instability and flux, and future population distributions will undoubtedly be affected by changes in political units and regimes.

Select Bibliography

BUCHANAN, K., *The South-east Asian World*, 1967.
CALDWELL, J. C., The demographic background, in SILCOCK, T. H. and FISK, E. K. (Eds.), *The Political Economy of Independent Malaya: A Case Study in Development*, Canberra, 1963.
CHANDRASEKHAR, S. (Ed.), *Asia's Population Problems*, 1967.
CHESNEAUX, J., *Le Viet-nam*, Paris, 1955.
COWAN, C. D. (Ed.), *The Economic Development of South-east Asia*, 1964.
DEMOGRAPHY 5 (1968), Special Issue: *Progress and Problems of Fertility Control around the World*.
DWYER, D. J., *The City in the Developing World and the Example of South-east Asia*, University of Hong Kong, 1968.
FISHER, C. A., *South-east Asia: A Social, Economic and Political Geography*, 1964.
FITZGERALD, C. P., *The Third China*, Sydney, 1965.
FRYER, D. W., The million city in South-east Asia, *Geog. Rev.* **43**, 474 (1953).
GINSBURG, N. S., The great city in South-east Asia, *Am. J. Sociol.* **60**, 455 (1955).
HALL, D. G. E., Introduction to *Atlas of South-east Asia*, 1964.
HAUSER, P. M. (Ed.), *Urbanization in Asia and the Far East*, Calcutta, 1957.
HO, R., *Environment, Man and Development in Malaya*, Kuala Lumpur, 1962.
HODDER, B. W., *Man in Malaya*, 1959.
INTERNATIONAL UNION FOR SCIENTIFIC STUDY OF POPULATION, 1967 Sydney Conference, Papers by J. C. Caldwell, H. J. Heeren.
JACKSON, J. C., *Sarawak: A Geographical Study of a Developing State*, 1968.
JONES, L. W., Malaysia's future population, *Pacific Viewpoint* **6**, 39 (1965).
JONES, L. W., *The Population of Borneo. A Study of the Peoples of Sarawak, Sabah and Brunei*, 1966.
LEE, Y. L., The population of British Borneo, *Pop. Studies* **15**, 226 (1962).
LEE, Y. L., The population of Sarawak, *Geog. J.* **131**, 344 (1965).
LENG, L. Y., Population changes in Sabah, *J. Trop. Geog.* **26**, 55 (1968).
LOUKA, K. T., *The Role of Population in the Development of South-east Asia*, Washington, 1960.
MADIGAN, F. C., Some recent vital rates and trends in the Philippines: estimates and evaluation, *Demography* **2**, 309 (1965).
McGEE, T. G., *The South-east Asian City: A Social Geography of the Primate Cities of South-east Asia*, 1967.
McTAGGART, W. D., The distribution of ethnic groups in Malaya, 1947–57, *J. Trop. Geog.* **26**, 69 (1968).
MYRDAL, G., *Asian Drama: An Inquiry into the Poverty of Nations*, 3 vols., 1968.
NEVILLE, R. J. W., Singapore: recent trends in the sex and age composition of a cosmopolitan community, *Pop. Studies* **17**, 99 (1963).
OOI, JIN-BEE, *Land, People and Economy in Malaya*, 1963. .
PASCUAL, E. M., *Population Redistribution in the Philippines*, Manila, 1966.

PELZER, J. K., *The Population of Indonesia*, Djakarta, 1963.

PURCELL, V., *The Chinese in South-east Asia*, 2nd edn. 1965.

ROBEQUAIN, C., *Malaya, Indonesia, Borneo and the Philippines*, 1954.

SENDUT, H., Patterns of urbanization in Malaya, *J. Trop. Geog.* **16**, 114 (1962).

SIMKINS, P. D. and WERNSTEDT, F. L., Growth and internal migrations of the Philippine Population, 1948 to 1960, in *Studies in the Geography of South-east Asia*, 1963.

SMITH, T. E., *Population Growth in Malaya: an Analysis of Recent Trends*, 1952.

SMITH, T. E., Population characteristics of South and South-east Asia, in WARD, B. (Ed.) *Women in the New Asia*, 1963, pp. 500–22

SPENCER, J. E., *Asia East by South*, 1961.

STERNSTEIN, L., A critique of Thai population data, *Pacific Viewpoint* **6**, 15 (1965).

SWEE-HOCK, SAW, The changing population structure in Singapore during 1824–1962, *Malayan Econ. Rev.* **9**, 90 (1964).

SWEE-HOCK, SAW, Fertility differentials in early post-war Malaya, *Demography* **4**, 641 (1967).

TAEUBER, I. B., The bases of a population problem: the Philippines, *Pop. Index* **26**, 97 (1960).

TAN GOANTIANG, Some notes on internal migration in Indonesia, *Int. Migr.* **6**, 39 (1968).

THOMPSON, V. and ADLOFF, R., *Minority Problems in South-east Asia*, Stanford, 1955.

THOMPSON, W. S., *Population and Progress in the Far East*, Chicago, 1959.

UN DEPT. OF ECONOMIC AND SOCIAL AFFAIRS, *Future Population Estimates by Sex and Age*, Report III, The Population of South-east Asia (including Ceylon and China: Taiwan) 1950–1980, New York, 1958.

UN DEPT. OF ECONOMIC AND SOCIAL AFFAIRS, *Population Growth and Manpower in the Philippines*, Pop. Studies No. 32, New York, 1960.

UN ECONOMIC COMMISSION FOR ASIA AND THE FAR EAST, *Report of the Expert Working Group on Problems of Internal Migration and Urbanization and selected papers* (held at Bangkok, Thailand, 24 May–5 June 1967), New York, 1968.

WERNSTEDT, F. L. and SPENCER, J. E., *The Philippine Island World. A Physical, Cultural and Regional Geography*, Berkeley and Los Angeles, 1967.

WILLIAMS, L. E., *The Future of Overseas Chinese in South-east Asia*, New York, 1966.

WITHINGTON, W. A., The distribution of population in Sumatra, Indonesia, 1961, in *Studies in the Geography of South-east Asia*, 1963.

WITHINGTON, W. A., The Kotapradja or King Cities of Indonesia, *Pacific Viewpoint* **4**, 75 (1963).

8

CONCLUSION

IN THIS volume a macroscopic view has been taken of the patterns of population in the six major regions of the world in which developing countries are preponderant. The scope has been broad for these countries comprise about 70 per cent of mankind, and owing to persistently high fertility and declining mortality their populations contribute about four-fifths of present world population growth. Unfortunately the rapidity of population growth in these poorer countries is generally not matched by rapidity of economic growth, and the gap between rich and poor countries is expanding. Few developing countries have enjoyed sustained economic growth; mineral rich states like Libya and Venezuela, relatively prosperous micro-states, like Hong Kong and Singapore, and states with considerable economic diversity like Malaysia and South Africa are exceptional. Hampered by illiteracy, ill health, malnutrition and heavy age dependency burdens, most developing countries have been able to do little to raise their standards of living and they still experience widespread poverty. To some extent they have also been hindered by the plethora of peoples within their boundaries, most of whom have preserved their linguistic identity and many of whom pose problems for national unity.

Developing countries are not, however, condemned to general stagnation, for all have poles of development and population attraction, although often they are scattered and peripheral. Urban centres exert attractions to migrants over wide areas, and urbanization is a process common to all developing countries. On the other hand, the levels of urban population are highly variable, being affected by numerous factors including the tradition of urbanism, the size of the country, the level of economic development and the degree of European impact.

Indeed, generalizations concerning developing countries mask substantial diversity among the major world regions as well as among the hundred or more individual countries. One obvious contrast is between the densely peopled regions of South and East Asia whose vast and mainly rural populations reflect the momentum of centuries of agricultural civilizations, and the less inhabited regions of Latin America, Africa, South-west Asia and South-east Asia where for one reason or another large concentrations of humanity never evolved until recently and where Europeans have had a greater impact upon patterns of population. The impact has been most profound in Latin America which had only a small population in pre-colonial times and which has evolved as the most Europeanized and most urbanized of all the major regions within the developing world. But in such regions the creation of export economies with "islandic" distributional patterns has encouraged patchy and coastal concentrations of population and in particular the growth of ports and primate cities, while immense areas remain almost uninhabited. In fact, many of these areas are inhospitable deserts, mountain ranges or tropical forests, but their low population densities are not entirely due to their environmental difficulties, and must be partially explained by local inability of peoples to overcome these difficulties despite the availability of technical means elsewhere in the world at least. Consequently, physical environments like the humid tropics exhibit marked differences in utilization and occupation, not only between regions like Amazonia and South-east Asia but also within countries like Indonesia.

The analysis of the major world regions has revealed that, despite certain common characteristics of population, great contrasts exist within them. All regions contain countries which for a variety of reasons . form exceptions to the generalizations: the countries of temperate Latin America, Puerto Rico, South Africa, Cyprus, Israel, Kuwait, Hong Kong and Singapore. Sometimes they differ more in growth than in distribution, but the existence of such contrasts within the major regions emphasizes the significance of political units in the geography of population. During this century the achievement of independence by many colonial territories and the spread of nationalism have had important effects upon migrations and natural increase of population. Boundaries have often become barriers to human movement. The size of a state has a considerable influence upon the mobility and growth of its population, and city-states like Kuwait, Singapore and Hong Kong are able to effect much more rapid changes in population growth than mammoth states like China and India.

Yet during this century the possibilities for human mobility are greater than ever before, especially with the evolution of road transport, introduced in some developing countries only since the Second World War. In most countries the improvement in transport facilities has stimulated internal migrations, notably toward cities, and rural–urban migrants have brought about great changes in the population map, much more than rural–rural migrants. The reasons for these migrations are extremely numerous involving "push" and "pull" factors of varied intensity, but their relative significance is often difficult to ascertain as migrations have their own momentum. Perhaps the most obvious result has been the emergence and rapid expansion of many large cities comparable in size with those of developed countries. Except in populous countries with long traditions of urbanism and little affected by colonialism, these large cities are often primate cities and capitals, and there is a lack of a well-developed urban hierarchy.

The rate of urban growth varies greatly in developing countries but the paucity of censuses sometimes makes it difficult to determine. Among the slower rates of increase in the level of urban population are the large, populous but relatively feebly urbanized countries of China and India. Other features revealed in previous chapters are the problems of urban housing, unemployment and excessive growth of the tertiary sector. Certainly employment within this sector is no guide whatsoever to the sophistication of the economy. Indeed, the concentration of services within cities, especially primate cities, has provoked accusations of parasitism and over-urbanization, which may not be easy to justify statistically but may in practice be abundantly evident. In many cases the accusation derives from the alien character of large cities and the concentration of ethnic minority groups within them, a fact which sometimes causes friction.

Urban growth in developing countries has been associated with increasing concentration or unevenness of population distribution. Poles of population growth are invariably the long-established centres of intense economic activity, often related to former economic and political conditions. Entirely new poles of growth, like Brasilia, Mindanao and Kuwait are rarities. During this century the earth's inhabited area has changed little in outline, despite the multiplication of mankind. According to recent estimates 63 per cent of the earth's land surface has less than five persons per square mile, and 63 per cent of the world's population live on less than 10 per cent of the land area. Despite much discussion about the reclamation of arid lands, the greater utilization of humid forests and the colonization of cold wastes, the uninhabited or negative areas have not been peopled and under present conditions of limited international migration and uneven population pressure it is unreasonable to expect their early habitation, at least on a large scale. With existing technological and economic conditions it may be expected that such areas will contain only scattered pockets of population concentration.

In other words, it seems likely that in the foreseeable future—and the ability to foresee appears to diminish progressively—the great majority of the world's population will remain within the ecumene or habitable area. Undoubtedly there will be pressures on its periphery in China, Brazil, Indonesia, Nigeria and elsewhere, but the broad pattern of the population map will probably not change imminently. Within the ecumene the bulk of people remain in rural areas, especially villages, despite the acceleration in urbanization. Most rural areas are remarkably stable in comparison with the great transformations in urban centres. The signs of modernity in villages in developing countries are few, but villages are experiencing substantial changes through increased educational, medical and transport facilities and migration, so that they can no longer be regarded as entirely traditional. The problem of increasing the productivity and quality of life of the rural populations of developing countries presents a greater challenge than the problems of urban growth. Our survey has shown that there is no simple panacea, as the problems vary from country to country and from region to region. In some countries urgent steps must certainly be taken, and among them family limitation offers immediate advantages, but there is no single demographic, economic or other solution to the manifold problems involved in improving the quality of human existence.

INDEX